Sport and Postcolonialism

Global Sport Cultures

Eds Gary Armstrong, *University of Reading*, Richard Giulianotti, *University of Aberdeen*, and David Andrews, *The University of Memphis*

From the Olympics and the World Cup to extreme sports and kabaddi, the social significance of sport at both global and local levels has become increasingly clear in recent years. The contested nature of identity is widely addressed in the social sciences, but sport as a particularly revealing site of such contestation, in both industrialising and post-industrial nations, has been less fruitfully explored. Further, sport and sporting corporations are increasingly powerful players in the world economy. Sport is now central to the social and technological development of mass media, notably in telecommunications and digital television. It is also a crucial medium through which specific populations and political elites communicate and interact with each other on a global stage.

Berg publishers are pleased to announce a new book series that will examine and evaluate the role of sport in the contemporary world. Truly global in scope, the series seeks to adopt a grounded, constructively critical stance towards prior work within sport studies and to answer such questions as:

- How are sports experienced and practised at the everyday level within local settings?
- How do specific cultures construct and negotiate forms of social stratification (such as gender, class, ethnicity) within sporting contexts?
- What is the impact of mediation and corporate globalisation upon local sports cultures?

Determinedly interdisciplinary, the series will nevertheless privilege anthropological, historical and sociological approaches, but will consider submissions from cultural studies, economics, geography, human kinetics, international relations, law, philosophy and political science. The series is particularly committed to research that draws upon primary source materials or ethnographic fieldwork.

GLOBAL SPORT CULTURES

Sport and Postcolonialism

Edited by

John Bale and Mike Cronin

Routledge
Taylor & Francis Group

LONDON AND NEW YORK

First published 2003 by Berg Publishers

Published 2020 by Routledge
2 Park Square, Milton Park, Abingdon, Oxon OX14 4RN
605 Third Avenue, New York, NY 10017

Routledge is an imprint of the Taylor & Francis Group, an informa business

Library of Congress Cataloging-in-Publication Data
A catalogue record for this book is available from the Library of Congress.

British Library Cataloguing-in-Publication Data
A catalogue record for this book is available from the British Library.

ISBN13: 978-1-8597-3544-2 (hbk)
ISBN13: 978-1-8597-3549-7 (pbk)

Typeset by JS Typesetting Ltd, Wellingborough, Northants.

Contents

Contents

Notes on Contributors

Alan Bairner is Professor of Sports Studies at the University of Ulster Jordanstown, Northern Ireland. He is the author of *Sport, Nationalism and Globalization: European and North American Perspectives* (New York: 2001) and co-author, with John Sugden of *Sport, Sectarianism and Society in a Divided Ireland* (Leicester: 1995).

John Bale is Professor of Sports Geography at Keele University, England, and Visiting Professor of Sports Studies at Aarhus University, Denmark. He is the author with Joe Sang of *Kenyan Running* (London: 1996).

Mike Cronin is Senior Research Fellow in History at the International Centre for Sports History and Culture at De Montfort University, Leicester, England. He is the author of *Sport and Nationalism in Ireland* (Dublin: 1999), and co-author, with Daryl Adair, of *Wearing the Green: A History of St Patrick's Day* (London: 2002).

Paul Dimeo is Lecturer in Sports Studies at the University of Stirling, Scotland. He is the editor, with James Mills, of *Soccer in South Asia* (London: 2001).

Grant Farred Assistant Professor in Literature at Duke University, USA. He is the author of *Midfielder's Moment: Coloured Literature and Culture in Contemporary South Africa* (Boulder: 1999) and the editor of *Rethinking CLR James* (Oxford: 1995).

Roy Hay is Senior Lecturer in History, Economic and Social Studies at Deakin University, Geelong, Australia. He is the author of a series of articles exploring the history of immigrant football in Australia, including 'Croatia: Community, Conflict and Culture: The Role of Soccer Clubs in Migrant Identity', in Mike Cronin and David Mayall (eds), *Sporting Nationalisms: Identity, Ethnicity, Immigration and Assimilation* (London: 1998).

Dong-Jhy Hwang is a postgraduate student at Stirling University, Scotland, and is researching into the area of sport and social development in China. He is currently the holder of the Taiwan Government International Doctoral Scholarship.

Greg Gardiner is based at the Parliamentary Library in the Victorian Parliament, Melbourne, Australia. He is the author of a series of reports exploring social issues and the Indigenous population in Australia, which include *Criminal Justice and Indigenous Victorians in the 1990s: Review and Analysis of Police Data* (Melbourne: 2001).

Grant Jarvie is Professor of Sports Studies at Stirling University, Scotland. He is the editor of *Sport in the Making of Celtic Cultures* (Leicester: 1999) and author of 'Sport, the émigré and a dance called America' in *Sports History Review* (2000).

Malcolm MacLean is Lecturer in Sport and Social Sciences at Cheltenham and Gloucester College of Higher Education, Cheltenham, England. He is the author of 'Of Warriors and Blokes: The Problem of Maori Rugby for Pakeha Masculinity in New Zealand' in Timothy Chandler and John Nauright (eds), *Making The Rugby World: Race, Gender, Commerce* (London: 2001).

James Mills is a lecturer in History at the University of Strathclyde and is the author of *Madness, Cannabis and Colonialism* (London: 2000).

Daryle Rigney is a lecturer in the Yunggorendi First Nations Centre for Higher Education and Research, at Flinders University of South Australia, Adelaide, Australia, and the author of 'Racialising Struggle: Indigenous Australians and the Sydney 2000 Olympics', in Susan Bandy *et al.* (eds), *Proceedings of the 6th Congress of the International Society for the History of Physical Education and Sport (ISHPES)* (forthcoming).

John Sugden is Reader and Deputy Head of Chelsea School at the University of Brighton, England. He is the author of *Boxing and Society* (Manchester: 1996) and, with Alan Tomlinson, *FIFA and the Contest for World Football* (Oxford: 1998).

Alan Tomlinson is Head of the Chelsea School at the University of Brighton, England. He is the author, with John Sugden, of *Great Balls of Fire* (Edinburgh: 1999), and with John Horne and Gary Whannel of *Understanding Sport* (London: 1999).

Jack Williams is Senior Lecturer in History at Liverpool John Moores University, England and the author of *Cricket and Race* (Oxford: 2001) and *Cricket and England* (London: 1999).

Bea Vidacs is a researcher at the Graduate Center of the City University of New York.

Introduction: Sport and Postcolonialism

John Bale and Mike Cronin

In 2001 a major Bollywood film, *Lagaan,* was released to much critical acclaim. The film was one the most expensive Indian films ever, and uniquely featured a large non-Indian cast. The film was set in an Indian village during the period of the Raj, and centred on the relationship between the locals and their colonial neighbours. In an attempt to settle a dispute between the two groups, the locals agree to play the British garrison at cricket – a game that none of the Indians have ever previously played. The film is illustrative of many of the themes that are central to this collection of essays, that is the relationship between post-colonial peoples and sport. For the villagers in *Lagaan* the cricket match gave them an opportunity to defeat the local representatives of their colonial over-lords. Such an opportunity to express the strengths of the local over the colonial was afforded by the shared space of a colonial game, in this instance, cricket. In the same way that postcolonial writers have used the language of the colonial to express themselves, so postcolonial sportsmen and women have largely used the bodily and sporting practices of the colonial in a similar fashion.

Postcolonialism can be regarded as one of a number of 'posts' that have assailed writers in a variety of disciplines in recent years. Initially the preserve of literary theorists, this particular 'post-' is now being embraced by scholars who – according to one observer – can hardly avoid doing so if they are 'not to lose out on their share of the spoils of the most exciting and innovative realms of contemporary theory' (Barnett 1995: 417). The size and scope of the scholarly output that has accompanied postcolonial studies is evident from the recent publication of a five-volume anthology of postcolonial writings (Brydon 2000). Despite the vast literature that accompanies and has analysed postcolonialism, there is little in this that has focused on the role of sport within the postcolonial. Brydon's five-volume collection is dominated, perhaps understandably, by considerations of theoretical and literary approaches to postcolonialism. The fifth volume contains a section headed 'Postcolonial Theory and the Disciplines', which looks beyond the canon of postcolonial literature, and embraces studies of film, music, gender, cinema, science and technology studies, and yet over-looks bodily practices such as sport. The absence of sport, one of the most globalized and commonly shared forms of human activity, from such an anthology of postcolonialism is a lacuna that this collection seeks to address. It appears that postcolonial theory has been dominated by a consideration of literature, an essentially subjective form that can be highly individual, placeless and contrived. Sport and bodily practices offer a potentially more fruitful vehicle for considering postcolonialism than literature, as they are mass hap-penings made 'real' through performance. This is not to say, however, that writers adopting a postcolonial perspective have totally avoided questions related to sports. Several references to the black athlete were made by Frantz Fanon (1986), and more recently allusions to cricket form central themes in the writing of, for example, Ian Baucom (1996) and Simon Gikandi (1996). Having said that, the allusions of these writers to sport, while proving useful insights, are marginal to broader objectives.[1]

Whereas postcolonial approaches and theory have had only a limited impact on sports studies, sport and postcolonialism share one vital theme in common – the body. The body is central to the study of sports, and it has been far from marginal in postcolonial discourse and analysis. David Spurr's *The Rhetoric of Empire* (1993: 22) stresses how, in colonial discourse 'the body of the primitive' was the major sign by which (s)he was represented. He observes that 'the body, rather than speech, law or history, is the essential defining characteristic of primitive people'. Nicholas Mirzoeff avers that the body of 'the African' has been rendered as 'visibly' different, confirming the perfection of the Western subject by '*this self-evident* difference of race' (Mirzoeff 1995: 3). And, as Mary Louise Pratt suggests, many descriptions in travel writing have traditionally been those of 'manners and customs', which *begin* with 'the body as seen/scene' (Pratt 1986: 239). From such representations of individuals it is a short step to fitting them into body-classes or groups and to ending up with stereotypes. This is especially appropriate in the context of sports, since physique was a partic-ularly important theme in the European construction of the athleticism of various groups of people in the colonized world. Contrasting groups such as travel writers and sports scientists were surely well aware of the significance of the African body for their respective readers. *The National Geographic* seems to have been a willing provider of bare-breasted African women for the great American male public – for entirely 'educational' reasons, of course. And in the body of the African male the sports physiologists and anthropologists antic-ipated the 'supposedly scientific ideas about the super normal physiologies of African athletes that haunt white athletes around the world today' (Hoberman 1997: 103).[2] It is the kinds of textual practices of colonial discourse that were marked by physicalities and performances whose recovery and re-reading should be central to any critical enquiry (Gregory 1994: 453). In the light of such advocacy it would seem fanciful, therefore, to suggest that 'there is no such thing as "the post-colonial body"'(Ashcroft, Griffths and Tiffin 1998: 183).

In this introductory chapter we seek to introduce approaches to the study of the sportized body from a postcolonial perspective. Like postmodernism – with which it shares several characteristics (such as opposition to master narrative; a concern with 'representation', a tendency towards relativism) – postcolonialism can be looked at in three ways. These are reflected in the structure of this chapter. First, we want to consider briefly postcolonialism as an epoch or time-period. Secondly, we look at what postcolonial sport might be – the postcolonial as content. Thirdly, we will make some introductory comments on postcolonial method in connection with sports. Finally we will exemplify a 'postcolonial approach' with reference to the contents of this book. Each of these may be dealt with in turn.

Postcolonialism and Sport – When?

Postcolonial sport could be said to have arrived when the first 'Third World' sports workers arrived in 'First World Sport' (Dirlik 1994). This, however, is only one way of arriving at the point when sport could be said to have experienced postcolonialism. A case could be made for going back to before the eighteenth century; but most works espousing a postcolonial approach deal with the period of colonization and imperialism during the nineteenth century. Postcolonial, literally, means 'after colonialism'. But studies taking in the period from the start of colonialism in a particular place are commonly found also. Sports were part of the colonizing process, and have remained in most colonized countries following independence. Given the presence of neo-colonial relationships, however, there is clearly no unambiguous division between colonialism and postcolonialism, and it can be argued that postcolonialism is something that has yet to be achieved, that it is, indeed, a scenario for the future (Quayson 2000). Indeed, the international governing bodies of sports are often still intent on a colonizing mission. For example, the International Association of Athletics Federations – one of the major governing bodies in world sport – seeks to promote in its member countries (which number 209) an 'athletics culture' that is an 'environment in which athletics must grow and develop. Every member federation must see that the athletics culture in its country is broadly based and as strong as possible.'[3] For this reason, it can be argued that it is the challenges to the present and the future that are most important in postcolonial studies.

In attempting to understand the present and future impact of postcolonialism, Stuart Hall, writing in 1996, argued that one of the biggest challenges for postcolonial theorists was their inability to conceive when 'postcolonial' was, how far the scope of its investigations and application should reach, and its problematic lack of engagement with the world of global capitalism (Hall 1996). Hall's arguments have great implications for our consideration of 'When'. Chronologically, what should we consider as postcolonial in relation to sport? Is sport and bodily practice an acceptable location for an interrogation of the concept of postcolonialism? As many international governing bodies of sport and the top performers are agents of global capitalism, how do we meet the challenge of understanding this role within the context of postcolonialism (Dirlik 1992)?

Postcolonialism and Sport – What?

On the basis of work by Bill Ashcroft and his associates (1998) in literary studies it is possible, we suggest, to consider seven types of postcolonial sports or sportoid forms. These are:

1. Pre-colonial body cultures that survived colonialism (for varying periods of time) and were never sportized – e.g. Rwandan 'high jumping'.
2. Indigenous body-cultures that were transformed into modern sports – e.g. lacrosse.
3. Body-cultures that were 'invented' by a former colony – baseball and basketball in the USA, for example.
4. Colonial sports that were modified by former colonies into distinctly 'national sports' – e.g. Gaelic and Australian football.
5. Sports that have been diffused by Empire and adopted, without rule changes, in colonized countries – e.g. soccer, cricket.
6. Sports initially introduced during colonization but that have (been said to have) adopted 'regional styles' of their own – e.g. Brazilian soccer; Kenyan running.
7. Hybrid sportoids – e.g. Trobriand cricket.

From a macro-perspective we could argue that sport *per se* is an eminently postcolonial phenomenon. After all, consider the composition of the British track and field team; observe the make-up of many Premiership football teams. Think about the presence of sports workers who are colonial extractions – and, following Quayson, we use the term 'extraction' advisedly – who, themselves or their forebears, have been extracted from somewhere before becoming British (Quayson 2000: 177). Consider also the origins of sports in some of the most successful sporting nations in the world. Kenya, the Caribbean and Cameroon owe their present-day sporting traditions to the implanting of modern sports by colonialists. Their sporting practices are, literally, post-colonial. While modern sports may serve to promote the modern postcolonial state, they initially served as a form of colonial social control. Colonialists were far from coy in acknowledging such strategies. 'A game of football in the afternoon', wrote one British missionary in Kenya, 'was played for moral benefit as much as recreational relief, . . . to stiffen the backbone of these boys by teaching them manliness, good temper and unselfishness – qualities amongst others that have done much to make them a Britisher' (Bale and Sang 1996: 77). It is clear that sport was part of the 'civilizing' mission of imperialism, and thus an essential part of the colonial experiment. Sport in its many forms is thus a legacy of colonization; yet because of the common need for sporting forms to have shared rules, governing bodies and international federations, the ways in which sport can be transformed to represent the postcolonial are in many ways actually quite limited. Therefore, while we look to national or regional playing styles as indicative of postcolonial sporting and bodily practice, we have to be wary that such forms are played out under the rules of international sporting bodies and in the context of a global sports business that both remain symbolic power structures indicative of a continuing informal imperialism.

In recent decades, postcolonial sport has been seen as a form of resistance – by colonies or post-/neo-colonies. A categorization based on ideas in *Post-Colonial Drama* by Helen Gilbert and Joanne Tompkins and based on the notion of performance suggests that a specifically postcolonial sport (performance) might involve:

1.   Dramatic body language;
2.   The arrangement of the sport's space and time;
3.   The manipulation of the conventions of sports.

Implicit in each of these is postcolonialism as resistance. It is worth speculating about the extent to which a distinctive body language reflects resistance. The extent to which the sportized body can deviate from a specialized standard is questionable. The same applies to the time and space of sports events. These are usually highly prescribed by rules and regulations, and for many sports they have to be identical, irrespective of global location. Vernacular architecture may exist; but this is beyond the actual confines of the field or track. It is in the third category, the manipulation of the conventions of sports, that seems most congruent with ideas of resistance. 'Conventions of sport' extend beyond the immediate site. So, for example, the black power salute at Mexico City in 1968 could be seen as such a contravention of convention. But to be unconventional during a sports event invites the risk of defeat. Game plans have to be adhered to. The Colombian goalkeeper's spectacular ('Latin'?) clearance with his feet behind his head could only take place because the opposing player was offside when he took the shot. Perhaps the sports arena can be thought of as a container of resistance rather than a focus for it; perhaps resistance and political action can more readily take place 'beyond the boundary'.

What might often appear to be resistance may be more akin to transgression – that is, being 'out of place'. The first Kenyan long-distance runners were 'out of place' because blacks were supposed to be sprinters. Likewise, the case of the early victories of the West Indian Cricket teams. Yet these victories are often hailed as forms of resistance by such different writers as C.L.R. James (1994) and Allen Klein (1991).

Sport and Postcolonialism – How?

A central theme of postcolonial methodology derives from the so-called crisis of representation, which is regarded as common to most disciplines in the social sciences and humanities. Representation, via the written word, has been crucial in colonial 'constructions' of the colonized athlete. Using a variety of texts John Hoberman has shown the way in which expectations were set up in the occident as a result of the colonial rhetorics communicated to it (Hoberman 1997). This is not to say, however, that there was a monolithic colonial gaze. Far from it. There were conflicting rhetorics, as the final part of this paper will demonstrate.

'Representation' is a key theme in both postmodernism and postcolonialism. It is a word that has multiple meanings and can be viewed as (a) interpretation, (b) communication, (c) visualization, (d) translation and (e) advocacy (James, Hockey and Dawson 1997). Representation is commonly undertaken via the written word. Traditionally, in most disciplines, language was thought to say what things meant and was thought to be unproblematic; it was considered to be transparent. This view reflected a form of naïve realism or, as Michael Curry puts it, 'traditional common sense' (Curry 1996). It is now widely felt that the claim of representation (or re-presentation) is disputable and simply cannot be taken for granted. It is also recognized that representations do not equate with simply re-presenting some original 'reality'. It is not about 'making copies', but is something that is always constructed by an observer (Gren 1994). What, for example, did 'sport' mean in colonial writing? A reaction against naive realism has resulted in the recognition that representations carry many meanings – Curry's 'new common sense'.

In recognizing that one's language limited one's world, writers have been 'driven by a desire for the words they do not possess [and] how conventional language did not furnish the words they most urgently wanted to express' (Olsson 1991: 174). Responses have included the destabilization of representation and engaging in the creation of Joycean neologisms and 'dazzling wor(l)dplay' (Gregory 1994: 73). It is not necessary, however, to play with linguistic conventions, and one can limit oneself to showing how the problem of an accurate and unambiguous form of representation can be exemplified by the deconstruction (meaning the way in which the instability of meaning in a text is revealed) of written and photographic 'texts'. According to this view, all representations can be said to be deformations, in the sense that all words or pictures are metaphors; they cannot be the same as the things they represent. This becomes particularly important in the exploring the ways in which colonists recorded and represented the native body cultures that they so often encountered in colonized regions.

In the context of sports and body cultures, postcolonial method can be seen as:

1. emphasizing aspects of colonial relations between the colonizer and the colonized;
2. providing alternative readings of conventional colonial wisdoms and dominant meanings;
3. showing a concern, through so-called 'postcolonial theory', with the re-writing of colonial texts;
4. displaying awareness of resistance to colonization in texts written during and after the generally accepted period of colonialism;
5. showing a willingness to seek out 'the density, contradiction and ambiguity of colonial discourses' (S. Ryan 1996: 15). 'Colonial discourse' can be said to 'refer to that collection of symbolic practices, including textual codes and conventions of implied meanings, which Europe deployed in the process of its colonial expansion and, in particular, in understanding the bizarre and apparently unintelligible strangenesses with which it came into contact' (Boehmer 1995: 50).

Among the iconic figures in postcolonial studies are Homi Bhabha, Gayatri Spivak and Edward Said. The work of each of these scholars has relevance to sport; but they barely touch on it in their work. Bhabha's notions of 'hybridity' and 'mimicry' have clear sporting applications, as do Spivak's concern with letting the subaltern speak – i.e. finding a voice for the colonized other in relation to sport. The ideas in Edward Said's (1995) almost canonized *Orientalism* can clearly be applied to sports.[4] By 'orientalism' Said means a Western style that makes statements about the orient (and, it could be added, other colonized regions), authorizing views of it, describing it by teaching it, speaking for it – in short, re-presenting the colonized world in a style suitable for dominating, restructuring and having authority over it (Said 1995: 3).[5] In recent years it has been widely recognized that dominance over the colonial world can come from writing and photography as much as from settling and ruling over it. Hence, texts can make worlds (often stating what they *ought* to be, rather than what they are) as much as representing them (Barnes and Gregory 1997: 138). This could lead to an agenda for a postcolonial study of sports that might include:

- the unveiling of the complicity of sport in the colonial domination;
- considering the possibility and potential of sport as a form of (neo-)colonial resistance;
- the examination of the nature of the representation of sport in colonial discourse, including an interrogation of the practices of authors, photographers and others engaged in colonial representation;
- the de-linking of sport from metropolitan theory and its totalizing systems of generalizations; and
- the recovery of the hidden spaces occupied, and invested with their own meaning, by the colonial and postcolonial body-cultural practices (Crush 1994).

The chapters that follow begin to explore these and other areas of the sport-postcolonialism nexus.

The Pattern of the Book

The chapters making up this book explore sports in several continental contexts. We have chosen to order them in regionally-based groupings. The first four chapters focus on Oceania, the next three on Asia, and the next two on Africa. The final two chapters look at aspects of sport in Ireland and sport on the global scale. There is only so much that a collection like this can cover. Geographically, the collection omits any consideration of Central and South American countries, and these areas offer fruitful and fascinating ground for future researchers. The essays also overlook, as much writing on sport unfortunately does, the question of gender and the role of women within the sport and postcolonial nexus. This was a topic that had featured, and was discussed at the conference that gave life to the book; but unfortunately it could not appear here owing to the speaker's other commitments. The exclusion of gender, and its place within the bodily and sportive practices of the postcolonial paradigm, is unfortunate, and an omission for which we can be criticized. That said, we offer the question of gender, and the issues that it raises, as another vehicle through which this text can be read, and trust that fellow scholars, thus inspired, will tackle the gender, sport and postcolonialism debate in future work.

The first chapter, by Roy Hay, builds on the editors' introduction by raising a number of 'postcolonial questions' in the context of Australia. Hay notes that Australia has both invented its own 'traditional' sport (i.e. 'Aussie rules' football) and has also successfully adopted the sports of the imperial power in the form of cricket and football (soccer, league and union). He draws some interesting distinctions between the invention of Gaelic football in Ireland and Australian Rules football. Significantly, he also alludes to the internal colonization by Australians of aboriginal land and indigenous body cultures. Hay's observations on sport and indigenous peoples leads neatly into Chapter 2 by Greg Gardner, who draws attention to the fact that indigenous Australians grow up in historical contexts of racism both inside and outside sports. The paradox remains, however, that sport has provided a rare avenue of participation, opportunity and success in mainstream culture. This comes at a cost, however – that of racial abuse. Following an insightful exploration of racial abuse in sports, Gardner focuses on sporting participation as a form of resistance, pointing to the iconographic significance of the Australian Rules football players Neil Winmer and Michael Long, each subjected to racial abuse on the field of 'play'. The chapter proceeds to examine the role of legislation in countering such abuse, recognizing the problematic nature of discourses of reconciliation and the ambivalent nature of reconciliation itself. Daryle Rigney (Chapter 3) examines more broadly the issues surrounding the indigenous peoples in Australia and their relationship with sport. Rigney demonstrates that sport, despite the many positive attributes that it is often given credit for possessing, has actually been a tool in the oppression of Australia's indigenous people. This chapter allows the exploration of sporting forms, practices and structures from the perspective of those who were the colonized, and who have, in recent decades, sought to empower themselves by critically assessing the legacy of colonization. This process, which is essentially an anticolonial exercise, has led to a broader requestioning of Australian history, and sport forms one part of this. The complexity for the indigenous population, as Rigney makes clear, is whether sport, as a legacy of colonization, should be rejected or used as part of the exercise of empowerment. Essentially, is the postcolonial process about the rejection of all colonial legacies, or is it the reshaping of colonial forms so that they are acceptable to colonizers and colonized alike?

Chapter 4 shifts attention from Australia to New Zealand. Malcolm Maclean, in a spatial approach inspired, in large part, by Edward Soja, and Henri Lefebvre, focuses on the 1981 South African rugby tour of New Zealand, drawing on a number of spatial metaphors, ranging from global to local, to inform his work. The distinction between rural and urban areas as loci of resistance to the tour is especially emphasized. Support for the tour was manifest in rural areas, where rugby is read as a form of cultural support for a threatened way of life. The anti-tour demonstrations in small, rural places were seen by the rural white population as yet another threat (along with native land rights and other government policies), especially given their accentuation of 'race'.

In Chapter 5 Dong-Jhy Hwang and Grant Jarvie take China as an example of a postcolonial state and undertake two fascinating readings of written texts on the history of Chinese sport. The authors initially explain why China can be seen as a subject for postcolonial analysis before proceeding to review premodern body cultures. The crucial part of the chapter involves readings of, first, *Sport in China* by Gu Shiquan, and secondly, Susan Brownell's ethnographic study *Training the Body for China*. In the former work, Hwang and Jarvie argue, Chinese 'sports' are represented as an example of official Chinese orthodoxy, playing down mass sports. Brownell's work is said to present an orientalist perspective that, in the authors' view, comes close to Said's notion of the Western inscription of mythologized views on the colonized. In other words, the authors focus explicitly on the problem of the writing of Chinese sport, both by (literal) outsiders and by a Chinese author whom they see as applauding the acceptance of Western sport as an agent of harmonization.

Jack Williams (Chapter 6) sets out to explore the postcolonial tensions that were evident in the cricket matches between England and Pakistan during the 1980s and 1990s. Although not providing the grand sporting stage of an Ashes series against Australia, the England–Pakistan matches offered the starkest illustrations of how the English coped, in the sporting environment at least, with the challenges of postcolonialism. The process was played out, as illustrated by Williams, in the pages of the British and Pakistani press, and against the backdrop of a large Pakistani population resident in England. Pakistan, as the 'other' on the field of play, were vociferously supported by a large crowd that, while British by birth or residency, supported the 'other' on the 'home' grounds. Williams uses the various scandals surrounding allegations of cheating to illustrate his chapter – scandals that were fuelled by mutually antagonistic postcolonial attitudes from the former colonizers and colonized. In examining the contemporary arena of international cricket administration, Williams is able to demonstrate, by means similar to those used in the later chapter of Sugden and Tomlinson, that the arrival of the colonized as an increasingly powerful player within the committee rooms and around the board tables of sport has raised fundamental questions about the collapse of the colonial management of sport in the postcolonial world.

In Chapter 7, James Mills and Paul Dimeo examine the place of sport and bodily practice in colonial and postcolonial India. They offer a considered appreciation of the existing available literature that relates to the body and Indian sport, and argue that while there is much of value, the available work is incomplete and lacking analysis of the colonial and postcolonial themes. In focusing on the game of football in India during its early decades, Mills and Dimeo argue that sport was originally a tool of colonization. Through football (and other sports), the British sought to transform the Indian body into a useful tool of Empire. By exploring the Indian reception and adoption of football, Mills and Dimeo succinctly demonstrate that the game, rather than being solely an agent of colonization, actually became a vehicle for resistance by the colonized, and eventually became a symbol of postcolonialism.

In Chapter 8, Grant Farred explores the embrace of football by black South Africans during the period of apartheid. He demonstrates that the Afrikaner government had dismissed football – itself an act of postcolonial defiance, as they believed the game was a marker of Britishness. Such a shunning of the world's most popular game allowed it to be wholly subsumed into the lives of the disenfranchised black population. The chapter argues that there was a linkage between the South African township footballers, in the last two decades of apartheid, and English football. The particular focus of the chapter, the Cape Flats townships, offers a window on the process whereby the resistance of the black African was afforded a means to mimic the footballers of the English industrial city. Such mimicry was in part a resistance to apartheid, in that it allowed teams to claim their own space and identity in a system that sought to deny them, and in part a product of postcolonial hybridity. The various themes uncovered in the townships of South Africa are revisited on the national scale in the next chapter.

The subject of Chapter 9 by Bea Vidacs is Cameroonian football. She specifically focuses on the way the postcolonial condition is experienced by Cameroonians. The chapter explores the Cameroonian view of their nation's involvement in the World Cup in soccer in 1998. This is a careful ethnographic study of the events following the game that led Cameroon to be eliminated from the competition and therefore to fail to find the opportunity to compete against France, the former colonial master. Such a prospect had been highly anticipated in Cameroon. The match that was seen as deciding Cameroon's fate was their game against Chile. As a result of obtaining a 1–1 draw the Cameroon team failed to progress to the next round. Blame for the elimination was placed squarely at the door of the white referee who had handled the Chile game. Riots and pandemonium occurred in Cameroon following the result. 'White racism' was blamed. Vidacs concludes her study by reading the Cameroonian discourse as one that recognizes that the 'ideal' world of football – the level playing-field – is a myth. Cameroonians had been temporarily duped, and the 1–1 draw served to remind them of the 'reality' of global power relations.

In Chapter 10, Alan Bairner assesses the role of sport in defining and shaping ideas about colonialism and postcolonialism in Ireland. As he demonstrates, there has been a wealth of publications, many in the fields of literature and politics, that have attempted to define whether or not Ireland has reached the stage of postcolonialism. Bairner uses the accompanying literature that has analysed sport in Ireland, most notably those works that explore the sports of Gaelic games and soccer. Bairner is careful to distinguish between concepts of Irish nationalism and identity as posited by residents of the Irish Republic, and those still agonized over by the inhabitants of Northern Ireland. The chapter illustrates the complexity of postcolonial ideas and theories when applied to contested regions such as Northern Ireland, and the often problematic stances taken by sporting bodies such as the Gaelic Athletic Association or the Irish Football Association. While his study is essentially one that operates at a regional level, and in the context of Irish sport, Bairner's focus on the part played in the postcolonial power struggle by sporting organizations does much to illuminate themes that emerge at the global level in the study of FIFA in the final chapter.

In the final chapter, John Sugden and Alan Tomlinson examine the role of football, in the shape of its governing body FIFA, both in promoting an imperialist or colonial standpoint and yet also simultaneously allowing for colonial resistance or the advancement of postcolonialism by non-Western footballing nations. While many of the other chapters in this collection do examine the role of sporting governing bodies in the postcolonial debate, they are predominantly national studies. Sugden and Tomlinson offer an analysis of an international governing body – one of the most powerful in the world – and in doing so open up a whole new area in the study of sport and post-colonialism. With such global power FIFA has the potential to support existing hegemonic and colonial power structures, that is, to support the West (most notably the European footballing nations), yet has, in recent years, increasingly functioned as an arena within which non-Western nations can forge a post-colonial future for world football. The work of Sugden and Tomlinson offers a window for future studies of postcolonialism in sport that transcends the national, and explores the historical and contemporary agents of imperialism and postcoloniality. Such an approach, will, it should be hoped, be applied to the International Olympic Committee and other global governing bodies.

In its entirety this collection offers a fresh, and it can be argued, a unique way of analysing the sporting world. While studies of postcolonialism have formed a dominant strand in recent years in literary studies, such theories have not been applied to sport – an arena of bodily practice that offers a wealth of national, global and chronological case studies and approaches. We hope that the material offered here will serve as an intellectual catalyst for new ways of thinking about sport specifically, and the history of imperialism and post-colonialism generally.

Notes

1. See, however, the special issue on Sport of the journal of postcolonial writing, *Kunapipi*, 23, 1, 2001.
2. Hoberman is principally referring here to the prominence of East African middle- and long-distance runners and of African-American and West African sprinters.
3. IAAF Development Strategy (http://www.iaaf.org/iaaf/dev.html).
4. In their embrace of postcolonial studies, scholars from a variety of disciplines may have been 'busy grabbing their share of colonial guilt'; they can hardly avoid doing so if they are 'not to lose out on their share of the spoils of the most exciting and innovative realms of contemporary theory': Barnett, 'Awakening the dead', p. 418. On the interconnections between postcolonialism, postmodernism, literary studies and anthropology see Gregory, (1994: 134–5). In that both postmodernism and postcolonialism 'refuse to turn the Other into the same' they can be said to be clearly allied: see During, 'Postmodernism or post-colonialism today', p. 125.
5. Prior to Said's usage of the term, 'orientalism' rarely carried any negative connot-ations: (Mackenzie 1995). The same applies to 'Africanism', which, in the usage adopted here, should be distinguished from its use by pan-African political movements that have sought to decolonize the continent.

1

The Last Night of the Poms: Australia as a Postcolonial Sporting Society?[1]

Roy Hay

What would it mean to describe Australia as a postcolonial sporting society? Where does Australia fit into the definitions of postcolonialism, if at all? There is nothing in Australian sporting history to match the denunciation of English sporting influence attributed to Croke of Cashel when he accepted the patronage of the Gaelic Athletic Association (see below), yet Australians have seldom seen themselves as simply and solely the British overseas. From Australian Rules Football as 'a game of our own' to the 'bodyline' tour and beyond Australians have always had an ambivalent relationship with the sporting metropolis, and this has developed further as United States influence has grown in the twentieth century. There are also questions of internal colonialism and postcolonialism, affecting Aboriginal Australians and ethnic minorities. A study of the evolution of Australian sport in the imperial and post-imperial context raises a host of empirical and theoretical issues about the notion of postcolonialism, and this chapter explores some of them.

Postcolonialism in Theory

Jane Jacobs, in her *Uncanny Australia*, argues that postcolonialism refers not to the state of being after colonialism, but to the processes by which we might reach that state (Gelder and Jacobs 1998). What would a postcolonial state look like? It would be tolerant of cultural diversity, non-exploitative, accepting of difference, not imposing any hegemonic influences. This is, of course, utopian, unhistorical and perhaps better left to the moral philosophers. When you contemplate the real Australia, if such a thing exists in a post-modern world, and if not, when you contemplate the various cultural constructs of Australia, do you celebrate or despair? The claim, for example, that multiculturalism has been a success in Australia in helping to forge a 'nation without nationalism' remains controversial (Castles, Kalantzis, Cope and Morrissey 1990). In 2001 Australia retains constitutional allegiance to the Queen, and the process of reconciliation with the indigenous population remains incomplete.

In the 1960s and 1970s there was considerable interest in the phenomenon of imperialism and the processes by which European hegemony was extended over most parts of the globe in the nineteenth century. Though Richard Koebner (Koebner and Schmidt 1964) argued 'imperialism was no word for scholars', partly because of the multiplicity of different uses of the word, he was also implying that the word had been so sullied by its political and ideological involvement that it had ceased to have any validity in scholarly usage. Not long after arriving at Deakin University in 1977, when we were preparing a course entitled *Imperialism: The Expansion of Europe,* I remember being asked by my Dean, Professor Francis West, 'Why do you want to bother with theories of imperialism, why don't we just tell the students what really happened?' It all seems a long time ago and a very different world. One of my students this year queried the absence of any independence movement in Australia in the aftermath of the Second World War, when the rest of the colonial empire was seeking to throw off the British yoke. One answer of course might be that Australia was to all intents liberated already, though the cultural cringe and the unwillingness to contemplate a republic might suggest otherwise.

Nowadays, with decolonization almost complete around the world, at least in the formal political sense, there is enormous interest in the legacy, for good and ill, of that period of human history that stretches from the latter part of the nineteenth century to the early 1990s, when the powers of Europe dominated the globe. The interest lies not just in 'facts' of history but in their interpretation and the kinds of relationship that are expressed in their analysis. Postcolonial theory has arisen as an umbrella term for a range of perspectives on the social processes of decolonization and its aftermath. As with imperialism, the term or terms have many meanings, with or without the hyphen. The formulation 'post-colonial' with the hyphen is sometimes interpreted differently from the word 'postcolonial' lacking the hyphen. According to that estimable little book by Bill Ashcroft, Gareth Griffiths and Helen Tiffin, *Key Concepts in Post-colonial Studies* (1998: 187): 'The heavily post-structuralist influence of the major exponents of colonial discourse theory, Edward Said (Foucault), Homi Bhabha (Althusser and Lacan) and Gayatri Spivak (Derrida), led many critics, concerned to focus on the material effects of the historical condition of colonialism, as well as on its discursive power, to insist on the hyphen to distinguish postcolonial studies *as a field* from colonial discourse theory *per se*, which formed only one aspect of the many approaches and interests that the term post-colonial sought to embrace and discuss.'

According to Dane Kennedy (1996: 346), 'Colonial discourse analysis refers to the examination and interpretation of particular colonial texts. Post-colonial theory refers to the political and ideological position of the critic who undertakes this analysis.' Postcolonial investigation began as a branch of literary studies, the literatures of the postcolonial societies. It was interested in the ways these were received, translated and interpreted in metropolitan centres. It was argued that this process emasculated and transformed the literatures, softening the oppositional elements and interpreting them according to Western capitalistic models. Or it essentialized the categories involved, such as the postcolonial societies, the third world, postcolonial women, and third world feminisms, treating as homogeneous groups who were distinct, and who had specific and unique histories and experiences (Mohanty 1991).

If the argument is that language is critical – that categories and relationships are constructed in language and specific discourses and have no meaning beyond those constructions – what are the implications of this methodological claim? Are the references then entirely internal, and is this formulation ultimately solipsistic? Or, as Edward Said argued, did 'orientalism' emerge as a means of controlling the peoples of the exterior world in the interests of the metropolitan centres. If so, the study must be historical and political and concerned with the relationships between theory and some other forms of material existence. Either way, is it the case, as Mongia (1996: 5) suggests, that 'The burden of post-colonial theory therefore is the burden of western philosophy, a rethinking of the very categories by which knowledge has been constructed?'

'Language is the key to emancipation from post-colonial modes of thought' (Kennedy 1996: 349). Does this mean inevitable exclusion for those who wish to maintain some form of indigenous discourse, assuming that this exists any more outside a postcolonial embrace? As the anthropologist Malcolm Crick puts it:

> Is culture a collective heritage from the past or merely a stage for contemporary conflicts about power and meaning? Do people actually have 'cultures', or are such substantivised entities merely the figments of anthropological imaginations or the reified by-products of historical encounters which produced ideological shadows which do not correspond to the substance of belief and behaviour at large? Such problems clearly run deep, but what can be said with confidence is that it is no longer possible for anyone to assert convincingly any pure or authentic cultural identity for the reason that there are no insular peoples or societies which have managed to escape the historical processes of, or contemporary expressions of, global entanglement. We are all mongrels now; we are all the products of a multiplicity of complex cultural influences; it is this hybridity itself that is the most evident aspect of cultural authenticity for most of us (Geddes and Crick 1994: 104).

The postcolonial critic must be in it to win it. The critic must take on the academy and the imperialists in their own terms, or at least in their own back yard and in their own languages. But then the price is inevitably some greater losses. Sad but inevitable? Or is there another way? Is Bhabha optimistic, with his effort to turn the pathos of cultural confusion into a strategy of political subversion?

If we accept that language is critical and forms of discourse determine patterns of power relationships, then what are we to make of the Australian case, where a common language and many overlapping discourses are shared between the mother country and the colony or postcolonial dominion? Indeed, we need to broaden the focus to include the United States, Ireland (North and South), Scotland, Zimbabwe and Kenya, where English acted as a common language around or out of which many discourses evolved. In all of these the language existed, with the potential for it to be turned back on its colonizing centre much like the concept of the rule of law, which in Edward Thompson's (1977) formulation was used as an instrument of class oppression in the eighteenth century, but which was turned into the basis of liberty of the free-born Englishman in subsequent generations.

Australia and Colonial Sport

Australia is an interesting example, standing at the intersection of first and third worlds. It is an offshoot of European imperial expansion, yet part of that expansion itself, with its own colonies such as Papua New Guinea and its internal colonization of its aboriginal (and there is a key term that we will have to disentangle in a moment) population. Given that sport played a not insignificant part in Australia's colonial relationships with Britain, it would be interesting to tease out how that set of relationships changed in the postcolonial period. At the same time we would be testing some of the versions of postcolonial theory against alternative readings of history (or, if you prefer it) histories.

When in the 1850s Australian Rules Football was invented as a 'game of our own', even though the term may not have been used so early, what was the central cultural reference of the concept of 'our own'? This is a question for the football historians (Blainey, 1990). Was it Australia? How could it be in 1859, when no such entity existed? It was not till 1881 that the editor of the *Footballer* talked about rewriting the book as Australian Rules. Could it be the fledgling colony of Victoria? But the Victorian Football League was a long way in the future, and even the Victorian Football Association did not come into being until 1877; and the focus in 1859 was much narrower. Was it a class-distinguishing moment? The game grew out of the Melbourne Cricket Club, whose membership was coterminous with the social elite, which in Victoria provided the controlling bodies for horseracing and cricket, and, through the Melbourne Club, the business and social life of the metropolis (Lemon 1987).

The game was played in the schools, or at least those schools in Melbourne and Geelong to which the sons of the local bourgeoisie were sent. It was to be a few years before the game spread into the suburbs and was taken up and eventually taken over by a broader community in which the working classes predominated numerically, if not in terms of effective control of the game and its organization. The game took time to be fully distinguished from the other forms of football extant at that time. One hesitates to use a word like 'hybridity' in this context, because it has a very specific meaning in postcolonial studies, meaning that culturally ambivalent space where relationships between the colonized and the colonizer are constructed, according to Homi Bhabha. Yet for a brief moment football did operate in that way in Melbourne and Geelong, before its trajectory carried it into a separate and distinct form that represented an alternative to the other codes of football. The choice was for a robust and distinct form, unique to this area, lacking a historical tradition or a leverage on the other codes. The price of a game of our own had become cultural isolation within a decade. And like the Upas tree, it was to stifle the growth of all other codes of football in Victoria until the 1950s or even the 1990s.

Having said that, football never developed the political dimension that Gaelic versions of the sport adopted quite explicitly from the 1880s onwards (Mandle 1979). There the sport was defined in nationalist terms – by Croke of Cashel, and again at the price of isolation and exclusion from international competition:

> . . . the ugly and irritating fact that we are daily importing from England not only her manufactured goods, which we cannot help doing, since she has practically strangled our own manufacturing appliances, but together with her fashions, her accents, her vicious literature, her music, her dances and her manifold mannerisms, her games also her pastimes, to the utter discredit of our own grand national sports, and to the sore humiliation, as I believe, of every genuine son and daughter of the old land.
>
> Ball playing, hurling, football kicking, according to Irish rules, casting, leaping in various ways, wrestling, handy-grips, top-pegging, leap-frog, rounders, tip-in-the-hat and all such favourite exercises and amusements, amongst men and boys may now be said to be not only dead and buried, but in several localities to be entirely forgotten, unknown . . .
>
> If we continue travelling for the next score years in the same direction that we have been going in for some time past, condemning the sports that were practised by our forefathers, effacing our national features as though we were ashamed of them, and putting on, with England's stuffs and broadcloths, her masher habits and such other effeminate follies as she may recommend, we had better at once, and publicly, abjure our nationality, clap hands for joy at the sight of the Union Jack and put 'England's bloody red' exultantly above the 'green' (quoted in Tierney 1976).

Since then the links with the political tradition have been maintained by a careful oppositional ideological programme outlined in the work of Mike Cronin. Grounds are named after the republican heroes Connolly, Pearce, Croke and so on (Cronin 1999; Davies 1994). There is no hint of this in Australian Rules Football.

But football's trajectory in Australia was not the only sporting one; indeed, it was virtually isolated in that respect. The same society that took football to its heart also embraced cricket, which, as various writers have demonstrated, had some claims to be Australia's national game from the 1880s to the 1970s at least (Cashman 1992). 'An appreciation of sportsmanship is the test for autonomy throughout the Empire. Australia had to defeat England at cricket before she was given a Commonwealth. . . . Australia's successes caused a sentimental mourning for "the Ashes of English cricket," and a form of flannelled crusade was despatched to bring them back again. . . . Sport remains the great unofficial department which permeates the Empire, and costs the nation half as much again as the navy', wrote the Anglo-Irish novelist, wit and raconteur Shane Leslie (1916) early in the twentieth century. Starting from a very low level Australian cricket pulled itself up to the point where it could be competitive with the metropolitan centre. The language here was not of exclusiveness, but of involvement and participation in a transnational project. Sometimes it was subservient, proving that the colonials were worthy of facing up to their masters. But soon it was assertive and triumphalist, but not in any sense separatist. (Haigh 2001) The cricketers were three or five day patriots, not republicans or revolutionaries (Jarvie and Walker 1994). As Alan Bairner puts it in another context in a review of Joseph Bradley's book on the Gaelic Athletic Association in Scotland, 'Beating the enemy, as opposed to simply conforming to its ways, is what Celtic [Glasgow Celtic Football, i.e. Soccer, Club] offers and Gaelic games cannot' (Bairner 1999). And indeed this was to be the model for the majority of Australian sports, including rugby union, league, netball, tennis, and even soccer, though its trajectory diverges somewhat in the 1950s.

It was not till well after the Second World War that the Victorian Football League reinvented an Irish connection, in part because of the superficial and unhistorical similarities in the codes of football, and in part to add an international dimension to a game that totally lacked it. It is true the game was played to a limited extent by Australians overseas. There was an Australian football league in Glasgow at the outbreak of the First World War, and certainly small groups of ex-pats and local aficionados played in England and the United States (Hedgecock 2000). The VFL/AFL also tried to export the game by playing exhibition matches in the United States and England. The game is also shown on a variety of cable television networks overseas, and broadcast by the ABC's international service.

Is there a pattern to all this in the Australian case? Richard Cashman (1995) has proposed a model in which the proselytization of the metropolitan centre is met by acceptance or resistance, following Mandle, but that resistance might take either the form of rejection, replacement or a more subtle infiltration and subversion. So some sports might be taken over as they stand and adopted and copied in Australia as an explicit adoption of British Empire values, leading sometimes, but not necessarily, to participation in these sports against the British in bilateral or multilateral competitions.

A more sophisticated taxonomy of types of body cultures and sports has been noted in this volume's introduction in which seven types of postcolonial sports or sportoid forms are outlined. Most Australian sports fall into category 5, 'Sports that have been diffused by Empire and adopted, without rule changes, in colonized countries'; Australian Rules is in 4, 'Colonial sports that were modified by former colonies into distinctly "national sports"'; and there are a few sports that have developed an identifiably Australian form, or at least method, at elite level, including women's hockey and netball.

Postcolonial Sport in Australia

In the twentieth century the focus of sporting activity changed from Britain to wider international competitions, sometimes, as with the Empire and later Commonwealth Games, the Davis Cup, and hockey and netball tournaments, within a recognizably British orbit, but often outside that in the case of the Olympic Games, where Australia was an accidental but early and consistent participant (Moore 1989). Even in the days of sea transport Australian sports participants were inveterate travellers, taking part in horseraces, boxing matches, pedestrian events, rowing and sculling around the world, in addition to the better-known cricket and rugby tours. In professional running, Australia's Stawell Gift inherited the mantle of Powderhall to become the premier event of its kind; as John Perry put it, quoting a local source, 'Stawell is the Mecca at Easter' (Perry 1993).

Now Australian sports make quite deliberate efforts to establish an international credibility. Australian Rules has, as we noted above, created and rebuilt links with Gaelic football and a hybrid form of the game for irregular international competition. It also made some, largely abortive it must be said, efforts to sell the pure form of the game in American and British markets. The Victorian, later the Australian, Football League under Allen Aylett, Ross Oakley and now Wayne Jackson has studied the National Football League in the USA very closely, borrowing marketing strategies, salary caps and draft systems, and the razzmatazz and hype for Grand Finals, which increasingly resemble mini Super Bowls (Alomes 1999). Rugby League did likewise with an extraordinarily successful campaign using Tina Turner; but more recently the influence has been more nefarious, with the now Americanized Rupert Murdoch's Super-league take-over.

But of the four major United States sports only basketball has established a deep presence among the Australian games. For a while it seemed that basketball would become the number one sport among the young on the back of the Michael Jordan phenomenon; but that bubble has since burst. Luc Longley collected trophies alongside Jordan with the Chicago Bulls, and Andrew Gaze got a championship ring with the San Antonio Spurs in 1999, though he was not activated in the finals series. Baseball is next in line, with the recent purchase of the national league by the returning Australian star Dave Nilsson and the sponsorship or purchase of young Australian talent by major league clubs in the USA. But the sport continues to struggle for recognition or support, and nearly all players are part-time professionals at best. Football and (ice) hockey have their devotees, but remain very minor influences. A couple of Australian Rules Footballers have made reputations in the NFL, most recently kicker Darren Bennett with San Diego, and overtures have been made to the Geelong superboot Ben Graham. A great deal of cant is spoken about the influence of America and globalization on Australian sports in the last years of the millennium (Cashman and Hughes 1998). But it is arguable that indigenous influences have been at least as important, witness the Packer revolution in cricket, the combined influence of Greg Norman and Australian television on golf, and the unsung but highly innovative work of the Special Broadcasting Service (SBS) television channel, especially but not exclusively in soccer and cycling. As has been noted by Kennedy (1996: 353) among others, totalizing or essentializing the West (globalization, or Americanization) is as misleading as totalizing the Orient.

Internal Colonialism

We ought to say something about internal colonialism and sport and the Australian Aborigines. The concept of aboriginality is clearly postcolonial in the Saidian sense. Kennedy refers to the colonial construction of collective identities, the creation of tribe and caste and hence, in our case, Aboriginality (Kennedy 1997: 353). So Aboriginality cannot be taken for granted, and the concept needs to be problematized and presented in the context of power. But what does power mean in this circumstance? What does this imply for post-colonial studies? Is postcolonial theory the ultimate colonizing discipline (Fine 1999)? Aboriginality lumps together very diverse groups, and is very closely bound up with concepts of control and interpretation.

In practice systematic discrimination over two centuries has operated to limit the participation of these groups and individuals in sport in Australia. Yet, as Colin Tatz and Richard Broome among others have demonstrated, members of these groups have triumphed over all cultural, linguistic, political and economic barriers to become exemplars in their fields since the middle of the nineteenth century (Tatz 1995a, b; Broome with Jackomos 1998; Tatz and Tatz 2000). The first Australian cricket tour of England in 1868 was by a team of Aboriginal players drawn from the western districts of Victoria. The star was Johnny Mullagh, leading batsmen and bowler, brilliant fielder and world-class high jumper. After the tour he was for a period a professional cricketer at the MCG. The subsequent history of cricket in Australia indicates that Aboriginal players have never been able to gain a regular place at the highest level. Some historians have attributed this entirely to racial bias, but the recent investigation by Bernard Whimpress, *Passport to Nowhere: Aborigines in Australian Cricket, 1850–1939* has a much more nuanced account (Whimpress 1999). Tatz was not seeking to create Aboriginal sporting heroes, though he did so, but to demonstrate the heroism of the Aboriginal peoples in the face of colonialism, racism, and prejudice and their collective attempts to triumph over such discrimination. What is of course problematic is whether the extraordinary performances of these athletes have been the significant driving force in the attempts to remove some of the grosser forms of that discrimination. Or have the sporting performances been a diversion? Do we need more people like Pastor Doug Nicholls or Charlie Perkins, who signally combined sport and politics, or more of those, like Lionel Rose, Eddie Gilbert, Evonne Goolagong-Cawley or Cathy Freeman, who concentrated on sporting efforts primarily? Or those like Tony Mundine, who devoted his life after boxing to supporting Aboriginal sporting activities at grass-roots level, seeking to create champions as role models. Fascinatingly, his son, after a meteoric career in rugby league, has turned to boxing, where his recent efforts show enormous promise, though whether he can live up to his latest claim that he will eventually be recognized as greater than Bradman remains to be tested. Or should we look to those who eschew sport completely?

Cathy Freeman's triumph in the four hundred metres at the Sydney Olympic Games in 2000 and her lighting of the Olympic flame at the opening ceremony may have been symbolic and possibly ephemeral, but the resonance of both events in Australian indigenous and non-indigenous societies was palpable. For those who are not directly involved in the minutiae of the debates over reconciliation between these groups in Australia the influence of Freeman's two moments in the spotlight probably did more to influence the attitudes of people than any other single episode in recent Australian history. The whole Olympic experience flowed on to the Reconciliation March across the Sydney Harbour Bridge, which isolated the forces surrounding the Prime Minister John Howard, at least at the level of ideology if not yet politically.

In April 2001 Howard, who is self-described as 'cricket tragic', co-hosted a cricket match in Canberra between a Prime Minister's eleven and a team of persons with some Aboriginal linkages backed by the Chair of the Aboriginal and Torres Strait Islander Commission Geoff Clark (Taylor 2001). The captain of the team, the test quick bowler Jason Gillespie, said that he had Aboriginal ancestors on his father's side, but admitted to knowing very little about them or their heritage. The Chair of the Australian Cricket Board, Denis Rogers talked in terms of an apology to indigenous cricketers through the match (McKew 2001). The former test spinner Ashley Mallett thought the match would symbolize an apology to indigenous cricket stars who had missed representative opportunities because of their colour: 'Australian cricket can say sorry through this reconciliation match for those guys not getting an opportunity, and point the way forward for people from now on getting every opportunity' (McKew 2001).

The relationship between Aboriginal anticolonialism and European academic studies has been intriguing. The history and archaeology of John Mulvaney and Rhys Jones, the palaeological economic history of Noel Butlin, and most recently the historical recovery work of Henry Reynolds have been significant with their shifting of the boundaries of political discourse in Australia, leading to Prime Ministerial interventions on the subject of 'black-armband history' (Mulvaney and Golson 1971; Mulvaney and Harcourt 1988; Jones 1985; Butlin 1983). There is little doubt that Reynolds' work has recaptured for blacks as well as whites in Australia a whole dimension of history of struggle and open warfare (Reynolds 1991; L. Ryan 2001).

Australian implicit colonization is not restricted to its Aboriginal population. Imperial attitudes die hard. Jack Williams demonstrates in this volume the English equivalent in his study of English and Pakistan cricket relations, which he thought of calling 'The umpire on which the sun never sets', but didn't, more's the pity. Australians can be very 'colonial' in their dealings with the various nations that make up the sub-continent in particular. The erstwhile Sri Lankan captain Arjuna Ranatunga is described as having 'unrivalled capacity to get under Western skins'; and 'the autocratic Sri Lankan captain who lifted the World Cup three years ago at Gaddafi Stadium in Lahore, is the master agent provocateur' (Blake 1999). Recent experiences of the Australian cricket team in Sri Lanka and India may produce a little more humility and perhaps respect. Perhaps.

The reactions to the death of Sir Donald Bradman have been intriguing. Widely mourned or celebrated in Australia and India, where he never played, Bradman's passing was noted in England. Michael Parkinson, who never managed an interview, only repeated a six-year-old piece on the Don's death.

In this chapter there is no discussion of ethnic minorities in Australia or about the history of soccer, for the author's views on these are fairly well known and can be found elsewhere (Hay 1994; Hay 1998). There is also nothing about issues of gender, though these are often central in the debates about postcolonialism, and to that extent a study that lacks such a focus may be inadequate (Ganter 1999; Burton 2001). Instead, two historical episodes are re-examined in the context of postcolonial studies.

The Reinvention of Australian Rules

A pivotal moment in what seems to be a post-modern and postcolonial reconstruction of Australian sporting history was the recent erection of monument to Thomas Wills at Moyston in western Victoria, with its stress on the aboriginal origins of Australian Rules Football. Taking this together with the AFL's official history of 1996, we seem to be witnessing a concerted campaign by the sport to rewrite its history; but instead it is engaged in mythmaking (Flanagan 1998; Ross 1996; Poulter 1993; Blainey 1990; Hibbins 1989; Grow 1998; Pascoe 1995; Mancini and Hibbins 1997). Wills spent much of his youth in contact with the indigenous peoples of the western districts, and there is some scanty evidence that the local youth took part in an activity that involved stuffed possum skins, which one Scottish settler described, in a book published in 1881, as 'similar to the white man's game of football' (Dawson 1981 [1881]: 85):

> One of the favourite games is football, in which fifty, or as many as one hundred players engage at a time. The ball is about the size of an orange, and is made of opossum-skin, with the fur side outwards. It is filled with pounded charcoal, which gives solidity without much increase of weight, and is tied hard round and round with kangaroo sinews. The players are divided into two sides and ranged in opposing lines, which are always of a different 'class' – white cockatoo against black cockatoo, quail against snake, &c. Each side endeavours to keep possession of the ball, which is tossed a short distance by hand, and then kicked in any direction. The side which kicks it oftenest and furthest gains the game. The person who sends it highest is considered the best player, and has the honour of burying it in the ground till required next day.
>
> The sport is concluded with a shout of applause, and the best player is complemented on his skill. This game, which is somewhat similar to the white man's game of football, is very rough; but as the players are barefooted and naked, they do not hurt each other so much as the white people do; nor is the fact of an aborigine being a good football player considered to entitle him to assist in making laws for the tribe to which he belongs.

That very description, if accurate, should give us pause. Which culture had ball games as part of its experience for a thousand years? – the existence of games with stuffed possum skins notwithstanding. What is the frame of reference? Surely not a suggestion that here is something in the local indigenous activity that can be borrowed to improve the moral standards or the fitness of Europeans? There is an anachronistic attempt to interpret the high mark as an Aboriginal importation; but this was not a distinguishing feature of the early versions of Australian Rules (Blainey 1990: 96–7).

Wills spent part of his schooldays in England, where he became a proficient footballer. He returned to Australia and survived a massacre of Europeans, including members of his family, by Aborigines in Queensland, a reversal of the normal in those days, before returning to Victoria to resume a sporting career. That was in 1861, though it was earlier, in 1857–8, that he proposed a domestic code of football to help cricketers keep fit in winter. But Europeans had been playing ball games long before this in Australia. The subsequent debates were, as we have already seen, conducted among the bourgeoisie of contemporary Melbourne, already on its way to becoming one of the cities of the nineteenth-century British empire. It might be pleasant and comforting to believe that Australian Aboriginals helped found Australian Rules football; but until some serious evidence turns up the only response of the historian must be scepticism.

Bodyline

No discussion of cricket, imperialism and postcolonialism can be complete without reference to the other great incident in Anglo-Australian cricket relationships, the bodyline tour of 1932–33. The symbolic significance of this series of events far outweighs its practical impact, which was negligible. Coming at the depth of the Great Depression, when financial relationships between England and Australia were very strained, with each side accusing the other of bad faith, the bodyline tour's events have been exaggerated out of all proportion. For those who only know of it through the television series, which was 'faction' at its worst, the reality was very different. Even the scholarly study by Rick Sissons and Brian Stoddart, *Cricket and Empire: The 1932–33 Bodyline Tour of Australia*, needs to be balanced by reading Douglas Jardine's own account *In Quest of the Ashes*, and especially John Arlott's foreword and the sections on Australian crowds and fishing. As Arlott makes clear, Jardine set out methodically and professionally (and Jardine was an amateur) to win a specific test series against a team that included the best batsman in the world at the time, the young Don Bradman (Sissons 1985). He did this by a mixture of psychological and physical tactics that nowadays would be taken for granted by a

Bobby Simpson, Kevin Sheedy, Ian Chappell or Steve Waugh, but that were fairly novel for the time. A coach at Winchester, where Jardine had been a pupil, is supposed to have said, 'Well, we shall win the Ashes – but we may lose a Dominion.' This typically glittering Wykehamist remark should not be taken as the considered judgement of England on the matter.

Australians, some on the field, but many more off the field as radio and the press, brought the details of the matches to an expanded audience and decided that the tactics were unfair, because they were effective and Australia lacked the means to retaliate – no Lillee and Thompson or Glenn McGrath were available. The Board of Control accused the English of unsportsmanlike behaviour, a heinous charge to level, and the reverberations rumbled up to Cabinet level in both countries. The urbane English offered to call off the tour, and the Australians capitulated, since there was a lot of money and much prestige at stake. The Empire hardly tottered, though much heat was generated and it helped to take people's minds off the depression for a little. It is reported that, in the later tests in the series, if the English team did not resort immediately to bodyline bowling the Australian crowd felt so deprived that they hooted and catcalled until it was adopted, whereupon the English were roundly booed for their perfidy.

While researching the history of soccer in Australia the author incidentally came across a reference to a soccer match between one of the local Australian clubs, Hakoah, the club of the Jewish community in Melbourne, and the visiting English cricket team (*Sporting Globe*, 11 March 1933). This was the last activity in which the team participated in Victoria prior to leaving for Sydney *en route* home to England. The symbolism of a match against a Jewish-backed team, given events in Germany in March 1933, may be a product of coincidence. It was not picked up in any of the press reports of the time that have been consulted so far. Jardine was not in the English line-up, needless to say; but otherwise most of the regular starting eleven were, including Ames, who played soccer for Gillingham, Hammond who skippered and had turned out for Bristol Rovers, and Duckworth, the wicket-keeper, in goal. Neil Tranter pointed out that many English test cricketers were all-round sportsmen of considerable ability, often reaching international standard in a number of disciplines apart from cricket. C. B. Fry and Patsy Hendren were outstanding examples. Hendren had actually played soccer against teams in Western Australia with Gilligan's and Chapman's touring cricket teams. He played for England at soccer in the Victory Internationals. The report in the *Sporting Globe* (11 March 1933) announcing the match appeared a couple of pages from a reflective article by E. H. M. Baillie under the heading that 'The Board must tackle Bodyline', pointing out that now was the time to do so, when passions had cooled, and noting that some of those who had been in favour of this form of attack had revised their opinions in the light of their experiences in Australia. This episode at least raises questions about the claimed strained relationships between the English and the Australians at the time, as of course does the reception of Harold Larwood when he emigrated to Australia several years later.

The Empire and the imperial spirit survived bodyline, and cricket controversies seemed to have no effect on Australian participation in the other kind of conflict that blew up only six years later. According to Jack Fingleton, who played in the series, and wrote his account *Cricket Crisis* many years later, the only effect of bodyline was to emasculate fast bowlers in the next generation. Anyone who bowled a bumper was accused of bodyline. Subsequently, though rivalry between Australia and England in test cricket has given rise to much hyperbolic writing about battles for the Ashes, this has never been more than an intense form of sporting activity with virtually no political significance.

If cricket was accepted by Australians and integrated into their cultural lives as part of specifically sporting rivalry alone, the other major team sport of the nineteenth century, soccer, was not. But that is another story (Hay 1997).

Note

1. Earlier versions of this paper were delivered to the Australian Society for Sports History, Melbourne chapter in June 1999 and the *Sport, Postcolonialism and the Body* Conference, and I am grateful to colleagues at both sessions for their helpful critical comments.

2

'Black' Bodies – 'White' Codes: Indigenous Footballers, Racism and the Australian Football League's Racial and Religious Vilification Code

Greg Gardiner

'Nigger, nigger pull the trigger' (White footballer's racial taunt – Smith 1995a: 1).

Even though it offers the excuse of blood, color, birth – or, rather, because it uses this natur-
alist and sometimes creationist discourse – racism always betrays the perversion of a man,
the 'talking animal.' It institutes, declares, writes, inscribes, prescribes. A system of marks,
it outlines space in order to assign forced residence or to close off borders. It does not discern,
it discriminates. (Derrida 1985: 290)

Introduction

During a game of Australian rules football in Melbourne in the early 1930s, a
young Aboriginal football player, Doug Nicholls, ran the length of the football
ground to castigate an opposition player, who had racially abused him moments earlier. According to Australian Football League records, Nicholls (later
to become Sir Doug, and the state Governor of South Australia), was the only
Indigenous player in the league in his era. This racial abuse incident – not the
only one Nicholls was to experience in a distinguished career in football (Sheahan
1995; Clark 1972) – went unreported in contemporary media.

Sixty years later, at an inner-suburban league football ground in Melbourne,
a young Aboriginal football player, Neil Winmar, star of the Saint Kilda team,
ran to the front of the main grandstand at the end of the match and in a gesture
of pride and defiance lifted his jumper high and pointed to his black skin.
Winmar was responding to an afternoon of being racially vilified and abused

by sections of the Collingwood crowd; his action culminating years of racial vilification by opposition supporters, players and officials. This incident was widely reported and discussed in all forms of local media.

In 1995, two years after the Winmar incident, the Australian Football League (AFL) introduced for the first time a code specifically prohibiting actions or speech that threatened, vilified or insulted another person 'on the basis of that person's race, religion, colour, descent or national or ethnic origin' (Australian Football League 1995: 19). It was the first such law to be drafted and implemented by a major sporting code in Australia. According to AFL records, at the time of its introduction, there were thirty Indigenous players in its ranks.

Bearing in mind the persistence, and centrality, of local forms in a global sports market and milieu (Rowe and Lawrence 1996: 10–11; Boyle and Haynes 1996), this chapter concerns itself with the narrative of race and identity in Australian sports culture; specifically, the campaign of Indigenous footballers that developed in the 1990s to end racial abuse in Australian Rules football. This chapter considers key aspects of this campaign and its aftermath, the racial politics of identity it unfolded, and the important role played by the media. It also investigates what this campaign has revealed about the operations of a traditional 'code' of Australian culture – namely racism, and the effect, if any, that the Indigenous players' campaign may have had in challenging it. In sport and elsewhere it is the code of racism that has historically limited Indigenous opportunity, and, in its form as speech, has been used persistently to vilify the black body.

This study is underpinned by certain key assumptions. In the postcolonial *polis* sports and sporting culture act as a primary locus of identity. Like the mass agonistic theatres of the Ancient West, sports events and genres, such as the Olympics and football, operate simultaneously as entertainment and as social catharsis (see Tomlinson 1996). As an enactment of citizenship on a mass participatory scale, they carry the narratives of their own physical contests, and other narratives; narratives concerning issues of national ethos, masculinity, and race, to name a few (Carrington 1998). The audiences to these mass sports events mediate these narratives in concert with the knowledges, and stereotypes, they bear with them to the arena. And importantly, local, national and global media also participate in the discursive construction, and replay, of these narratives of identity (Maguire 1999; Teo 2000: 7–46; Baker and Boyd 1997; Jakubowicz, Goodall, Martin, Mitchell, Randall, and Seneviratne 1994).

In Australian popular culture the most powerful, performative myths concern sport, and sporting heroes. The links between sport and national identity in Australian culture, and the important role sport has played in the developing mythology of the colonial nation – robust, egalitarian, fair-minded, harmonious – are frequently cited as fundamental (Jobling 1988; Cashman 1995). Less observed, until recently, is the manner in which sport and its attendant media have traditionally been involved in constructing racialized national sporting identities – that is, have produced narratives that *racialize* as they *nationalize* – and the central role that issues of 'race' continue to play in the politics of popular representation (Jaireth 1995). From this perspective, the Australian sporting hero is traditionally produced as a racial hero; exemplified in white culture for several generations by a white man in a white uniform – cricketing hero, Donald Bradman.

When Indigenous people gain entry to the realm of elite sport they enter a world that represents, in Hoberman's words, a neo-colonialist enterprise, 'both as an economic operation and as a cultural time capsule in which the colonial ideology of race lives on' (Hoberman 1997: 120). Tatz (1995a) has shown that the achievements of Indigenous sportsmen and women occur in a historical context of racisms surviving both within and without Australian sport. Paradoxically, sport has provided Indigenous people with one of the few avenues for participation and success in mainstream culture. Since the 1960s Australian sporting culture and its media have produced Indigenous athletes and sports stars as cross-racial 'egalitarian' role models (Kell 2000). In this context, Tatz (1995a,b) identifies a process whereby successful Indigenous men and women are celebrated as 'Australian' heroes – and as icons of national unity – but re-characterized in popular discourse as 'Aboriginal' when success wanes. This particular trope in national sports discourse is not confined to Australia (Rowe 1998: 248–9). From Jim Thorpe and Jesse Owens to Tommie Smith and Ben Johnson (Jackson 1998) there is a history of Indigenous and black sports stars who have performed, and been acclaimed, as national heroes: non-white athletes who are paradoxically configured as 'standing in' for national identities in dominantly white cultures. In his famed epigram the US athlete Tommie Smith captured this process whereby black is (temporarily) glossed as white: 'When we're winning we're Americans. Otherwise, we're just Negroes' (Tomlinson and Whannel 1984: 28).

This study follows writers such as Garland and Rowe (1999), Jackson (1998) and others (e.g. Outlaw 1999) in viewing the notion of 'race' as a shifting social construct, one that is produced and reproduced discursively (Parisi 1998), and historically allied to the project of colonialism. The term 'racism' is deployed here with an understanding of its plural, non-static character (Garland and Rowe 1999: 36), and as a social practice historically connecting politics, law and institutions. Most important for the question of racial abuse is the determination of racism as a discourse, which for Derrida (1985) inscribes, codifies, sets boundaries and marks and delimits space – this perverse *speech*. In the

Australian context such speech can be considered normative (Augustinos, Tuffin and Rapley 1999).

Racial discourse can also be construed as a mimetic mode – as a form of representation. Anderson has argued that this colonialist discourse on Aborigines was predicated on the latter's construction as a radical otherness (I. Anderson 1993: 23–5). As the opposite of the knowable and the familiar, this radical otherness 'became the principal organising feature of their [Indigenous] representation by non-Aborigines' (I. Anderson 1993: 24). As Anderson maintains, the non-Aboriginal construction of Aboriginality remains deeply embedded in Australian identity generally.

Background

Australian Rules football is an extraordinary amalgam of colonial, Indigenous Australian and postcolonial influences (Sandercock and Turner 1981; Flanagan 1998; Fitzgerald and Spillman 1988). Despite the early Indigenous contribution to the form of the game, known in Victoria as *marn-grook* (see Atkinson and Poulter 1993; Dawson 1981 [1881]; Thomas 1838–9), in its first hundred years Aboriginal players were virtually excluded from participation at the elite level. As Colin Tatz (1995b: 152–9) has argued, an effective race barrier existed in the AFL preventing Indigenous entry. Only four known Aborigines are listed as players in AFL records for the period up to and including the Second World War, an amazingly low figure given Indigenous success in other sports such as athletics. While the number of Indigenous players participating slowly increases from the 1960s, it is only in the 1990s that the numbers grow dramatically, an increase that can be partly attributed to the inclusion of new teams in the expanded 16-team national competition. By the start of the 2000 football season there were 50 Indigenous players listed at the elite level, representing 8 per cent of total players, about four times the proportionate rate of Aboriginal people in the community (Niall 2000), making Australian rules one of only two team sports in the country with an over-representation of Indigenous players at the elite level. Thousands of Indigenous men and boys participate in the lower leagues and junior ranks. In the Northern Territory entire teams composed of Indigenous players are the norm, and despite a serious lack of resources Indigenous football is vibrant across the country. For the business-oriented AFL Indigenous players today represent an important asset, commanding huge attention and acting as a powerful drawcard to the game; a game which is far and away the most popular team sport in Australia, with almost two million adults attending annually (Australian Bureau of Statistics 1995: 1).

Pandora's Box

'Boong . . . Abo . . . Coon . . . Go back to your own country . . . Have another flagon . . .':
Opposition supporters to black player (Howell 1995: 15)

'Racism denies people the fundamental human right to be judged by their character, by
what is inside. This is why it's not easy to experience a lifetime of racial abuse, be constantly
reminded of it and yet be expected to simply ignore it': Aboriginal footballer, Michael Long
(1997: B16).

The media debate in the 1990s surrounding the introduction of the race abuse
rule and its aftermath has led to revelations about the extent to which Aboriginal players have been subjected to racism and racial abuse. Indeed, one football
journalist claimed that when the Indigenous player Michael Long named
Damian Monkhorst as a racial abuser in 1995 he had opened up a Pandora's
box (Sheahan 1995: 13). It is an instructive metaphor. The ancient aetiological
myth is about transgression: about the revelation of the unseen, the undesirable
and the unspeakable. Some former players and commentators laid claim to
these woes as they took flight: the Collingwood player Tony Shaw was on record
to the effect that he would make racist comments every week if it gave him an
advantage (C. Wilson 1991: 6) – comments later retracted. The former player
Mal Brown said that Long should have been around in his day, the 1970s, when
common racial taunts directed at Aboriginal players by white players frequently
contained references to killing, such as: 'Nigger, nigger pull the trigger' (Smith
1995b: 1). Derek Kickett, an Indigenous player with Sydney, responded that
during the preceding weekend's game a supporter had yelled at him: 'Get off
the field, you nigger!' (Australian Associated Press 1995: 2).

The debate revealed that the West Coast Indigenous player Chris Lewis had
received racist hate mail and death threats. Michael McLean's experiences as a
young Aboriginal player mirrored those of other Aboriginal players. Notwithstanding the camaraderie of team-mates, he was subject to racial abuse on a
weekly basis, both by opposition players and, often with incredible menace, by
supporters. In his first game in 1983 McLean supporters yelled at him to, 'Go
back to your own country', an amazing reference for a person with a heritage
stretching back 40,000 years! (Howell 1995: 15; see also McNamara 1998).
Jim Stynes, originally from Ireland, described his astonishment at the level of
racial abuse he had experienced over the course of a 12-year career, which began
in the mid-1980s (Davis 1997: 22). Other non-Anglo players also provided
examples of the abuse they had habitually received. In 1990s cases of racial
abuse the most common racial epithets reported and represented by print

media involved the phrase 'black bastard', usually printed as such, or its racist and sexist double, 'black cunt', printed with dashes following the 'c'. Television reportage of racial abuse events is oblique or euphemistic in commentary, but close-up video replays in such reports are explicit for anyone capable of a modicum of lip-reading. In one case, and in an attempt by the perpetrator to subvert the rule and avoid being put on report, a non-Indigenous player repeatedly called an Indigenous player a 'green cunt' throughout a match.

In interviews and documentaries Indigenous former players, such as Graeme Farmer and Syd Jackson, who played in the 1960s and 1970s respectively, have confirmed the relentless nature of this abuse through their careers (Hawke 1994: 25–6; Graham 1994: 1–2). In an era that lacked any legal mechanism by which Aboriginal players could lodge a complaint, and with a football culture that told Aborigines to turn the other cheek, many Aboriginal players took this denigration in silence. However, some Aboriginal players did (and do) retaliate to on-field abuse, and their actions have often gained them a suspension. Retaliation to racial abuse has not been considered a mitigating circumstance. A common response from racial abuse apologists, including at least one current player, was that what was said on the field should stay on the field; that forms of so-called sledging are in some way undifferentiated. As one letter-writer to a daily newspaper put it: 'In the good old days, footballers were called "wog", "bludgers", "poofters" and whatever else came to mind' (George 1997: 20). Michael Long and other Indigenous players have countered by arguing that racial abuse is both morally wrong, and connected to history and power.

Racial abuse is of course a form of coercion: it represents, dehumanizes and objectifies its target. Constructed of and through imaginary stereotypes, it projects both fantasies and fears of difference, and Michael Long (1997) is correct in drawing attention to its innate immorality. As Jones (M. Jones 1994: 306–12) contends, racial vilification has enormous potential power to harm its victims, even to the extent of precipitating physical illness. In Australia this speech-in-excess that is racial abuse is highly loaded, as the abuse directed at Michael McLean demonstrates. In an era of debate on native title issues, questions of who 'owns' and who 'belongs' are at the centre of national identity discourse and politics. Racial abuse therefore looks back, and forward; it is one inflection or mode of a colonialist racial discourse expressing both power and history: a discourse that has attempted to inculcate codes of conduct in Indigenous people for 200 years.

An Indigenous player with Port Adelaide, Che Cockatoo-Collins, speaking about his own family's experiences in the stolen generations, has referred to the importance of non-Indigenous people's understanding the historical and cultural context in which racial abuse occurs (Connolly 1997: 17). As Langton (1994: 96–7) observes, this white Australian code has been obsessional in its desire for classification of the 'other'. From the early 1800s on, over seven hundred pieces of legislation were passed by white parliaments in the states and territories that effectively constructed codes of conduct for Aboriginal existence and the Indigenous body; the legal definition of an Indigenous person was amended sixty-seven times (McCorquodale 1987; Gardiner and Bourke 2000: 7–8). The various state protectorate boards were handed authority over all aspects of Indigenous daily life: over marriage, employment, language, dress, travel, residence and cultural practice. Aboriginal communities have been under constant surveillance, by managers of reserves, overseers, police, welfare, and their agents, in what Sackett (1993) has described as a colonialist Benthamite experiment. This procession of white codes that attempted to regulate existence was capricious, draconian and, in the years when child-stealing became a central preoccupation of white authority, a source of terror. In 1997 the report of the Human Rights and Equal Opportunity Commission (1997: 3) into the removal of Indigenous children from their families, *Bringing Them Home*, revealed that between one in three and one in ten Indigenous children were removed from their families between 1910 and 1970; a policy affecting entire generations. As the debate on racial abuse widened, football audiences learnt that some of the best-known AFL Indigenous players, both in former times and currently, were directly affected by child removals, either having been removed themselves and placed in institutions, or as the children of parents who were removed (Stone 1999). The publication of Indigenous players' personal stories revealed a complete alternative narrative of Australian life for white audiences.

As was noted above, the code of Australian racism runs deep and wide, shaped by imperialism, nationalism, class and sexism (Hazeldine 1994). It is a text without borders, a boundless text in the Derridan sense. Yet as Derrida (1985) points out, racism paradoxically seeks borders, limits, controls. As the stories of Indigenous players reveal, in a multitude of ways Indigenous people have always resisted this text, and these controls. By speaking about the racism in their lives, and in sport, Indigenous sportsmen and sportswomen in the 1990s, including the sprint champion Cathy Freeman, have proffered a counter-discourse, and have provided white Australians an opportunity to examine the unexamined, and to understand and connect verbal abuse with other abuses of human rights, including the forced removal of children. Michael Long's transgression, if such it was, was to confront a code that would have had him act as silent victim.

The Winmar and Long Incidents

'I think a lot of people now understand why I did it. It has made Aboriginal people stand up tall. We've been in the shadows for so many years': Aboriginal player, Neil Winmar (Rees 1994: 5).

These comments of Neil (Nicky) Winmar's were made in 1994, a year after the now (locally) famous photo was taken of him lifting his shirt at the Colling-wood Football Club's ground, Victoria Park, at the end of St Kilda's match with Collingwood. Winmar, now retired from football, is a veteran of over 200 games played for the St Kilda Football Club and the Western Bulldogs, where he spent the last years of his career. Since 1993 the defiant image of Winmar pointing to his skin (and depicted on this book's front cover) has been endlessly re-presented, in all forms of media, and has achieved iconic status. It has also inspired one of the great portraits in the Melbourne-based genre of football painting, by Martin Tighe, and was used in promotional material for the Aboriginal and Torres Strait Islander Commission elections in 1996. And until the Aboriginal sprint star Cathy Freeman lit the cauldron at the Sydney Olympics, this image of Winmar was rivalled as iconography only by an earlier image of Freeman at the Commonwealth Games in Victoria, Canada, holding the Aboriginal flag aloft in triumph (Given 1995). Print media regularly use the Winmar photo as a visual drawcard, not just to stories concerned with race abuse incidents in football, or sport generally, but for articles focusing on race relations, reconciliation and identity.

Winmar's act represents the first of two defining moments in the modern Aboriginal footballers' campaign against racial abuse. In the photo Winmar is depicted facing towards an unseen subject(s), towards whom he gestures. Video footage reveals that he is facing the main grandstand at Collingwood football ground, a sea of white faces, and he reportedly yells up at them as he points: 'I'm black and I'm proud of it' (Rees 1994). St Kilda has won the match, for the first time in years at Collingwood's home ground, and Winmar has been unstoppable, beating several opponents. Throughout the afternoon he has been repeatedly vilified and abused by sections of the crowd. From comments he has made after the event it is clear that Winmar was aware that his gesture would be remarked, aware of its strategic value, its *semiosis*, since both TV cameras and photo-journalists surrounded the arena. Winmar has also connected his protest with the Mabo decision in the High Court in 1992, which overturned the colonial myth of 'terra nullius' – no one's land – noting that Mabo had enabled people to understand the meaning of his action (Rees 1994: 5).

The image touched off a large scale media 'event' (on such events see Deutch-man and Ellison 1999). The President of Collingwood Football Club responded, just days after its dissemination throughout the country, that Indigenous people would be all right if only they conducted themselves like white people (McAsey 1993: 7). This response attracts critics from many quarters, and Collingwood earned themselves in return a traditional Indigenous curse, which they attempted to expiate later by playing a 'friendly' against an all-Aboriginal team, who thrashed their white opponents in front of a largely black crowd in the Northern Territory. Some Collingwood supporters are reported as having written personal apologies to Winmar.

Winmar's deictic gesture produced one of the most profound and influential, multi-layered images on race in sport, indeed on race *per se*, in Australia in the 1990s. It has its status because it fundamentally shocked Australian sporting culture, and because it spoke directly in visual form to history, and to the embodying of race and its representation. His transgression was threefold: first, in an elementary way, by raising his jumper Winmar exposed the body of the actor, the player in the drama. Like the theatre, football relies equally for its success on the suspension of disbelief, and Winmar's act momentarily breached this convention. But more importantly, Winmar's action exposed his *blackness*, a blackness traditionally ridiculed, obscured, locked away; the colour traditionally conceived of in dominant culture as a sign of negativity or absence and, as Tatz (1999) shows, a target of 'breeding out' campaigns by white society. With this gesture, and if you were in earshot, with his accompanying language, Winmar turns these traditional signs upside down. It is a gesture of self-representation, of self-*mimesis*, wherein the black man points to himself, and signifies his proud ownership of blackness. In this one gesture Winmar pointed to a whole history, and the white codes, including racial abuse, that would define and confine Indigeneity are challenged and confronted. It also immediately signified to the football and wider community that Aboriginal footballers were literally adopting a new stance, a new visibility, in contrast to the past: one that would confront the issue of racism in football head on. In the debate that followed, the AFL promised to introduce a code of conduct on racism.

The second decisive moment in the campaign to confront racial abuse in football occurred two years later. Essendon and Collingwood Football Clubs played before a full house of over 90,000 people at the Melbourne Cricket Ground on Anzac Day 1995. Michael Long, the 1993 Norm Smith Grand Final medallist, claimed after the game that he had been racially abused in the presence of an umpire. The Essendon club supported Long and lodged a complaint with the AFL, naming Collingwood ruckman Damian Monkhorst as the offender. After more than a week of intense media attention, including commentary, TV replays of the incident, talkback radio, academic and legal opinion, and letters to the editor on the subject (some of which condemned Aboriginal players for their 'thin skin': Viti 1995: 15), the AFL held a press conference, at which it was declared that the complaint had been successfully settled, but that there would be no penalty imposed. The terms of the settlement were to remain undisclosed. Officials of the Essendon Football Club, and sections of the media, were openly critical of the process employed by the AFL and the outcome of the complaint. However, it was the Aboriginal players, led by Michael Long, who demanded that strong penalties be introduced for players found guilty of racial abuse. The Aboriginal players also called for league umpires to have the power to report racial abuse, for an educational and cultural awareness programme to be set up for players and clubs by the AFL, and that they should have a direct input in the drafting of the new code (De Bolfo 1995: 2).

It was in the midst of negotiations with the AFL that the Aboriginal players directly entered the media discourse on the issue, with interviews to media outlets around the country. Indigenous players, such as Long, Michael McLean and Derek Kickett, told their stories about the history and continuing verbal abuse experienced by them both from the terraces and on the field. They argued their case on moral grounds, in historical terms, and in relation to workplace practices. They threatened that they could not currently encourage their sons to enter football if racial abuse continued.

Two weeks following the Long case another racial abuse complaint from an Aboriginal player was lodged with the AFL, providing a new round of media speculation, comment and interviews. From the AFL's perspective the issue had become a public relations disaster, and it issued an open letter to the community accepting that racism in football was a major problem, and that a code was forthcoming. Two months after Long's complaint the AFL's racial vilification rule (Rule no. 30) was unveiled. The release vindicated the courageous public stand that Michael Long had taken two months earlier, and Winmar's protest two years before. Notwithstanding the absence of stipulated individual player penalties, and the presence of some other flaws that would soon reveal themselves, many provisions of the rule were in substance what Aboriginal players had been demanding. The Aboriginal players and Indigenous community groups applauded its introduction. Collingwood Football Club, however, was less sanguine in its response – six weeks later the Collingwood Cheer Squad's banner pre-game carried the message 'Sticks and stones may break my bones but names will never hurt me', in response to which one letter writer to a daily newspaper proposed that Collingwood change its acronym from CFC to KKK (B. Blake 1995: 16).

The Rule

The Racial and Religious Vilification rule was directed at the on-field behaviour of players, but also covers the behaviour of club officials, coaches and other staff entitled to enter the football arena. The rule provides for complaints to be lodged by an umpire, player or club with the AFL; for the AFL to conduct a confidential mediation process involving the parties with an independent mediator; for a Tribunal hearing of the matter if mediation is unsuccessful; and for fines of up to $50,000 (AUS) to be applied to the player's club in guilty cases. While the rule has been since amended, elements of the code bear a strong resemblance to the articles and processes contained in the Commonwealth's Racial Hatred Act, 1995, where mediation is also given central prominence, and which continues to provide the context of a civil law specifically prohibiting racial vilification. This Act amended the Racial Discrimination Act 1975, which implemented Australia's obligations under the International Convention on the Elimination of All Forms of Racial Discrimination (ICERD). Article 4a of ICERD declares as 'an offence punishable by law all dissemination of ideas based on racial superiority or hatred, incitement to racial discrimination, as well as all acts of violence or incitement to such acts against any race or group of persons of another colour or ethnic origin' (Barker 1997: 103). The Australian states, with the exceptions of Tasmania and Victoria, have also enacted legislation aimed at racial vilification, mostly within the purview of civil law.

The Handshake

The AFL launched the new rule with fanfares. The league's match-day publication *Football Record* was devoted to its introduction, with details of various AFL anti-racism initiatives, including education programmes for all staff, players and officials, and photos of Indigenous and ethnic players above the words, 'There's never been any place in Australian sport for racism and the new AFL rules make that official', and the slogan: 'Racism. The game's up' (Australian Football League 1995). The same slogan appeared on the cover of the *Record*, flanking black and white hands clasped in a handshake. At the Melbourne Cricket Ground, the giant electronic screen displayed the same message before the game. The AFL was subsequently awarded a peace prize for its anti-racism by the United Nations Association, and for many sports in Australia the league's code has been used as a model for the introduction of anti-racial abuse measures and laws.

In the first four years of its operation there were twelve complaints lodged with the AFL under the new rule. Two of these complaints were heard at the league's quasi-court, the Tribunal, while the rest were resolved through mediation. Only one player had a penalty imposed, and no club was fined. Despite confidentiality provisions applying to the rule, the majority of cases attracted intense media coverage, from the moment of their recorded enactment on-field to replays on TV broadcast news and sports programmes, print media discourse, radio discussion and letters to major daily papers. Newshounds actively pursue the parties to disputes, including player managers and club representatives, for doorstep interviews, even at supposedly secret mediation venues, which are filmed by TV crews. Many of the disputes have concluded with large-scale media conferences, with the parties delivering prepared statements, and question-and-answer sessions. In news parlance, racial abuse cases have made good copy. It is important to note that not all these cases have involved Indigenous players. At the time of writing, the last public case in 1999 involved a player of Italian background lodging a complaint.

In the light of the massive media appeal of race abuse cases, the AFL's decision to inaugurate the rule with the image of the handshake of reconciliation is significant. The handshake is a resonant traditional gesture in Australian male sporting culture. After an afternoon of contesting and sledging each other, football players – and players in other sports – shake hands with their opposition. The handshake thus operates as a sign of transition and closure. In racial vilification proceedings the handshake has also operated as a sign of closure: the parties to the dispute emerge from mediation, and to the assembled media, clasp hands. In this way the image of the handshake mediates our understanding of the process. It signals that an agreement or understanding has been reached, a reconciliation, and that the racial politics that have consumed the media for the previous two or three days or the previous week can be safely re-interred. The normative football discourse – of bad knees, torn ligaments, and rising stars – can re-emerge. It is an apparently clear and clean image.

However, as Godwell (1999: 11) points out, in most mediated cases of racial abuse such consummating handshakes are highly problematic gestures, and particularly where no fines or penalties of any sort are being imposed on the perpetrator, amount to little more than phatic symbolism. From the earliest cases heard under the rule in 1995 Aboriginal players have been critical of the central role of mediation and the absence of penalties. Che Cockatoo-Collins and others argued that the abused player was being twice victimized by the process (Masanaukas, Heaney and Probyn 1997: 3). Following a string of racial abuse cases in early 1997, Indigenous players called for mediation to be scrapped entirely at senior level, for the public identification of all racial abuse offenders, and for an individual player penalty system to be introduced. AFL officials agreed to review the rule and its operation. However, the modifications introduced at the beginning of 1998 effectively ignored the position of the

Indigenous players, with heavy penalties introduced to apply *not* to offenders, but to any party breaching the rule's confidentiality provisions. Only one senior white official has publicly backed the Indigenous position. The then coach of the West Coast Eagles, Mick Malthouse, said in 1999: 'Let players guilty of racial vilification say sorry and then sit it out in the grandstand for two or three weeks. Then you'll find out how sorry they really are' (Malthouse 1999: 18). To date the Aboriginal players have not succeeded in changing in a substantial manner the provisions of the rule they find inadequate. Other sporting codes have since adopted more stringent player-centred penalty regimes for racial and other forms of abuse.

In early 1999 a case of racial abuse became another large-scale media event. This case made a mockery both of the confidentiality provisions of the rules, and of the absence of individual penalties. In a strange twist, the player against whom the complaint had been lodged resolved after a drawn-out mediation process covering several days to impose a penalty on himself. The St Kilda player, Peter Everitt, announced at a media conference that he had agreed to a settlement that involved a self-imposed four-week suspension, a $20,000 (AUS) fine, a racial awareness training programme and loss of match payments. Everitt publicly apologized to the player he had abused, Scott Chisholm, to his family and to the Aboriginal community. He and Chisholm then shook hands (Hadfield, Pegler and Burke 1999: 67). Everitt thus became the first white man in any capacity – player, coach, administrator, president, boot studder, supporter – associated with an AFL football team in its entire history to incur any form of censure for racial abuse; with the considerable irony that it was not the AFL itself that imposed the penalty.

The sporting handshake as a metaphor for racial reconciliation in sport is therefore highly problematic, and as the AFL's visual counterpoint to the Winmar image, clearly inadequate. Like much of the reconciliation discourse conducted in white society, it raises the prospect of a historical need for public dialogue and redress and, at that very point, smothers the gap necessary for that dialogue to take place. However, these two images – the lifted shirt, the handshake – also underline the paradoxes contained within the term 'postcolonial'. As Appiah (1997) shows the prefix 'post' here is problematic, signalling as it does a radical break from the past. In reality, the 'postcolonial' represents a contest between ideas and practices received, and new emergent ones. The AFL's position on racial abuse demonstrates the conundrum: on the one hand, the AFL has conducted a loud, public campaign condemning racism in football; on the other hand, its rule prohibiting racial abuse mandates that all cases be mediated in total secrecy. The AFL wants to be seen as doing the right, progressive thing – but it does not want the racism in its ranks to be seen. The obsession with secrecy is indicative of a desire to control the process, to foreclose public scrutiny and the articulations of abused players. It is a position destined to failure. Notwithstanding the encroachments of corporatism, football remains a public document and a voyeurs' palace. Tens of thousands of people witnessed the Everitt–Chisholm confrontation in real time, while hundreds of thousands consumed it in virtual space, where it was continually re-enacted. And while some cases of abuse may escape detection from this collective panopticon, there will inevitably be cases that don't.

Nicky Winmar's gesture in 1993 revealed the body of the actor, a reference to football's dimensions as theatre. In performance theory terms, football is a meta-theatre that relies upon an aesthetics of distance, both physical and imaginary, between players and audience. The tension that exists between this distance and the potential for its fracture or crossing is, in part, what provides a sense of danger and attraction; the perennial threat of injury, outbreaks of violence. In 1990s AFL football the traditional form of 'fracturing distance', the unsanctioned violence of the all-in brawl, has been virtually eliminated. It was perhaps no co-incidence that racial abuse cases have attracted such major attention over this period, when the sport itself is increasingly sanitized of its capacity to cross the threshold between security and danger. This is particularly so for a media that require conflict as a means to production and discourse. But the effects of Winmar's gesture indicate another dimension.

In AFL football, a predominantly white citizen audience – for the most part having little direct personal contact with Indigenous people – has in the 1990s, been witness to both the face-to-face confrontations of racial abuse events, and the playing in to the game's wider discourses of an Indigenous perspective on those events, whatever the motivations of media outlets for their inclusion of those accounts. The introduction of a counter-narrative to the formerly impervious colonial narrative of football, a sport that was racially exclusive for over a hundred years, has at the very least provided an opportunity for the testing of beliefs, and takes place in the context of other revelations concerning the country's history and race relations. For many in this football audience, it has been Indigenous players that have been the principal source for these revelations, providing a singular and unique perspective on Australian society and new versions of Australian identity. Indigenous players themselves have reported that the level of racial abuse hurled at them from both within and without the arena has generally declined since 1995 (M. Davis 1998: 20). At AFL games in 2000 the Aboriginal flag is a regular sight in the outer, and interestingly, is waved by supporters from different teams. The writer has personally witnessed racial abusers at AFL matches having their views loudly contested by other supporters, with arguments flaring that cross team allegiances.

Such shifts in behaviour are not universal. In March 1999 John Elliot, President of the Carlton Football Club, made a speech to a group of accountants containing a series of racist remarks, including the comment that Aborigines were a 'forgotten race' (F. Maguire and Gordon 1999: 1). The AFL Chief Executive, Wayne Jackson, declared Elliott's remarks were totally out of line with AFL policy on racism, and the AFL subsequently indicated that it would review Rule 30 so as to include the off-field remarks of club officials (Smith and Lyon 1999: 1). Shortly thereafter, Elliott publicly apologized for what he called his 'offensive comments'. In the context of AFL history and its race relations, and notwithstanding the continued inadequacies of its rule, this statement condemning racist language in policy terms by the major football institution in the country does represent a remarkable shift in Australian sports administrative culture – a policy adoption that it would have been hard to see forthcoming from the AFL in 1993 and unthinkable in the previous decade. Such reductions in the levels of racial abuse do not imply that other forms of racism are no longer prevalent in the sport. For example, in a recent study of position assignment by racial status in the AFL, the authors concluded that a continuing covert structural racism persists in the AFL based on racial stereotyping (Hallinan, Bruce and Coram 1999). Indigenous people continue to be under-represented in many major sports, such as cricket, and they are in general players in sports, not managers, coaches or administrators.

In gaining a code, a text, that will (with the inclusion of player penalties) work consistently to player benefit, Indigenous players have had to confront a sports culture in which, traditionally, white codes attempt to dictate, order and define black bodies. Here, for once in sport, the rules of engagement have had Indigenous input. In speaking back to racism's talking head they have therefore created a contested space, and this arena of contest relates to and feeds into a broader contest of ideas about country and history, identity and ownership. The texts that have emerged from Indigenous people in the last twenty years – in history, literature, poetry, dance and music, and sport, to name a few – have produced a completely different picture of the history and future possibilities for Australian culture. And, just as the scripts for football are contested and the results unknown, so is that future.

3

Sport, Indigenous Australians and Invader Dreaming: A Critique

Daryle Rigney

> Aboriginal intellectuals are working hard at producing history and sociology from a black perspective. Their fight is a tough one: how to wrest control from the non-Aborigines who do all the writing and talking about them (Tatz 1995b: 5–6).

One of the ways to colonize a people is to control their ability to represent themselves. One of the ways to subvert colonization is to retain or recapture the process of representation, to set the scene for counter-hegemonic anti-colonial narratives. This chapter aims to contribute to the field of anti-colonial scholarship by exposing the relationship between Australian colonial knowledge and Australian colonial power, in and through sport.[1] In doing so it is possible to name the examination of such a connection between Indigenous Australians and other Australians as postcolonial, particularly if the nature and practice of sport is viewed within wider social and historical contexts and struggles. For many Indigenous peoples, though, this assertion is problematic, particularly in a society that remains both historically and politically racialized and where our subjectivity is framed within colonial discourse.

In Australian cultural life, sport has long held a reified standing. As a result sport has often escaped critical examination, and thus Australians have failed to see the extent to which it is socially conditioned and influenced by the political and economic power of the nation-state.

In framing questions about sport and its relationship to power, McKay (McKay 1990) writes that there are essentially three positions in the literature on inequality in sport in Australia. The first relates to a popular myth in which Australia's sees itself as an egalitarian society that is inherently democratic, meritocratic and classless. Sport, it is argued, is a microcosm of this egalitarian society and thus opportunities are freely and equally available to all who employ them provided one has the drive and desire to seek them out (McKay 1990). The second position argues that inequalities do exist in Australia, but that sport possesses particular qualities that enable participants, administrators and controlling bodies to transcend such disparities. Proponents of this position voice loudly and strongly those popularly expressed qualities captured in the discourse: sport is an equal-opportunity employer; sport is colour-blind; sport does not discriminate; and sport and politics do not mix (McKay 1990). The third position argues that, contrary to popular and academic myths, sport in Australia is shaped by structures of social inequality. This is consistent with historical, sociological and anthropological evidence that demonstrates that social characteristics (gender, age, ethnicity, 'race', income, wealth) have been, and continue to be, major factors in systematically reproducing unequal access to education, health, employment and other social formations, including sport (McKay 1990).

In openly adopting the third of the positions I wish to engage in the struggle against oppression and respond to the systemic process of cultural domination through the imposition of colonial structures of power. By exploring the processes of colonization, in and through sport, I allow particular issues to emerge: whose culture(s) are represented; whose policies set the agenda for sport; whose sport are we, as Indigenous Australians, engaged with? Such an agenda projects an oppositional stance on the one hand; but it also enables a practice of possibility on the other, if Indigenous Australian agency is to be recognized, embraced and empowered.

Sport as a Site for Cultural Struggle

The location of Indigenous people and sport in a historically and politically racialized context enables insights into the historical construction of dominance and the roles of political, economic and cultural institutions in society. Privileged elite social groups control the critically important economic and political institutions of society, and thus have the principal access to society's ideological institutions. The control of access allows these groups to 'write' the rules of society in the form of norms, values and beliefs; and the rules they 'write' enable them to continue to 'write' the rules, thereby reinforcing and reproducing their structural advantages.

The key to understanding sport as a cultural phenomenon, then, is found in the nature of the relationship to broader societal forces of which it is a part. As Colin Tatz in *Obstacle Race* (1995b: 6) argues:

> The enduring realities of racism, discrimination and race classification, of philosophies on race, of restrictive laws and of past legacies need to be understood

and

Sport is indeed an effective way of illuminating the prevalent and prevailing social and political values of . . . eras, whether in the 1860s or the 1990s.

As a Ngarrindjeri[2] I was often subjected to racist behaviour throughout my sports career. The use of racist remarks by players and spectators in attempts to diminish the effectiveness of Indigenous players is commonplace. This practice of personalized racism occurs in one form or another both on and off the field. Having experienced racism at this level, I was shocked and angry that the Physical Education pre-service teacher-training course I studied at an undergraduate level did not examine racism in sport and physical education as a component of its curriculum. My shock should hardly have been surprising, given that 'the sociology of sport in Australia is underdeveloped conceptually, methodologically and theoretically' (Stokes 1985: 13), particularly with respect to Indigenous Australians, even though 'sport has traditionally occupied a prominent place in Australian society and culture' (Stokes 1985: 1). In recent years there has been a shift and advancement with respect to research into the sociological aspects of sport. The issue of racism in sport, however, is still undertheorized, even though on the international stage writings on sport, and racism in sport, have increased. As Tatz (1995b: 1) notes, writings on Indigenous people in sport are 'a frustrating omission'.

While issues of racism in sport are of great concern and need to occupy a prominent place in the research and writing of sports sociologists, of even greater concern is the limited level of understanding of the phenomenon of racism on which much of the discourse is based. This assertion inevitably raises questions about how you research racism in sport. What sort of things do you look at? Susan Birrell suggests that sports sociology should 'move from a generally a theoretical approach to race and sport to a critical analysis of racial relations and sport' (Birrell 1989: 212). Certainly in the Australian Indigenous context there is an ongoing need for an adequate analysis of Indigenous people in sport, because overall sports history and sociology remain the domain of colonial sport, communicated by the colonial voice.

An Anti-colonial Critique: Approaches to the Study of Racism and Sport

When theorizing an anti-colonial critique it must be remembered that racism is a concept for which there is no homogeneous, clearly accepted understanding (Anthias and Yuval-Davis 1992; Hollinsworth 1997). As a historical and political movement the boundaries are particularly problematic and fluid. In sport, popular beliefs about 'race'[3] and racism have had a major impact on how sport is organized, theorized and understood. These popular beliefs have led to largely narrative or descriptive writings that generally focus on either involvement or attitudes with respect to racism in sport.

Indigenous sports history and sociology intersect with Indigenous history, and the literature on Indigenous sports history/sociology has until very recently been limited in its quality and interpretation. There needs to be a political contextualization of Indigenous people in sport that acknowledges the historical invasion of Australia and the effects of the worldwide racist movement.[4] The basis for any anti-colonial critique of racism in sport must, therefore, be predicated on challenging the colonizers as to their confidence in the superiority of their social formations, which is what ensures a racialized society and serves the interests of the colonizers to the detriment of Indigenous people (Rigney 1997).

The rise of modern sport can be explored as a site for defining and reinforcing 'racial' differences, where the differences, were 'supported' by 'scientific' discourse. In the context of a movement towards Indigenous liberation the powerful arguments developed by the scientific community that focused upon the supposed inherent inferiority of Indigenous people, including the form our sporting and/or recreational activities took, need to be challenged.

In order to challenge popular understandings of racism in sport and to explore racism in sporting practices further I emphasize the importance of revisiting and rewriting the events, processes and history from an Indigenous perspective. The crucial point in Indigenous perspectives of history lies not only in the method, but in the questions asked and the perspectives provided (Vertinsky 1994). A failure to challenge the assumptions by not looking critically at the characteristics of modern sport places restrictions on how we understand sport, and thus '. . . explanations are imposed . . . and questions, which might have resulted in new insights, are unasked' (Struna 1984: 129). These questions and perspectives are never neutral: they are based upon personal, political and intellectual decisions. Moreover, sports scholarship must aim to do more than simply write Indigenous people into sports history. It should also develop new understandings about the social construction of 'race' and its relationship to sport, because the racialization[5] of sport and the unequal power relationships between Indigenous society and dominant society are and will continue to be reconstructed and contested (Vertinsky 1994).

Sports sociologists have increasingly asked questions about the nature and practice of sport and its relationship to power and domination (Jarvie 1985, 1991; Hargreaves 1986; Sage 1990). Culturalist or colonial theories focus on power relationships that are created in the relationship between 'minority' and 'dominant' groups. Researchers who adopt such positions have attempted to understand where power comes from, how power works (in different situations and different forms) and how power shifts as people struggle with issues that affect them. These researchers have focused upon 'cultural suppression and cultural hegemony on the one hand and cultural regeneration and cultural survival on the other' (Birrell 1989: 219) and have sought to politicize the nature and practice of sport by asking questions about:

1. why sports have taken on particular forms and ways of being organized;
2. what values and ideologies are being communicated (Brock and Kartinyeri 1989; Daly 1994);
3. who stands to benefit from these explanations (L. Davis 1990; Churchill 1994);
4. what sports could be in society (Coakley 1994);
5. how opportunities in sport vary from group to group (Fleming 1991, Krotee 1988);
6. how sports could be changed to reflect the interests of participants (Leviatin 1993); and
7. when and how sports are able to be sites for transforming social relations (Foley 1990).

The aim is, therefore, to problematize the concept of sport and open up alternative ways of thinking about, defining and doing sport as a central plank in an anti-colonial critique.

Racializing Australian Sport

Australia's racist history is embedded in the well-established ideas of 'race' and 'racial' theory imported from across the globe by the worldwide racist movement. While the racist movement in the Americas, Europe and Africa was about the struggle for political power in Europe, the economics of slavery, and the debates between pro-slavers and anti-slavers, this was not the situation in Australia (Moore 1994). The purpose of Australian racist ideology was to legitimate and justify the invasion of Indigenous land and to seize and occupy those lands. Racist ideology was then employed to exonerate the decimation of Indigenous society and to determine the place of Indigenous people within colonial society (Reynolds 1987). 'Racial' ideology as a framework for understanding Indigenous people ensured in the thought of the colonialists a complete belief in their own superiority, and this ideology significantly influenced the form sporting practice took in Australia.

Birrell (1989) argues that the critical formative years for modern sport were from 1880 to 1900. These two decades represent the most successful period of ideological consolidation of dominant sport forms and practices, and occurred at a time when the racist movement worldwide had either begun to or already had established itself across the globe (Stepan 1982). It would be extremely naive to believe that the movement had no impact on sport. A comparative analysis of 'race' and racism during this period would aid our understanding of the cultural meaning and power of sport, and would help us to examine ways in which sport is used to legitimate and consolidate colonial privilege.

Guttmann (1994: 2) supports such a position when he states that '. . . modern sports are to a large degree British inventions and from the British Isles, modern sport went forth to conquer the world.' Sports development, therefore, finds its roots and cultural base in the traditions of either England or Europe, and it is significant that the evolution of sport in Australia and the development of sport in the industrial world occurred during a high point in European Imperialism (Mangan 1986). The fusion of the prevailing racial ideology of the time and the development of 'modern sport' resulted in the total disregard and eventual delegitimation of Indigenous Australian sporting practice.[6] In this manner sport is a significant cultural form, because as new technologies were formed and as the worldwide racist movement came into power it resulted in new forms of 'sanctioned' sport that 'symbolically affirmed the correctness of the social order that fostered them' (Mandell 1984: 15).

Australia Constructing an Invader Dreaming through Sport

In Australia, the years 1860–1940 were dominated by colonial society's constructing an invader Dreaming.[7] During this period, commonly known as the Protection and Segregation era, colonial society continued to build upon its established foundations. Indigenous land continued to be stolen as the frontier expanded, Indigenous resistance was subdued, and Indigenous social systems were struggling to survive against the imposition of colonial legal, political, health, education, religion and sports social systems.

Social Darwinist racial ideology informed the argument that Indigenous people were a dying 'race' in a battle for survival against superior 'races', and that this was part of nature's plan – for humanity to evolve to higher life forms (Markus 1994). Evidence of Indigenous inferiority was everywhere. Indigenous people had not developed weapons and military power capable of resisting the invader. 'Indigenous people were unable to resist diseases introduced by the invader. Indigenous people did not have, in the eyes of the invader, social systems for ordering society and Indigenous people were locked into heathen superstitions' (Crotty *et al.* 1993: 72). The laws of nature were being affirmed for the invader by these events of history and confirmed their systematically learnt racist ideology: 'Social Darwinism carried a message of struggle, competition and violence. These were not only inevitable but necessary to progress itself' (Reynolds, 1987: 128).

The 'problem' for the colonist was what to do with the dying 'race'. The solution resulted in the forced removal of Indigenous people from their lands to be incarcerated in the invaders' racial palliative care centres commonly known as missions (see Jenkin 1979; Reynolds 1987; Moore 1994; Hampton and Mattingley 1988). The deportation and incarceration of Indigenous people from colonial society served to clear the land further for the colonists and to remove Indigenous people from the consciousness of colonial society. As Henry Reynolds (1987: 129) declares:

> Racism furthered the material interests of most settlers. It made it so much easier to take Aboriginal land without negotiation or purchase, to crush resistance to the dispossession and then keep the survivors 'in their place'. Frontier squatters and other entrepreneurs could pursue their economic objectives, could invest their capital, free from restraint. . . . As long as the whites continued to believe the blacks were primitive savages, it could all be done with a clear conscience.

The dispossession of Indigenous lands provided colonial society, during this period, with a time of economic and social growth along with increased urban and rural development. Further, the development of improved transportation, communication and technological capabilities influenced the sporting movements of colonial society. Sport could now be played at night following the introduction of the electric light, and sporting results could be communicated faster and more widely (McKay 1990). Transportation developments allowed inter-town and inter-colonial sports competitions to become possible, and thus the number of colonial competitive sports being played increased significantly. Underpinning these events, however, was the continued racial ideology and policy that maintained the racialized forms sport took in Australian society.

The colonizer, having won the struggle for possession of the continent and the racialization of Indigenous social systems, used sport as a weapon in the creation of an invader Dreaming. Sport was a tool in the building of a different image from that of the colonial invader. It shaped the way the invaders began to see themselves. A transformation of image away from a 'settler convict society' to that of a nation culminated in Federation on 1 January 1901.

Sport provided opportunities for Australia to present an image to the global community and take its place in the modern industrialized world. The fostering of national pride was developed by the interplay of sporting, social, political, economic and geographical features. The features of 'Australianness', including courage, independence and mateship, were evident in the success of Australian sportspeople on the international sporting scene. Australians could compete on an equal footing with other nations. These successes in colonial sports led to mass participation by the Australian populace and provided an escape from the economic realities of life during the Great Depression of the 1930s (J. McKay 1990).

The role of sport in the creation of an invader Dreaming is significant in the portrayal of 'the good life' of Australian society. Eric Wilmot, commenting on the construction of the invader Dreaming, says: '. . . they became in a sense a living image of their own deception. This is why they were so quick to grasp the idea of the "lucky country" and the debilitating mentality which that produced' (Wilmot 1991: 7).

Moreover, the creation of invader Dreaming ignores the reality that 'these people were caught up in an expansive movement of political power and also in religious proselytisation in a kind of Christian "jihad"' (Wilmot 1991: 4). What is even more frightening is that the creation of a false consciousness through the construction of an invader Dreaming lives with us today: 'Colonialism in its time was inevitable, and the British colonialism was the most gentle and civilized of all colonialisms. The Aborigines were lucky that the Dutch, the Portuguese, or the French did not stake an effective claim before the British' (McGuinness 1992, cited in Markus 1994: xi).

In addition to incarcerating Indigenous people as a response to the 'dying race's' situation colonial society was also confronted with the problem of an increasing 'part-Indigenous' or 'mixed blood' population. Social Darwinist evolutionary racist theory created a problem for colonial society with regard to 'mixed blood' people. Could you rescue those with some of the 'blood' and genes of the superior 'race'? The Eugenics movement argued that racial interbreeding was to be avoided, as it tainted the genes of superior 'races'. The response of colonial society to such a problem was to remove 'mixed blood' children from their parents, families and communities and place them in institutions such as orphanages or in foster care. Those affected are today known as the Stolen Generation (Human Rights and Equal Opportunity Commission 1997). This form of cultural racism was supported by most Christians of the time, who believed that the only hope for the 'half-castes' was to remove them from the influence of their parents and their own 'traditional' cultures. Government policies officially sanctioned efforts to destroy Indigenous identity, culture and language. Indigenous people were expected to adopt the same customs, values and attitudes as colonial society, as well as to take on, in theory, the racialized social systems of the colonizer. In essence Indigenous people were expected to use the tools that were instrumental in structuring Indigenous oppression.

Sport again played its role in the construction of invader Dreaming – particularly the perceived benefits of sport in healing the wounds of Indigenous people created by ideological policies of segregation, 'protection' and assimilation.

During this period colonial sport benefited from the effects of the Second World War. It was a time of general prosperity, growth and expansion that enabled many Australians to experience a higher standard of living.

In the late 1940s colonial lifestyles were bolstered by the introduction of the forty-hour, five-day week, with four weeks of annual leave. It was a boom time for colonial sport, with the population now enjoying more leisure time than ever before (McKay 1990). Australian society entered its 'golden age', with many of its athletes becoming Olympic and World champions, culminating in the successes at the 1956 Melbourne Olympic Games. Australia became acknowledged as one of the great sporting nations, and this set the platform for contemporary Australian ideology. Australians were constructed as healthy, bronzed, muscular athletes who developed these skills in the 'free', 'settled', 'democratic', 'lucky country' of popular imagination.

Indigenous access to and success in sport, it is argued, is evidence of the 'harmonious' nature of 'race' relations in this country. Sport, in addition, provided a model for the assimilation of Indigenous society into the broader Australian society. Even as colonial society has created its Invader Dreaming, however, through racialized sport and ideology, sport has also been a site of ongoing struggle. Tatz (1995b: 342) alerts us to the potential of sport in the struggle against racism:

> Sport is a vehicle for many things, including the promotion of nationalism and ideology and for demonstrating attitudes, such as dislike of apartheid. Sport is not the sole preserve or domain of governments or officials to use in this way. It is logical and legitimate for groups to use sport to make political and social points in a dramatic way.

By the end of the 1960s it was becoming clear to colonial society that ideas for an assimilated and integrated Indigenous population that gave up its cultural identity were not going to be realized (Lippmann 1994). The actions of resistance groups in response to the oppression of Indigenous people helped shape the movement away from official assimilatory government policy. Concepts of cultural diversity began to germinate in the consciousness of Australian society. The racializing invasion of Indigenous lands would however, ensure that notions of cultural diversity would not include the incorporation of Indigenous legal, health, political, economic, social or sporting systems or the rejection of colonial ways of organizing society.

Indigenous Australian resistance to colonialism, grounded in principles of self-determination or relative autonomy, and the validation and legitimization of cultural aspirations and identity, along with the struggle for land rights, continue to sustain the contemporary reshaping of the political agenda.

Indigenous voices have not and will not be silenced, despite attempts to stop the consciousness-raising efforts to rewrite colonial Australian history in all its forms. Indeed, all attempts to delegitimate or invalidate Indigenous under-standings and rights continue to be met with fierce resistance. Sport does not escape the process of Indigenous peoples writing back in resistance to coloniz-ation.

Toward Indigenous Australian Sports History: An Anti-colonial Reconstruction

The study of racism in sport in the Australian context has begun to examine institutionalized racism in sport.[8] It has also started to explore the use of sport as a means of social control and the imposition of colonial norms and values upon Indigenous people.[9] The majority of writings, however, persist with a theoretical paradigm that situates the understanding of racism at the person-alized individual level and thereby concentrates on the attitudes and values of racists.[10]

Despite this important literature on Indigenous people and sport, there has been, overall, a scarcity of research that focuses on 'race' and/or racism in an Australian context. Colin Tatz's text *Obstacle Race: Aborigines in Sport* (1995b) is an important text in the scholarship of Indigenous sport history and soci-ology because it focuses substantially upon analysis rather than description. This text places Indigenous people in sport within a history, politics and sociology of racism in Australia, with an emphasis on racial and social trends, civil rights and the forms of genocide perpetrated in Australia. Tatz moves some way towards filling the gaps in our knowledge of Indigenous experiences in sport, even though he seems unwilling to ask critical questions about the construction of sport and what impact colonial society had on Indigenous sporting practices. Nevertheless, Tatz asks Australians to examine critically the prevalent attitudes, values and folklore about sport. This is important, because Australians, in the main, do not critically examine sport, and thus fail to see the extent to which it is socially constructed and influenced by the political and economic forces of the day (Sage 1990). Moreover, as I contend, the shaping of a critically conscious body of work in sports sociology must be built upon an agenda that begins with Indigenous Australian experiences and that places Indigenous Australians at the centre of writings on Indigenous Australians, racism and sport. Our cultural freedom requires the addressing of issues of structure and power by beginning in the places where Indigenous Australians live their lives, where meaning is produced, represented and contested in the relationships between Indigenous and other Australians.

Conclusion: Survival, Reclamation and Transformation

There has been no shortage of 'privileged' colonial sporting analyses, but very little in the way of Indigenous Australian sporting analyses. Depriving Indigenous Australians of our own history, from our perspectives, is an instrument of oppression. Attempts to deprive Indigenous people of Indigenous knowledges or ways of being have made it more difficult to sustain an individual and collective identity. However, we have survived, and will continue to do so; but there is a need to continue the struggle through reclaiming our knowledges and resisting the further racialization of our social institutions. It is for this reason that critical analyses of 'race' relations in sport that emphasize Indigenous perspectives are needed. Understanding how Indigenous people construct racism in sport and how they experience it could help to deconstruct taken-for-granted socially constructed notions of racism and sport.

A critical approach to racism in sport from an Indigenous perspective should be interested in change in and transformation of the roles and structures that control us. If we agree that Indigenous peoples are oppressed, then we must ask: 'What are we as Indigenous people in sport to do about this? Are we a part of the solution or are we a part of the problem? Can we even agree on the problem? Sports may contribute to a healthier physical self and provide role models to other Indigenous people, but to what extent do they politicize us and empower us to challenge and change dominant hegemonic processes? What is the value or point in being fitter, stronger and faster if we do so only in ways and within limits set for us by those who oppress Indigenous Australian people?'

Notes

1. Sport in this paper is defined as competitive, organized and institutionalized, and is governed by constitutions, by-laws, rules and codes of practice.
2. The Ngarrindjeri nation are the Indigenous Australian people whose country includes the Murray River and Lakes, Coorong and Encounter Bay of what is today known as South Australia.
3. I subscribe to the view that 'race' is an ideologically loaded, socially constructed term, which has no scientific status. I use inverted commas around the word to indicate a refusal to legitimate its claimed status.
4. When I refer to the worldwide racist movement I am using the term 'movement' as a social movement in the same sense as Touraine (1985, 1992) and Cohen (1985). I am not referring to an organized and structured political movement.

5. By 'racialization' I mean the use of the concept 'race' to oppress groups of people systematically (racism) and establish the social, political and economic systems that govern a society.

6. See Atkinson and Poulter (1993), who argue that Australian Rules Football is derived from an Indigenous Australian game known as Marngrook.

7. 'Dreaming' is a concept or term used by some Indigenous Australian communities to refer to all that is known and all that is understood. It is central to the existence of Indigenous communities (though it may be named differently in particular communities), their lifestyles and cultures, and explains origin(s), values, beliefs and relationships with life and land.

8. See Tatz (1995b); Vamplew, Moore, O'Hara, Cashman and Jobling (1992); Whimpress (1992); Hallinan (1991); Nadel (1993).

9. See Broome (1979); R. Howell and Maxwell (1986); Daly (1994).

10. See Harris (1989); Walker (1992); Chryssides (1993); Coolwell (1993).

4

Making Strange the Country and Making Strange the Countryside: Spatialized Clashes in the Affective Economies of Aotearoa/New Zealand during the 1981 Springbok Rugby Tour[1]

Malcolm MacLean

Picture the scene if you will. You are in Eltham, Taranaki on 3 July 1981. This country town of around 2,400 people is a service centre for the local dairy region. The biggest annual event is the Christmas parade, and rugby success is one of the few grounds on which local men feel that the local professional elite respects them (de Jong 1986, 1987). July 3 was the only time that people in Eltham opposed to the planned 1981 South African Springbok rugby tour of Aotearoa/New Zealand sought to make their opposition public. On Friday night the shops were shut and the town was usually quiet. This Friday was different. A small group of around a dozen gathered to march against the tour. Hostile groups from the local hotels confronted them once they entered the main street. They were showered with eggs, stones, glasses – not all of them empty. Participants speak of feeling as if the whole town was bearing down on them to snuff them out.

To the tour supporters, the issue was rugby. As the march entered the main street it was greeted with a chant – 'We want rugby.' One young man ran up to the marchers, shouting 'We support apartheid. We support racist teams. Give us rugby'. Other cries: 'Traitors! Look, they've all got beards! Go back to Russia you Communist pigs!' One man, the local school guidance counsellor, whose children had joined the march, was singled out to jeers of 'You coward.

Hiding behind your fucking kids.' The roadside crowd thickened, became more aggressive, and finally showered the marchers with debris. It may not sound like much, but the marchers were few in number. Most had never marched before. They faced the wrath of the town, a 'fundamental force . . . so common as to be anonymous' (Chapple 1984: 50). In Eltham, the anonymous force was challenged and threatened with exposure by fewer than 20 anti-tour marchers. Its representatives fought back. The next day no one mentioned the march – it seemed that all had returned to normal. The challengers never marched again.

Eltham is in rural Taranaki, scene of some of the most protracted fighting between Maori and Pakeha (New Zealanders of European descent) during the nineteenth-century colonial wars. Land is a precious and contested commodity in the area. During 1997, Pakeha leasehold farmers claimed rights akin to ownership when new legislation allowed the revision to market rates of lease payments on certain Maori-owned land (rather than the pittance of the last 120 or so years). In Taranaki there is a cultural substratum, a subtle undercurrent stemming from the wars and land confiscation that is seldom exposed but is hotly contested and denied by those who contend that 'We are all New Zealanders.' The substratum, although an ideological underpinning to the response by Eltham's many tour supporters, was not an explicit factor in their hostile response. The protesters were, in themselves, no threat. They were few in number, and not likely physically to threaten the majority of Eltham's people. They were the local Methodist Minister, the school guidance counsellor and members of a Church youth group. The cultural threat was far more profound, and the response packaged much more than the question of rugby.

This chapter explores the spatiality of Aotearoa/New Zealand's 1981 Springbok tour as a crucial moment affecting the conditions of life and cultural security of the dominant cultural formation. There are two converging strands in the argument. In the first, the question of fandom is explored to consider the ways that supporters and opponents of this tour maintained differing affective relationships with the world around them. In the second, the notion of 'lived spaces' will be examined to consider reasons for the spatialized pattern of responses. (Lefebvre 1991; Soja 1989, 1996) The convergence of these strands will provide the framework necessary to understand the context within which this particular response to the tour took place by showing the connections between contested structures of subjectivities. In spatializing rural protesters' and tour supporters' affectivities in the context of an emerging post-colonising tendency this paper explicates the structural context of both affectivities to argue that affectivity provides a means to 'release the co-ordinates of subjectivity from static, uniform, transparent notions of place and being' (Pile and Thrift 1995: 5).

This chapter therefore focuses on means to link structure to agency, rather than explore an emphasis on agency itself.

The anti-tour campaign tapped three strands of political discontent (MacLean 2000). There was a growing dissatisfaction with the National Party government under the leadership of Robert Muldoon. The second was the impact of feminist politics: like much of the rest of the First World, Aotearoa/New Zealand had witnessed over a decade of active feminist campaigning around a diverse range of issues. The third was an emerging Maori land rights movement, asserting a different history of Aotearoa/New Zealand. The land rights movement found an ontological ally in the anti-tour movement through their common prioritization of the politics of 'race': this ontological kinship presented a profound critique of the dominance of (colonial) New Zealand over (indigenous) Aotearoa. In this chapter I use three different terms to refer to the islands in the south-west Pacific known as 'New Zealand': 'Aotearoa' is used to mean the Maori cultural and historical space within those islands, 'New Zealand' refers to the dominant colonial, gendered and classed political entity, and 'Aotearoa/New Zealand' is an inclusive noun.

The land rights movement is vital to understanding the rural spatial politics of the anti-tour campaign. The Treaty of Waitangi in 1840 legitimated the colonization of Aotearoa by New Zealand. This allowed Britain to claim territorial sovereignty and assert its power to govern. The nineteenth-century history of the colonial North Island is one of widespread, but sporadic, warfare involving almost all the Maori on one side or the other. Twentieth-century Maori–state relations had been characterized by work within the terms of a Westminster system. During the early 1970s a shift took place when a new generation of activist Maori leaders emerged. The tensions over land became more intense and had catapulted to public awareness with the occupation of Takaparawha (Bastion Point) – in central Auckland, the largest city – in 1977 and 1978. The effect of this newly assertive Maori politics stressing land alienation, while also drawing attention to the decline of *te reo Maori* (Maori language) and demanding new social policies, was an emerging reinterpretation of New Zealand's colonial history. By the middle of the 1980s the politics of colonialism had transformed itself into a state-supported policy of biculturalism. In this context, the anti-tour movement, and the wider anti-apartheid movement, appear to have had quite different meanings for Maori and Pakeha involved in the campaigns. As a result, this discussion deals primarily with Pakeha engagements with and responses to anti-tour politics (MacLean, forthcoming).

As a colony of settlement, a fundamental historical tension in Aotearoa/New Zealand is one of land and of space. This is not to deny the socio-cultural and historical significance of gender and class, but to assert that the key factor affecting the historical and socio-cultural specificity of Aotearoa/New Zealand is spatial and colonial. The question of colonial and post-colonizing relationships and tendencies underlies the more explicit tensions in Aotearoa/New Zealand during 1981 – the struggle over the tour, the cultural centrality of rugby union, the growing economic crisis. The commingling of dissident forces in the anti-tour campaign made it a key factor in the emergence of a post-colonizing trend in Aotearoa/New Zealand. Considering the particular forces contextualizing rural responses to the anti-tour movement can expose this post-colonizing tendency.

Rural New Zealand is valued and valorized in the dominant world-view. The ontological significance of the rural world cannot be underestimated in assessing the political and cultural assertions of nationhood: the rural community, the farming man, the taming, shaping and controlling of the land to produce the modern nation and economy are crucial signifiers. The dominant view is that New Zealand is expressed through relations with the land as a farming nation that articulated a way of belonging to the nation and to the remnants of empire; but 'belonging is a way of remembering and constructing a collective memory of place, . . . such constructions are always contestable' (Parkin 1998: ix). The land rights movement was telling new stories about the land, so that new ways of belonging needed to be found.

In the late 1970s and early 1980s these local circumstances existed alongside a dissentient set of forces that can be conceived of as a nascent post-colonizing tendency. Contemporary means of understanding post-colonial identities emphasize metaphors of diaspora, mobility and transculturation. These experiences of ex-colonials in the metropole are of minimal use in a colony of settlement such as Aotearoa/New Zealand. Diaspora may, however, be suggestively adapted to inform an analysis of Aotearoa/New Zealand. During the late 1970s both Maori and Pakeha can be seen as diasporic: Maori from rural to urban dwelling, and as dispersed from cultural and communal bases including the ability to exercise enough social power to deal with the dispossession effected by colonization; Pakeha from a still powerful notion of Britain as 'home', although this was weakening significantly. Both Maori and Pakeha were likely to occupy more than one home (both were in Aotearoa/New Zealand, but Maori also tended to occupy Aotearoa and Pakeha occupied New Zealand, as well as retaining an attachment to the British 'home'). Maori and Pakeha were like a rain-forest's sympatric breeds: within the same space but occupying different niches, with Pakeha largely unaware of the existence of Aotearoa. The nascent post-colonizing of Aotearoa/New Zealand relied on Pakeha awareness of the oppressiveness of (Pakeha) New Zealand. There was a willingness among a few to 'make some kind of difficult settlement with the new . . . cultures with which they were forced into contact, and . . . [succeed] in remaking themselves and fashioning new kinds of cultural identity by, consciously or unconsciously, drawing on more than one cultural repertoire' (S. Hall, 1995: 206). In Aotearoa/New Zealand this is now referred to as 'biculturalism', but during 1981 was barely considered outside Maori activist circles and a tiny number of Pakeha activist supporters. The prioritization of 'race' and the ontological challenges presented through the challenge to history and national self-image during the anti-tour campaign shifted the terrain to provide more fertile ground for the growth of this post-colonizing tendency. The cultural disruption resulting from this shifting ground is apparent in the responses to anti-tour activity in rural areas, where the struggle was largely seen as one over rugby union.

The traits of rugby union are seen to embody a number of defining national characteristics. The classic image of the New Zealand man is the rugby fanatic: he follows the game closely after childhood inculcation, and aspires to be like the paragons of rugby-hood. Despite his obvious passion for the game, he is not unseemly or excessively emotional about it. He is subdued and stands quietly in support of the local team, just as he stands quietly to support the All Blacks. His support is restrained, but intense. Despite all this, Robin Winks could note in 1953 that New Zealanders (undistinguished by gender) 'go raving, frothing mad when football season arrives' (Winks 1954: 100). At times this is true, and nothing would get the male going like a visit by the Springboks – South Africa's national rugby team.

The most successful of these visits was the Springbok tour of 1956. There are men in their 50s who can still recite all the names of the touring party. These men would certainly not classify themselves as fans, but they might call themselves *aficionados* – men who were connoisseurs of or enthusiasts for rugby union. If pressed, they might admit that there might just be something unhealthy about this devotion. One of these men who can still recite all 32 members of the touring party ironically claims to have become a member of Rugby Fanatics Anonymous, which provides 'therapy to cure people of this overblown addiction to the game of rugby football'.[2] In suggesting that there might be such a thing as an 'overblown addiction' to rugby this man points to ideas of excessiveness and deviance.

In refusing to see themselves as fans, many of these men are acting in a way that Jensen sees as allowing the assertion of normality (Jensen 1992). For Jensen, many discussions of fans include a tendency to pathologize fans so that their excessiveness becomes a way to construct the fan as deviant. This notion of the pathological fan can help explain the cultural power of the excesses of emotion associated with much masculine sporting fandom. In the case of rugby union in Aotearoa/New Zealand, the cultural site in question is at the heart of the moral landscape in its associations with masculinity, with the nation and with the dominant colonial fraction. Fiske excludes the association of sports with masculinity from his more general observation that fandom is more typically associated with denigrated cultural forms and with the cultural tastes of subordinated social formations (Fiske 1992). In his vision of fandom it is outside of or oppositional to official culture, while also expropriating and reworking official cultural values and characteristics. His exception of sports and masculinity from this conceptualization allows us to consider rugby fandom in Aotearoa/New Zealand as an -Other that is not outside or oppositional, but is fundamental to official cultural values and characteristics.

Fiske points to fans' enunciative productivity, where a range of verbal and non-verbal discursive codes talkfandom. This enunciative productivity remains hidden, masked or obscured when the identity being asserted is a core element of the dominant value system. It is also likely to be highly naturalized within habitual bodily and other mundane practices and within habitual verbal codes. Connerton suggests that habits are 'affective dispositions'. As such, they are more than mere dispositions (Connerton 1989: 93). In his view, a disposition implies a degree of latency or potentiality, whereas an 'affective disposition', a habit, implies operativeness through a continually practised activity. It is the affectivity of the disposition that shifts it from a potentiality to an operative force. The masking of this enunciative productivity within ritual and habitual bodily practices naturalizes the identity being asserted, so that challenges to sites of identity assertion are met with fiercely defensive opposition.

This bodily practice links the pleasures and meanings of fandom to place. The notion of proprioception relates to the reception and interpretation of information by non-visceral means. This suggests that the orientation of the body and its movement through either physical or cultural space can result in the making of particular meanings. For instance, Kirshenblatt-Gimblett (1998) sees different bodily movements through a museum as effecting the construction of different stories.[3] A similar analysis can be applied to the orientation of the body within 'natural' space – although the notion of 'natural' space obscures the cultural meanings of spaces and places. As specific bodily practices acquire and develop particular meanings specific to the place in which they occur – in which they take place – a second layer of naturalization is effected. The 'natural' body overlays the 'natural' place in such a way that neither is critically examined and that both remain relatively uncontrolled. The result is that enunciative productivity is masked through the naturalization of space and the construction of a series of common-sense meanings, or affective dispositions. In instances such as rural New Zealand in 1981, where the cultural meaning and interpretation of space was in dispute, spatial (re)configurations challenge this naturalization of space as the orientation of the body to cultural (existential) space is reshaped. This partial denaturalization (exposure) of enunciative productivity accounts in part for the intensity of the localized response to the anti-tour movement.

Affect binds these components of fandom so as to account for the depth of feeling manifest in Eltham. Grossberg contends that neither the audience nor the texts themselves are sufficient to distinguish fandom or to explain why fans emerge (Grossberg 1992). In his view, analysts need to look at the relationship between the fan audience and its texts. Fandom, for Grossberg, goes beyond a consumer sensibility that produces and prioritizes structures of pleasure, and must be understood as a sensibility within a domain of affect or mood made difficult to identify because of its very mundanity. This mood, this affectivity, includes both the extent of feeling and the sites of affective engagement. It is characterized by both quantity and quality while also directing emotional investment to particular (multi)textual sites of 'absorption'. This makes specific sites important as places of identity formation to prioritize different differences that become arenas of ideological struggles. Fandoms are therefore overlaid by other forms of difference, to be augmented and reshaped, resulting in affective alliances that vary according to context. In this sense, affectivity makes certain practices/things matter and thus become textual representatives of the fan, as authorized to speak on the fan's behalf. This is the process that results in a situation where rugby union is allowed by many New Zealand men to enunciate their relationships with the world on their behalf. Affectivity, therefore, is an action-creating imperative that shapes quotidian practice.

In speaking these relationships, rugby union interpellates other images and sites associated with the dominant culture's favoured national image. This interpellation includes identities associated with masculine and settled colonial cultural economies. Bell's discussion of images used to depict and promote Aotearoa/New Zealand shows a popular imagery of New Zealand where urban life is not considered to be 'real New Zealand' (Bell 1996: 10–11). Despite its overwhelmingly urban population, over 80 per cent in the 1981 census, New Zealand remained economically dependent on land-based extractive industries and tourism – itself premised on the spectacularity and splendour of the New Zealand landscape. Each of the dominant economic sectors is non-urban in its material base. Although agriculture fell from 35 per cent of GDP in 1936 to 10 per cent of GDP in 1976, wool, meat, butter and cheese remained the major exports – making up 80 per cent in 1936 and 50 per cent in 1976 (Rice 1992: 596, 598). Despite attempts to protect and encourage local manufacturing, the sectoral shift in the composition of the GDP was between agriculture and services; manufacturing remained static.

The economic importance of the rural sector in a country that saw itself as Britain's farm in the South Pacific, and responded to the UK's entry to the European Economic Community by seeking to retain privileged access to British markets, only later seeking new markets for agricultural produce, gave farmers and the rural world an iconographic place in New Zealand's self-image. This translated into political importance and power, and to a political discourse where the two major parties at least recognized the political importance of the farming sector (Bremer 1993). The economy was subject to major strain during the 1970s. Although the agricultural sector grew in volume by 2.1 per cent per annum between 1971 and 1983, it was seriously affected by the high inflation during that period (Rose 1985: 34–35). Agriculture's income grew by significantly less than costs during the 1970s. Between 1971 and 1983, output prices for agricultural production grew by 291 per cent while input prices grew by 367 per cent. The result of these shifts in input and output costs was a sector-wide falling operating surplus.

This rural identity is hailed and made by the dominant iconographies of both the nation and of masculinity. Grossberg stresses that affectivity can never justify itself, but needs an ideological justification. In fandom this justification is provided by an ideology of excess: because something matters, it must have some excessive characteristic that justifies affective investment. Fans' investments in particular practices and texts grant them a means of asserting control over their affective lives and allow new investments in and creations of meaning. In this way, the association of rugby union with the dominant cultural formation of New Zealand grants the people who have joined that formation, but are not members of the socio-cultural elite, a means of controlling their lives and of articulating their membership of the nation. In criticizing rugby's connections with South Africa, anti-tour activists were calling into question the legitimacy of that dominant affective economy. In Grossberg's words 'the organisation of struggles around particular popular languages depends upon their articulation within different affective economies, that is, upon the different investments by which they are empowered and within which they empower their fans' (Grossberg 1992: 65). In other words, the conflict in 1981 should be seen as a clash of affective economies shaped in part by different post-colonizing identities.

An affective association with rugby union empowered affiliates of the dominant cultural formation in the same way that an association with the anti-apartheid movement empowered opponents of the tour. In Taranaki, this dominant affectivity rests on an embodiment of a particular socio-historical cultural mood that is barely ever exposed or challenged. Eltham exists because of its place in the rural economy. It is part of the cultural core, both intellectually and spatially. There is a material basis to Eltham's core location. The rural sector is the iconographic core of the national economy, first providing wool exports and then frozen meat and dairy products. The nineteenth-century colonial contest for land is primarily seen in this materialist frame – as competition between Maori and Pakeha for control of a key element in the means of production. This was a vital element, but this contest was shaped by Victorian attitudes into a struggle for sovereignty and for the assertion of a particular cultural form (Belich 1986: 311–55). The final success of the colonial forces, after military efforts between 1842 and 1916, was not a military success but a victory through building a regime reliant on the maintenance of Maori colonized dispossession.

A core ideological element of that regime was the myth of 'the best race relations in the world'. This combined with myths of military chivalry by both Maori and colonial forces and with the pioneer myth to create for New Zealand a heroic tale of development and a noble past and present. The modern form of this super-myth, in 1981, was the persistent notion that 'we are all one people' and a populist valorization of 'the working man'. This notion of all working together to build a nation is a key element of the populist politics of the era. It was a time when war was not available as a nation-building tool, when unemployment was beginning to emerge as a significant problem for the first time since the end of the Second World War, and when work became fundamental to the maintenance of the dominant conceptualization of the nation. As Webster has pointed out '[s]weat is to populism what blood is to nationalism, an almost mythical fluid that preserves tradition' (Webster 1988: 70). Work and sweat are linked to the work ethic and to gender. The populist politics of the era retained a deep-seated endorsement of the status quo, and appealed to the popularly held myths of nation contained in the image of the hard-working (rural) man.

During the mid-1970s Taranaki was the site of a significant development of petrochemical industries developed within a state strategy to make New Zealand self-reliant in energy supplies. This strategy was presented as the solution to the nation's economic woes. In Taranaki it represented an unstated but significant cultural blow. This was a dairying economy of small holdings, where wealth depended on high-quality milk production. The prioritization of industrial production threatened the cultural and economic significance of Taranaki's farming world. For people in towns such as Eltham, the late 1970s was not only a period of threat from non-workers, those who did not sweat in their jobs – including those in their own town who dared break ranks on 3 July; but also from a new sort of worker without the cultural matrix that is a settled agricultural community. The agricultural sector (and with it the rural economy) was under increasing strain throughout the 1970s as world commodity prices placed considerable pressure on agricultural output prices at a time when input prices were rising rapidly. Farmers in Taranaki who were feeling the pinch as a result of these economic shifts appeared to respond ambivalently to the new petrochemical industries, as economically important and significant, but also as culturally threatening. The dominant national imaginary was particularly strained in Taranaki.

In towns such as Eltham, the historical and material reality needed considerable finessing to comply with the dominant mythology. The colonial history of Taranaki is obscured behind a noble mythology emerging from the stories of war elsewhere in the country. Taranaki's first outbreak of fighting, at Waitara in 1859, was engineered by the governor of the day to break Maori resistance to land sales. In general, colonial and imperial troops performed badly in these wars, which lasted until 1874 – with an epilogue at the destruction of the Maori community at Parihaka in 1881. In the late 1870s over a million acres of land were indiscriminately confiscated from Maori, all of whom were deemed to be 'rebels', whereas previously land had be 'bought' through a process of negotiation. This seizure of land both destroyed Maori social organization and provided the material basis for the development of a Pakeha-dominated economy in the area. The land was cleared and burned, and almost all traces of Maori occupation were destroyed to allow the construction of the agricultural economy that is now Taranaki (Waitangi Tribunal 1996). This destructive history is obscured behind the more generalized heroic mythologies. It is also obscured by the sense of naturalized proprietorship Pakeha farmers have come to claim, as they did during the debate over the Maori Reserved Lands Amendment Act 1997. The sense of proprietorship is common among farmers in colonies of settlement (Read 1996: 52–74).

The potential discomfort caused by the history of the acquisition of Taranaki was obscured by the populist politics of sweat and by the framing of the landscape within a discourse of beauty. The broad rolling fertile band surrounding the near-perfect cone of Mt Taranaki is strikingly beautiful in content and contrast. Whereas once it had been an inhospitable and difficult bush-clad environment, its post-confiscation agricultural image is of a landscape (along with the rest of the native environment, including the natives themselves) tamed by human efforts and the skills of civilization (Park 1995). Taming the natural world controlled its dangers. This tamed landscape was generally conceived of as a natural landscape, obscuring the cultural implications of seeing it as tamed. Taranaki is, as a result, seen as a naturally beautiful place where its people were, in the late 1970s and early 1980s, satisfied with the place in which they lived (Terry 1981: 17). This perceived natural-ness of the

Taranaki landscape is vital, because the landscape is not seen as conquered: a perception that parallels the historical amnesia of colonial war. During the late 1970s, as the Maori demands for land rights grew, rural Taranaki found itself in a context of growing existential uncertainties that grew from challenges about the land and its history. The effectiveness of the beautiful landscape where the 'sitedness of belonging' is continually re-en-acted to transcend these existential uncertainties was weakening as it became a site of struggle that allowed and asserted those existential uncertainties (Lovell 1998: 10).

The weakening ideological effectiveness of the landscape threatened to facilitate that small step from the awe inspired by the experience of Beauty to the threats and dangers that make the Sublime, which must be carefully controlled to prevent the Beautiful slipping through the Sublime to the Monstrous (Zizek 1999: 34–50). Taranaki's Sublime had become the cultural dangers presented by the telling of another story about the land. The rural landscape, and the relationship with the land where farmers see themselves as 'of' the land, has become a fundamental element of the hegemonic national imaginary. The land, therefore, occupies a similar iconographic position to rugby in the dominant national cultural matrix. The legitimacy of the position held by land in this matrix was coming under attack through the 1970s as an increasingly strong Maori land rights movement emerged. As the legitimacy of land ownership was challenged, the rising women's movement threatened to unsettle the established gender politics of the matrix as well. The lived nature of the dominant cultural formation in rural Taranaki meant that the emerging state of cultural siege was intensely felt.

Taranaki's Sublime, controlled by its discourses of Beauty, was threatened with full exposure by the growing Maori land rights movement. The anti-tour movement intensified that threat by accentuating the question of 'race'. Not only was the myth of the best race relations in the world under threat, but opposition to playing rugby against South Africa alleged New Zealand complicity in the maintenance of apartheid, the most reprehensible race relations regime in the world. New Zealand was at risk of being seen as much whiter and less moral than it liked to see itself. The debate did not threaten to expose the Sublimity of the Taranaki land, or even to deny or dispute the Beauty. The debate threatened to expose the masculinist and colonial mechanics of the topographic Sublime. The Sublime carries with it a sense of rapture. The position of land(scape) in the dominant cultural matrix is premised on this sense of rapture itself, as the matrix is both trapped by and engorged with the land(scape) as iconic.

Cultural analysts, historians and geographers are not adept at readings of the Sublime. It is, however, a major element in treatments of Romantic fiction, especially the Gothic. Sayle (1999) has noted that a key distinction within the Sublime is between a masculine Sublime, seeking to control the objects of its rapture, and a feminine Sublime encountering (and in part exposing) the mechanics of gendered (or in this case colonizing) power. The discourses of Taranaki's Beauty operate within the masculine Sublime as controlling discourses. The anti-tour movement's largely unarticulated critique of the dominant cultural order threatened the controlling elements of those discursive frames through a perceived connection with a Maori land rights movement to threaten the position of both land and rugby in that matrix. What is more, in exposing the control of the objects of rapture, the unarticulated alliance of the anti-tour movement and the land rights movement was gendered feminine. The dozen or so people on the street in Eltham on 3 July were therefore the physical manifestation of every threat to Eltham's way of life and location in the cultural matrix that was.

In the medium term, this unarticulated threat saw the control of the Sublime fail as the control of the objects of rapture was exposed and weakened by the reinscription of New Zealand history that has led to a growing awareness of Aotearoa/New Zealand as post-colonizing. New Zealand is still at the stage of confronting its Monstrousness, the hidden histories underlying the acquisition of land and the domination and appropriation of the indigenous. The state's active role in seeking to address and atone for the breaches of the Treaty of Waitangi is generally failing to meet the full range of Maori aspirations and demands, but it has provoked a widely based debate and a shifting awareness of New Zealand's history. The commission of inquiry into Maori claims of breaches of the Treaty has prompted a rapid expansion in historical research and has granted a considerable degree of legitimacy to Maori histories of their encounters with colonizing forces (Ward 1997). It is an awareness with which many remain extremely uncomfortable. Whereas the threat to the controlling forces of the Sublime was largely unarticulated in 1981, by the middle of the 1990s in Taranaki the dominant Pakeha understanding was submitted to an assault by the Monstrous as the result of the Waitangi Tribunal's inquiries' leading to an interim report that infamously describes the colonization of Taranaki as 'a holocaust' (Waitangi Tribunal 1996: 312). The tensions underlying this conclusion were present in Taranaki and provided the sedimentary basis of Maori–Pakeha relations and discourses of 'race' in the province well before 1981. They were, as such, the fundamental unarticulated tension that Eltham's protesters threatened to expose.

The events in Eltham were among the worst to be reported. In smaller towns and provincial centres protest organizers tended to play it safe. They organized meetings, street stalls where literature was distributed, or static rallies, perhaps recognizing the cultural danger they posed. Almost all were during daylight hours. In Eltham they had braved the night-time wrath of the locals – and risked excommunication, in the same way that the rugby community shunned the All Black captain and Taranaki farmer Graeme Mourie for years after his refusal to play the Springboks in 1981 (McTaggart 1982; Knight 1990).

The imbrication of rurality with the dominant cultural view as an intimate element of the hegemonic existence meant that an apparent attack on rugby led to a struggle over the place where that cultural orientation had meaning. Soja contends that spatiality must be added to historicality and sociality as a 'third existential dimension'. His analysis parallels and develops Lefebvre's three concurrent spatial forms (Soja 1996: 3; Lefebvre 1991). Lefebvre proposes a perceived space of materialized spatial practice, a conceived space as representations of space, and lived spaces of representation. These spaces of representation are not a combination of perceived and conceived space, but are a third level of spatial existence. Soja's extension of this categorization is to develop a more explicit spatially-linked epistemology, and point to the existence of a spatialized ontology. Spaces of representation destabilize the predominant theoretical tendency in the social sciences to immobilize space. This approach does not eliminate sociality or historicality, or any other social dynamic: it brings them together in such a way that space is not an inert medium for history and society, but is active as an instrument and as a goal. Space and, more particularly, spatiality therefore becomes a subject of struggle and political contention, not just an object or an inert site.

As space can then be read as a subject of struggle, the rural political dynamics of the 1981 tour take on a new layer of meaning. Anti-tour campaigners were not only challenging the politics of sporting contact with South Africa, they were challenging many of the vital elements of the dominant cultural identity. It is likely that they failed to recognize the spatiality of this cultural identity, given the general tendency to denigrate space as a factor in affective economies. In staging its critique of this dominant affective economy, the anti-tour movement was seeking an implicit reterritorialization of Aotearoa/New Zealand that would weaken the rurality of prevailing cultural iconography. A corollary of Gupta and Ferguson's call to disrupt the idea that cultures are correlated with discrete spaces can be read in de Certeau's notion that resistive acts inject other meanings into space defined by relations of power (Gupta and Ferguson 1992; de Certeau 1984). These relations of power – be they state power or cultural power – thus seek to isolate and exclude resistive space through effective border maintenance, but continually find that spatial purity is disrupted, or more accurately dislocated, by resistive acts. Resistive spaces are, as a result, multiple, dynamic and weak – but the dislocation remains. The hostility of the response in rural areas must be understood as the result of reterritorialization and associated cultural dislocation.

In the case of the anti-tour movement, a mass movement that sought to challenge extant cultural forms confronted the relations of cultural power. In mounting this challenge in rural areas, the anti-tour movement sought to dislocate the metaphorical sites of cultural power by reinscribing other elements of the cultural *mélange*. A vital element of this cultural dislocation is the divergent foci of the competing tendencies. The dominant cultural force among Pakeha looked to the countryside, primary industries (especially farming) and the local. The resistive cultural formation had an urbane, metropolitan and internationalist perspective. In places such as Eltham the local was barely challenged or threatened; in cities such as Wellington and Auckland urbane internationalism found more fertile pastures. This clash of cultures is then a clash of co-located spatialities. In the one, a priority is given to the rituals that maintain the current body corporate – to rugby and the cultural codes it signifies. In the other, priority is given to a series of rituals and practices that seek to subvert and dislocate that body corporate by attaching other meanings to rugby games against South Africans. In many ways, each group misunderstood the other. The tour defenders were certain that, despite the issue's being apartheid, the challenge was to their local way of life. In this sense they were correct – but the local way of life should be seen as more than national; it must be seen as local and specific, it must be spatialized and firmly attached to this place and places like it.

The differing tour responses must be read in the context of the spatiality of dominant and dissident cultural forms. Each affective economy carries with it a particular spatialized cultural dynamic woven through and connecting its sites of significance. This imbues each lived space with a pattern of significances that shapes and is shaped by the practice of everyday life, its social memory and habitual/affective dispositions. In rural New Zealand, the ambience surrounding the tour was far more hostile than in urban New Zealand, because in the provinces the people affectively embody the national mythology – it is a potent form of (cultural) proprioception within an (ideologically totalized) sympatric niche. Their spaces of representation were those valorized and vaunted by the prevailing mythological regime. The anti-tour movement coupled with the land rights movement threatened to make strange the country and make strange the countryside. Support for the tour was therefore support for a way of life seen to be under challenge.

Notes

1. I am particularly grateful to Loykie Lomine for helpful comments.
2. Interview, 30 August 1999.
3. I am grateful to Professor Kirshenblatt-Gimblett for her advice on references to proprioception.

5

Sport, Postcolonialism and Modern China: Some Preliminary Thoughts

Dong-Jhy Hwang and Grant Jarvie

Introduction

Sport as an important part of Chinese culture has been the subject of an increasing amount of attention (Brownell 1995 and 2000; Fan 1996; Knuttgen, Ma and Wu 1990; Riordan and Jones 1999). Central to some of the most recent interventions has been the suggestion that since at least the 1980s China has entered a period of neo-coloniality or postcoloniality. In this particular aspect of the work of postcolonialism, a number of writers have been critical of Western Universalism as a basis for explaining non-Western problems (Bhabha 1994; Said 1993, 1995; Spivak 1987, 1990; JanMohamed 1985). Said has been critical of what he sees as cults such as post-modernism, discourse analysis, new historicism, deconstruction, and neo-pragmatism, all of which afford an astonishing sense of weightlessness with regard to the importance of history (Said 1993: 366–7). Although this chapter is deliberately eclectic, if there is a single strand running through it, it is to recall Said's attention to the historically variable, complex and distinct set of processes at play in imperial and colonial articulations of the non-Western world. Following on from the work of Said (1993 and 1995), which has made a significant and sustained contribution to the debate of postcolonialism, the argument at the heart of this chapter is that the analysis of the development of sport in Modern China continues to be heavily influenced by Western thought. The issues outlined in this chapter emphasize the extent to which sport in China has developed under the influence of postcolonialism since at least the 1980s. This provides the context for a preliminary discussion of sport and postcolonialism in Modern China.

Postcolonialism in China

Although China was never directly colonized by any Western imperialist power, Mao Zedong frequently referred to China as a colonial, semi-colonial and semi-feudal society in the first half of the twentieth century (Mao 1975: 341). Neo-colonialism can be best seen through the lens of the Chinese people in the 1980s. Since the beginning of the 1980s, multinational capital and post-modernist culture have made a significant impact upon the Chinese mode of production and communist ideology. In terms of both economic and cult-ural production, China has been increasingly commercialized. The 'Green Revolution' spread new ideas and social relations into the most rural areas. American dollars, televisions, refrigerators, and video machines were increas-ingly popular in the Chinese countryside. Yet fresh memories of material poverty and political suffering in the past may suggest that the Chinese people competed with one another within a culture of hedonistic materialism. At the same time, post-modernism has manifested itself within popular culture. Imbuing the market of mass culture are rock'n'roll, Karaoke, *Kung fu* movies or videotapes, mysteries and best-sellers, and mixtures, all of which literally emulate Western cultures. A recent withdrawal from traditional ideology together with a crisis in traditional values has in part motivated the Chinese people to accept almost uncritically 'Western' ideas and values. This neocol-onialist invasion of China cannot be properly grasped except in a historical context, and it might be suggested that this is, at least, the second time the Chinese have experienced a general crisis of national identity following the May Fourth Movement[1] of the twentieth century (Xie 1997: 12–13).

On the one hand, Westernization has acknowledged an explanation of mod-ern Chinese history; but, on the other, this negotiation of Chinese cultural identity has yet to be historically connected. The most dramatic instance of this new cultural situation is the effort over the last two decades to reconcile cap-italism with the so-called Confucian values of East Asian societies, which is a reversal of a long-standing conviction that Confucianism was historically an obstacle to capitalism (Dirlik 1994: 328–56). In that cultural hybridity and in-betweenness, Chineseness as a signifier needs to be situated and substantiated within the liberated practices of both national and individual identity in relation to both 'tradition' and 'the West' – that is, in relation to both the modern Chinese historical imagination and the social and cultural imagination emerging out of the experience of otherness. If modern Chinese culture, as Chow claims, 'is caught between the past as culture and the present as real-politik' (1993: 133), then what is needed is a rediscovery of 'the experience of uneasy translations between cultural traditions that are mediated by the possession and lack of power' (1993: 141). In this respect, the postcolonial strategy of opposition to mainstream Western culture can easily be identified with the Chinese attempt to struggle against imperial hegemony politically, economically and culturally.

There have been in contemporary Chinese cultural and literary circles various approaches to postcoloniality. First, post-modern studies in China have aimed to illustrate that post-modernity is not an exclusively Western product. Second, post-Chinese studies have adopted a strategy of 'decolonizing' Chinese culture and literary discourse; and yet the approach that these scholars adopt is still a 'colonized' one. In using Western theory or ways of thinking to reconsider and reinterpret Chinese culture, this body of work has rather unconsciously produced an 'otherness' opposed to the West. Finally, Third World criticism has attempted to help in demarginalizing Chinese literature and criticism so that it could merge into the mainstream of world literature or promote interventionist dialogues with international critical circles on an equal footing. All these developments may easily be taken as illustrations of the way in which different cultural critiques within contemporary China challenge Western culture. Chinese scholars living outside China have indeed themselves been influenced by Western thought (Zhao 1998: 137–56).

In many references to the 'Chinese people', 'Chinese intellectuals', 'Chinese culture', 'Chinese cultural studies' and 'Chinese sport', 'China' is often assumed to be a more or less stable and unquestionable signifier, which has hardly been subjected to careful study. This, in part, is what this chapter attempts to address. The preoccupation with respect for the West, symptomatic of doubt as it may be, has served as a convenient means of postponing a much-needed examination of China's own hegemony – namely Chinese cultural centrism. It is important to disengage from the solid notion of China as one culture; and yet this does not mean that Chinese intellectuals should adopt a 'pluralistic' cultural approach, for in the 1990s even the Chinese government itself developed a form of pluralism. Many previously forbidden 'cultural' subjects may now be openly discussed, except political issues. In this limited permissive 'cultural' climate, the support for the most declining forms of postcolonialism or the most pioneering forms of art cannot be regarded as real agencies in Chinese centrism. In the most 'subversive' representations or experimentations (of literature, music, art, sport, painting, photography, and journalism) from the People's Republic what often remains is China's own cultural dominance, chauvinism, and indeed internal imperialism.

In *China Can Say No* (Chiou, Song and Zhang 1996) the authors argue that what we face is no more than a reproduction of a dead form of 'Third World' nationalism, itself a vengeful echo of 'First-World' imperialism. One of the authors states that he became a nationalist when China lost the right to host the 2000 Olympic Games. What is disturbing about this claim is much less its apparent extremism than the fact that it refers to the West. In particular, the United States remains an imaginary enemy of China. Contemporary Chinese centrism, in other words, relies for its own connection on a continuing reactive relationship to the West. Consequently, any discussion of cultural studies and China could be easily misunderstood without any attempts to address the issues of China's relation with those regarded internally as being politically and culturally subordinate. It is important not to forget China's internal relationship with Tibet, Taiwan and Hong Kong. Among these regions and social formations, their own cultures and histories are simply denied an identity and authority under the beliefs of the People's Republic. These other 'Chinese' cultures, in so far as they constitute China's repressed cultures, are and should be a vital part of any consideration of vibrant 'Chinese cultural studies' (Chow 1997: 147–51).

For Chinese intellectuals to face up to the realities of these other 'Chinese' cultural spaces would mean that they would need to abandon the essential reactive position *vis-à-vis* the West that they have usually occupied. While it places them in a distrustful relation to the West, this reactive position also brings the comfort of an unreal victimhood, making it illegitimate to question their own power and their complicity with a centrist regime. Even today as China opens her doors to the 'cultural' influences of capitalism, the Chinese government continues to state what it means to be 'Chinese' and to suppress, imprison, exile, or execute those who dare question those claims. For example, more than a hundred Falun Gong followers have died in police custody since the Chinese government banned Falun Gong in 1999. The Chinese leaders call Falun Gong an evil cult. They believe it intends to overthrow the Chinese Government, and have accused it of links with separatists in the western regions of Tibet and Xinjiang (*The Times*, 15 January 2001: 14; 24 January 2001: 14). From the perspectives of many people in Tibet, Taiwan and Hong Kong, the important question is not how and why China can say no to the West, but 'Can one say no to China?' Hence, there are two types of postcoloniality in the Chinese context when we discuss postcolonialism in China. First, domestically, it may refer to undermining the so-called 'Chinese narrative' of official ideology. Second, and internationally, it speaks to the deconstruction of Western imperialism and its dominance over world culture and discourse. These are the two crucial points of departure that help to shape the thinking and questioning that underlie the discussion of sport in this chapter.

Sport in China: Some Preliminary Critical Observations

One of the essential terms within postcolonialism is 'reading'. The act of reading in postcolonial contexts is by no means a neutral activity. How we read is just as important as what we read (McLeod 2000: 33). The notion of post-colonialism has not been extensively active within existing works on sport in China, and it is possible to re-read some of the relevant literature and re-examine Chinese sport. In order to address this objective the discussion that follows emerges from a central consideration of the current dominant inter-ventions that have helped shape contemporary thinking in sport and cultural studies.

Published in 1990, *Sport in China* provides a substantive amount of empir-ical data on the development of physical culture in China. The main empirical base for this research draws upon anthropological material, reports, national documents and letters. It is not necessary to discuss the whole book in order to establish the point that the folk origins of modern Chinese sporting culture developed out of a number of traditional practices that existed prior to about 1860. There is some evidence that a thriving physical culture existed before the birth of Christ. In some cases the available evidence is used to establish the ancient origins of Chinese physical culture. In some instances, however, the authors, we believe, have attempted to hypothesize beyond the scope of the evidence provided. Arguably ancient China had no forms of physical culture that corresponded directly to such practices as formal Western gymnastics or sport. Yet it would be misleading to argue that ancient Chinese culture possessed nothing resembling sport. Some ancient Chinese forms of physical culture such as *wuyong* (martial valour), *quanyong* (boxing valour), *xi* (games), *jiji* (the art of attacking) and *yangsheng* (the art of keeping fit) are described in sufficient depth by Gu Shiquan (1990) to illustrate that physical culture was experienced in numerous forms by the ancient Chinese. The most distinguish-ing characteristic of these forms is that they were all closely associated with some form of social activity, such as military training, symbolic rituals, sacrifices, medical treatment or artistic creation, to name but a few of their most common functions.

Gu emphasizes that two ball games were popular in China during ancient times: *cuju* or *taju* (a kind of football game) and *jiju* or *daqiu* (a kind of horse polo). Both were forms of military training. A variety of football game was first played in China during the periods of Spring–Autumn and Warring States (770–221 BC). In the beginning, this was essentially a folk game, but it dev-eloped into a kind of military art. During the Han Dynasty (206 BC–AD 220), the game involved two teams, each of which guarded six goals. During the Tang

Dynasty (AD 618–907), the number of goals was reduced to two, one for each side, to form a game similar to modern soccer. Polo was probably introduced into China from Central Asia. It became a highly developed sport during the Tang Dynasty, owing to the wars that the Tang Empire waged against the Turks and other minority nationalities, many of whom were extremely skilled riders. Polo provided military training for cavalrymen as well as entertainment for the nobles. The evolution of *chuiwan* (a variation of golf) was in turn influenced by polo. However, the popularity of these ancient forms of football and polo had begun to decline by the Ming and Qing Dynasties (AD 1368–1911) (Gu 1990: 7–10).

This initial discussion of sport in China has been instrumental in establishing that various forms of physical culture existed in ancient China. Gu points out that traditional sports and Western sports form a sort of Yin and Yang, being both antithetical and yet complementary to other. Furthermore, this research suggests that the mass of labouring people became masters of the land as well as of their own physical education and culture when socialist New China was founded on the Chinese mainland in 1949. Gu's writing offers a lot of material on the history of physical education and sport in China before 1949; and yet the text may be fundamentally flawed in the sense that the research fails to acknowledge the influence, for example, of Yin and Yang philosophy upon the development of sport in China. Gu totally disregards the relationship of sport development between China and the West through the thought of Yin and Yang and the ancient Chinese philosophy of balance or harmony. In fact, there were very few culturally harmonious situations within the development of sport in Modern China. If we use Said's words to examine Gu's view here 'we are still required to ask where, how and with what supporting institutions and agencies such studies take place today?' (Said 1995: 342). The mass of labouring people have never been masters of their own land or physical culture, and in some sense, Gu's work merely represents an example of Chinese official thought: it sustains and reproduces a form of orthodoxy that does not highlight mass sports and forms 'the other' in the development of sport in China.

The book by Susan Brownell contains personal experience and observation of sport in Chinese culture and society. In *Training the Body for China*, Brownell (1995) outlines three main assumptions. First, that sport should be analysed as part of the entire culture of the body. Second, that power affects the culture of the body. And third, that sporting events can be viewed as cultural performance of the body (1995: 8). Her approach to sport acknowledges that there is something unique about sports compared with other body techniques. In discussing the concept of body culture, Brownell believes that the Western walking style, which was no doubt influenced by Western forms of physical education, is a clear style that expresses broad cultural differences. By contrast, she considers that the typical Chinese walking style was rooted in and influenced by the traditional martial arts. However, Brownell (1995: 9) was very surprised by the fact that the walking style of some Chinese students in Beijing was more like that of Westerners:

I was often struck by the fact that the students walked more like Westerners, with their chests pushed out and bouncing on their toes. Western visitors to the Institute often commented that the students there looked more European. Once, while training at the Beijing City team centre, much to my surprise I saw a group of European women athletes approaching across the field. I watched them until they reached me, when I suddenly noticed their black hair and Chinese faces. Their sudden metamorphosis was as shocking to me as if I had been hallucinating.

It is arguable whether or not Brownell overstated the influence of Chinese martial arts and Western physical culture on Chinese walking style and whether Chinese walking style is fundamentally different. As Said (1995: 348–9) argues, it is impossible to distinguish radically between different cultures and civilizations:

One of the great advances in modern cultural theory is the realization, almost universally acknowledged, that cultures are hybrid and heterogeneous and, as I argued in *Culture and Imperialism*, that cultures and civilization are so interrelated and interdependent as to beggar any unitary or simply delineated description of their individuality. How can one today speak of 'Western civilization' except as in large measure an ideological fiction, implying a sort of detached superiority for a handful of values and ideas, none of which has much meaning outside the history of conquest, immigration, travel and the mingling of peoples that gave the Western nations their present mixed identities? . . . And this was one of the implied messages of *Orientalism*, that any attempt to force cultures and peoples into separate and distinct breeds or essences exposes not only the misrepresentations and falsification that ensue, but also the way in which understanding is complicit with the power to produce such things as the 'Orient' or the 'West'.

Images of 'Chineseness' emerge frequently in Brownell's research. Moreover, Brownell (1995:15) focuses on sports as daily practice (Bourdieu) and as cultural performance (Turner). She argues that the concept of body culture can be used to analyse any level of differences, such as ethnicity, nationality, class, and gender differences, because it draws our attention to the practical differences that really matter. Bodies are immensely important to the people to whom they belong. Pain, hunger, fatigue, sexual desire, and so on, are central to the people experiencing them. An ethnographic account that overlooks the body omits the centre of human experience. According to Brownell, the human body's feeling should be more real to life than power. Yet this contradicts her second assumption of the power and body culture relationships that are strongly shaped by power relations, including state, society, class, gender, and ethnic relations, as well as the international relations between nations (1995: 8). While the senses of the body are easier to satisfy than the feelings of the heart, it is important to bear in mind the relationship between imperialism and psychology when we discuss sport in Modern China. For example, Frantz Fanon (1986; 1990) constantly exposed the interplay of psychological and political factors, showing that colonialism affects individuals as well as societies. Fanon's work forces us to take psychoanalysis seriously and attend to the pervasive influence of empire in fantasy, fiction, ideology and sport (Moore-Gilbert, Stanton and Maley 1997: 12).

Body techniques, in Brownell's thought, have occupied a very important position in the cultural context of China since the late nineteenth century. She avers that there are two lessons to be learnt from the history of body techniques and their public dramatizations. First, body culture is never as simple as it is depicted in such performances as the National Games, and therefore transforming it is never as easy as is often assumed. The second lesson is that modern sports have occupied a definite place in the Chinese moral order, but that place has been constructed differently at different times in history. Reformers and revolutionaries, for instance, emphasized newness and foreignness in their attempt to break with the traditions of the imperial past. Modern sports were perceived as being in opposition to martial arts, which were hailed by traditionalists as essentially Chinese and attacked by reformers as outmoded and feudal (Brownell 1995: 62). Furthermore, Brownell claims that Chinese people could cut the queue (pigtail) and throw off the long gown and the footbinding, but that these were only the most visible artefacts of an entire orientation to the world that was not so easy to transform. Uniquely, Chinese conceptions of nation, class, gender and social change still shape bodily practice in ways often mysterious to Westerners (Brownell 1995: 62). Within Brownell's dogmatic views, which are based more or less upon some notion of a sovereign Western consciousness, it seems that 'Chineseness' is a kind of ideal and unchanging abstraction. Perhaps Memmi's (1970: 83–5) notion of the colonizer and the colonized may address the reflections behind Brownell's words:

> The point is that the colonized means little to the colonizer. Far from wanting to understand him as he really is, the colonizer is preoccupied with making him undergo this urgent change. The mechanism of this remolding of the colonized is revealing in itself. It consists, in the first place, of a series of negations. The colonized is not this, is not that. He is never considered in a positive light; or if he is, the quality which is conceded is the result of a psychological or

ethical failing . . . It seems to him that strange and disturbing impulsiveness controls the colonized. The colonized must indeed be very strange, if he remains so mysterious after years of living with the colonizer.

The otherness of the colonized can be found in Brownell's analysis of the Western notion of 'fair play' and the Chinese notion of 'face' (1995: 289–311; 2000: 49). Brownell (2000: 49) accepts Barnett's (1990) and Fei Xiaotong's (1985) assumption that the English concept of 'fair play' does not seem to have a significant equivalence in the Chinese language. Hence, it was not easily understood by Chinese students. Brownell believes that 'the concept of fair play is loaded with connotations derived from its background in English culture, specifically in English sport'. She goes on to suggest 'I do not think that fairness was a key cultural concept in China in the 1980s' (1995: 292–5). In Brownell's discussion, the concept of fair play represents a central moral value of Western sports; but there is no similar meaning to fair play in Chinese culture, and Chinese people do not accept defeat easily because of the Chinese notion of 'face'. Nonetheless, Brownell disagrees with Fei Xiaotong's view that the Chinese character *li* (rites; ceremony) is the closest equivalent of Western 'fair play', and explains that although the concepts of *li* and 'fair play' are central in Chinese and Western morality respectively, while *li* may have been functionally equivalent as a guiding principle, it cannot be considered to be a concept similar to that of 'fair play' (1995: 294).

At least 2,000 years ago, one of the most influential Chinese classic books – the Confucian *Analects* (*Lun Yu*) describes an archery competition among gentlemen in China:

> The master [Confucius] said: 'Gentlemen have nothing to contend for. If an exception must be cited, it is perhaps in archery. They cup their hands and yield the way to each other before ascending and descending. Then they drink. Even in contention, they are gentlemanly' (Huang, 1997: 60).

In Confucian philosophy, the competition was in a ritual archery tournament with an ancient form of salutation. While it is not necessary to argue for differences or similarities between Western and Chinese sporting cultures here, it is important to illustrate that Brownell's conclusion has re-established Western imaginary ideas on the 'otherness' of Chinese culture. As Said argues in *Orientalism*, the scholarly discovery, philological reconstruction, psychological analysis, landscape and sociological description not only create but also maintain a certain will or intention to understand the obvious different world (Said 1995: 12). In addition, all the faces of Western hegemony carry the multiple character of both a contribution to the human repertoire and an expression of the imperial domination which spread across the globe with the effect of Western power. The effect of Western power has been built into the notions of race, progress, evolution, modernity and development as hierarchies extending in time and space (Pieterse and Parekh 1995: 1). Indeed, Brownell's argument on Chinese culture in sport appears to be a kind of 'mythical portrait of the colonized' that corresponds to the incomprehensible Western stereotype of the alien Chinese culture (Memmi 1970: 79–89).

Furthermore, on the notion of fair play, C. L. R. James (1994: 227) explained how British power unfairly affected cricket games in the West Indies:

> In Jamaica in 1953 the umpire was threatened when Holt was given lbw at 94. Stollmeyer was threatened when he refused to ask the English team to follow on. None of this faintly resembles the situation in Melbourne in 1903. Again: none of this was a political demonstration against an imperialist Britain. The 1953–4 M.C.C. team was actively disliked. This was not due merely to unsportsmanlike behaviour by individuals. There is evidence to show that the team had given the impression that it was not merely playing cricket but was out to establish the prestige of Britain and, by that, of the local whites.

In James's argument, the notion of fair play was seldom seen in the cricket history of the West Indies. In particular, the notion of fair play did not exist between imperialists and Third World people. Cricket was not only a sport, but was also a facet of imperialism in the West Indies. Here Brownell's discussion of fair play in China may be compatible with Western imaginary ideas of Chinese athletes and coaches today. This common belief is evident in Western sports media and communities in regard to the Chinese. For example, during the 1996 Atlanta Olympic Games, the media proclaimed that drug use produced Chinese sporting triumphs (*The Daily Telegraph*, 5 August 1996; *International Herald Tribune*, 7 August 1996). *Time* (12 August 1996: 29) commented that steroid or other medication could be used to help Chinese divers recover from their punishing routines – repeated plunges from 10m platforms are particularly brutal – but no Chinese diver has ever tested positive for drugs. Furthermore, in the 2000 Sydney Olympic Games, *Time* (18 September 2000: 80–1) quoted Lindstedt, an anti-doping expert: 'China's athletes have a big historical burden to overcome' and concluded that China might need something stronger than a shot of steroids to outrun its dubious sporting past. Drug use has been a critical problem in international sports arenas, and is not merely China's problem. This will be discussed further in the next section.

To sum up, Brownell's work provides an insightful contribution from personal experience and observations of Chinese sport and body culture. Nonetheless, it is still a form of Western academic analysis. She overlooks the notions of power, hegemony and imperialism. Especially, Brownell's arguments on Chinese walking style, Western sport in China and the notion of fair play hint at an unbridgeable chasm separating China from the West. Brownell uses Western discourse analysis to represent a Chinese body culture that does not correspond to the reality of Chinese body and sport culture, and some of her assumptions of cultural differences between China and West are questionable.

Both Gu and Brownell believe that Chinese sport culture has been strongly influenced by Western sport. In particular, Gu argues that Western sport was introduced to China by imperialism after the Opium Wars in the nineteenth century. However Mao's slogan of the 'New Physical Culture' was essentially anti-imperialistic and anti-feudalistic from 1949 to 1978. True, after the Open Policy of 1978, Gu accepts uncritically the notion of Western sport as the harmonizing counterpart of Chinese sport, applying the classic concept of Yin–Yang. This displays a Western influence upon the attitudes of the Chinese academics towards Western civilization. Brownell's work unconsciously proclaims Western images of Chineseness that match those of Orientalism, if only partially. Their works on Chinese sport have highlighted the problematic of postcolonialism. Though their analyses of Chinese sport are made from contrasting cultural backgrounds, the former Chinese and the latter Western, both coincidentally agree on a strong Western contribution to Chinese sport culture. It is a question whether both writers are under the dominating influence of Western hegemony. This merits further discussion under the notion of postcolonialism.

Sport and Postcolonialism in Modern China: Some Preliminary Thoughts

To write developmentally about Chinese social formation in Modern China is extremely difficult. Not only does this period of development merge with what many writers refer to as a politically socialist and economically capitalist society, but there is also a relative lack of sociological material and research that emanates from the unique patterns of tension and struggle experienced by Modern China. Western scholars in particular have asked when sociologists in China are going to wake up to the possibilities of their unique situation? With specific reference to the analysis of Chinese and Western forms of sporting culture, there is relatively little evidence of such important features as social transformation and control, or any concrete analysis of the complex way in which forms of sport are mediated by relatively complex and specific forms of postcolonialism and cultural domination. The major discussions on postcolonialism remain within the reading of colonial discourse, nationalism, the question of representation, re-reading and re-writing Western literary theory, feminism, a diaspora of identities and the question of class. However, the notion of post-colonialism may bring new possibilities of explaining how sport has developed in Modern China. It is not necessary to discuss all aspects of postcolonial possibilities here, since our purpose is to provide some preliminary thoughts in relation to sport and postcolonialism in Modern China after 1978.

The notion of postcolonialism can be used in different ways in different contexts. This reflects contingent historical, cultural and geographical conditions, while offering ways of thinking across these differences to global and transnational operations, such as multinational capitalism and American military aggression, which inevitably link together in many disparate locations. Postcolonialism has an inseparable relationship with the expansion of Western capitalism and imperialism. According to some, postcolonialism services the requirements of Western capitalism in its contemporary global and multinational operations, just as surely as colonialism served capitalism in an earlier period (McLeod 2000: 254–5).

In China, sport has been widely promoted following the spread of capitalism since 1978. The development of sport has come with political change. For example, the famous term 'Ping-Pong Diplomacy' was coined when the United States of America took a team of table-tennis players to China during Richard Nixon's historic visit in 1972. Since then China has been gradually opening her doors and improving Sino-Western relations through sport. On the other hand, Western capitalists have set up sports-related businesses in China since at least the 1980s. These include Trans World International[2] (IMG/TWI) in sports marketing and sports television, News Corporation in broadcasting, Nike and Adidas in sporting goods, and some multinational sponsors, especially from tobacco, beverages and communications, such as Philip Morris, British American Tobacco, Coca-Cola and Ericsson.

Soccer is now acknowledged as the number one sport in China. The 14-club premier league has been sponsored by Marlboro – a sponsorship that could not have happened in the West. The Chinese FA cup competition has been sponsored by Philips, and the league has also attracted sponsorships offering perimeter-board exclusivity from Budweiser, Clarion, Canon, Ericsson, Ford, Pepsi, Samsung, Fuji Film, General Motors, JVC, Korean Air, Olympus, Santafe and Vinda (a Chinese paper manufacturer). Soccer's dominance is only a recent development, and in team sport it is competing with basketball, in particular, in the minds of Chinese consumers. Basketball was popular throughout the 1990s; NBA basketball was popular, and Michael Jordan was recently voted the 'Greatest Man in the World' by Chinese students. Recognition of the NBA brand logo among Chinese teenagers is over 79 per cent (Glendinning 1999: 20–1).

In this postcolonial context, the development of global capitalism in China is similar to Ahmad's (1995: 1–20) description of the economic and social situation in some Third World countries. Ahmad points out that 'we should speak not so much of colonialism or postcolonialism but of capitalist modernity, which takes the colonial form in particular places and at particular times'. According to Ahmad, the contemporary global economic situation can be seen as a neo-colonial condition. Multinational capitalist companies are increasingly able to expand their new territories easily in China. Western sports media bypass national borders and transmit Western ideologies and desires for Western cultural products direct to the Chinese people. It is recognized that Western capitalism as a form of neo-colonialism has been successfully changing China's economy, culture and society.

The idea of the nation emerged with the growth of Western capitalism and industrialism, and was a fundamental component of imperialist expansion. The issue of nationalism as discussed by Frantz Fanon is an important marker in the field of postcolonialism. As Fanon's work contends, sport could have played an important role in the construction of a national consciousness in Modern China. The People's Republic of China (PRC), in the decade following the death of Mao Zedong in 1976, experienced a cultural and ideological transformation unprecedented in the history of communist societies. Sport, like the arts, is a political subculture that expresses prevailing ideological trends; and, for this reason, the new modernization in China necessitates a new ideological interpretation of sport. Contrary to appearances, the ideological content of the Maoist sport doctrine has actually been retained in post-Maoist sport ideology. What has changed is the relative degree of emphasis accorded to four specific ideological elements, namely competition, high-performance sport, sporting ethics, and scientific sport (Hoberman 1987: 156–70). Under the banner of these four primary ideological elements, China seeks to 'break out of Asia and advance on the world', and this gives a strong political purpose to Chinese nationalism in the international arena. Accordingly, we may see hybridity and ambivalence of sports development in China. For instance, Chinese leaders intend to appropriate Western sports as a tool to promote Chinese nationalism against Western imperialism. At the same time, they also resist Western culture in their fear of encouraging the Western idea of democracy. More recently, for example, after NATO's mistake in bombing the Chinese Embassy in Belgrade on 8 May 1999, the Chinese government temporarily banned NBA basketball games on television as a strong protest at the bombing.

In 1979 China rejoined the International Olympic Committee (IOC) after an eleven year absence following an unsatisfactory resolution of the 'Two Chinas Problem'. Beijing hosted the Asia Games in 1990, but lost the right to host the 2000 Olympic Games. China has now succeeded in its bid for the 2008 Olympic Games. The increasing importance of sport in China reflects the international importance of the Olympic Movement. In China, sport has been fought over by many different groups, and it is relatively easy to demonstrate sport's role in promoting Chinese nationalism and its importance to the power elite. Under their inflexible ideology of Chinese centrism (Sinocentrism) Taiwan is regarded as part of China. China bans the Taiwanese from using their official national name, flag and anthem in all international competitions. Since 1984, Taiwanese athletes have competed under the name of 'Chinese Taipei' in international arenas, but the Chinese domestic media consistently name Taiwanese sport teams as 'China's Taipei'. The sports relationships between China and Taiwan can be critically viewed as a symbol of Chinese internal imperialism and hegemony. Today, the majority of Taiwanese people continue to resist attempts by China to promote unification under the Chinese official nationalist slogan of 'one country, two systems'.

Chinese official nationalism involves the imposition of cultural homogeneity from the top through state action. One of the Chinese official actions is to force Taiwanese sports organizations to accept that the PRC is the only central government and that Taiwan is merely a provincial state. Under the continuing threat of the PRC, the Taiwanese people are struggling and searching for their own self-definitions, rather than allowing themselves to be defined by the Chinese government. Therefore, to a certain degree, the debate over the 'Two Chinas Problem' has shifted to a debate on the 'Two Nationalisms Problem' through the notion of postcolonialism.

Though one postcolonial criticism is the lack of attention given to the problem of class, Spivak's work 'Can the Subaltern Speak?' may be seen as one of the few relatively postcolonial discussions on the issues of class and feminism by postcolonialists. As Spivak's (1995: 25–8) argument on the question of the subaltern in India has it:

> Let us now move to consider the margins (one can just well say the silent, silenced centre) of the circuit marked out by this epistemic violence, men and women among the illiterate peasantry, the tribals, the lowest strata of the urban subproletariat . . . On the other side of the question of the international division of labour from socialized capital, inside and outside the circuit of the epistemic violence of imperialist law and education supplementing an earlier economic text, can the subaltern speak? . . . If, in the context of colonial production, the subaltern has no history and cannot speak, the subaltern as female is even more deeply in shadow.

Similarly, the voices of the Chinese subaltern class and of women have been disregarded during China's economic boom over last two decades. Mass sports development has been ignored and limited because of a lack of access to sports facilities. Among the reasons for the lack of sports facilities in China are: (i) the Chinese government did not pay attention to building sports facilities in public places; (ii) the rate of increase of population was much greater than the rate of increase in building sports facilities; (iii) most sports facilities in sports committee systems have often been closed to the public; (iv) some sports halls are used only for competition; (v) school sports facilities have not been actively used by local residents; and (vi) a large number of sports facilities were swallowed up by factories and enterprises. Some activities that require a low skill level and few facilities (such as walks, running, traditional Chinese exercises, disco dancing, etc.), remain the most frequent and popular forms of physical activities (Wang and Olson 1997: 69–85). *Qigong* has become one of the most popular mass sports in recent years. It is one of the oldest ancient Chinese physical fitness and breathing exercises, which can be traced back to at least the Spring and Autumn period (770–476 BC). Throughout Chinese history *qigong* has been considered an important means of curing diseases, prolonging life, and improving the skills of participants in *wushu* (martial arts).

A very special case of *qigong*, in Beijing on 25 April 1999, was when more than 10,000 members of Falun Gong (the 'Way of the Law Wheel' or 'Buddhist Law Cult') staged the largest silent demonstration since the student democracy movement (1989). The Falun Gong protesters were angry because a number of cult members had been arrested in Tianjin; they also wanted to demand their legal status for the cult. The leader of Falun Gong, Master Li Hongzhi, said that Falun Gong was based on the belief that human beings can harness their *qi* (vital energy) by meditation and physical exercise. The Falun Gong spokesman also claimed that they have about 70 millions members in China and another 30 millions or more elsewhere (the Chinese Communist Party has 60 millions). However, the state body in charge of *qigong* claimed that Falun Gong cannot be officially recognized (*The Economist*, 1 May 1999: 83–4; *The Guardian* 26 April 1999: 13). On 28 April 1999, the government stated that 'This kind of gathering affects public order . . . and is completely wrong'. Punishment, it said, would await those who 'damage social stability under the pretext of practising martial arts'. The Chinese government banned citizens' practising Falun Gong in the public area of Beijing, with effect from 5:00 a.m. on 26 June 1999 (*Central Daily News*, 29 June 1999: 7).

There are several reasons to explain why Chinese citizens practise Falun Gong. First, Falun Gong followers believe *qigong* can fulfil their wish to enjoy good health. Second, the cult advocates truth, goodness and patience, which meets the needs of those seeking moral and spiritual life. Last, Falun Gong followers practise *qigong* collectively, allowing them to make friends. If such needs of Chinese citizens could be readily satisfied by other means, Falun Gong would not have spread so quickly. Falun Gong is even practised by government officials, party members and intellectuals. Li's charisma is only one of the factors that encourage the common people to join the cult. In China, more and more workers have been laid off since the government began to restructure the economy, the health care system is in poor shape, and traditional values have collapsed. Many people feel empty and crave support and consolation. With such material and spiritual problems, Falun Gong has spread like a prairie fire started by a single spark (*Ming Pao Daily News*, 23 July 1999: A2, A13–15 and 24 July 1999: A2–A4). Unless these problems are solved, though Falun Gong organizations have been outlawed, similar groups will sooner or later appear. It is impossible to prevent people from having material and spiritual needs by enforcing strict laws or imposing severe punishment. Sport in Modern China contributes to this process.

Postcolonialism can recognize the continuing agency of colonial discourses and relationships of power in the contemporary world in various contexts. We have made a critique of texts on Chinese sport and pointed out that some of the sport scholars have been critically influenced by Western discourse. Said's argument is that Western views of the Orient are not based on what is observed in Oriental lands, but often on the Western dreams, fantasies and assumptions that this radically different place contains (McLeod 2000: 41). While we have discussed Chinese sport and postcolonialism, we should provide an illustrative example of Orientalism as it appears in the imaginary psyche of Western sport authorities and media.

A recent study by Darcy C. Plymire (1999: 155–73) concludes that, from the evidence of athletics drug tests, there is no single group that is innocent and not a single group that is to blame for the problem. Drug use is a common problem in Western athletics. It will not disappear by blaming the Chinese and the other communist nations. It is possible that Western sports communities unfairly discredit Chinese athletes and coaches. Plymire argues that when the PRC's women set a number of world records in track and field events in 1993, some Western journalists insisted that Chinese women could only have succeeded by taking steroids. Furthermore, Plymire (1999: 169) points out some unsubstantiated assumptions about Chinese women within the Western track and field communities. These are as follows:

1. Women are naturally unable to run as fast as Chinese women have done.
2. Steroids make Chinese women more like men and so allow them to run unnaturally fast.
3. Women from communist countries are more likely to use steroids than women from Western nations.

4.   Women from communist nations are compelled by state-supported sports 'machines' to take steroids.
5.   The Chinese are incapable of developing a knowledge of the human body and its potential that is superior to that produced in the West.
6.   The Chinese must be using illicit knowledge gleaned from the East German sport 'machine'.

On the basis of this logic of the Western imagination, the conclusion is clear. Chinese women have borrowed (or stolen) the scientific and technical knowledge of the West (represented by steroids) and have used it in illegitimate ways to produce unnatural performances. Plymire's argument has vividly exposed stereotypes of Chinese people that are produced and reproduced by the West. In particular, some American images portray Chinese men as small, weak, cowardly, sensual and deceitful. Furthermore, the Chinese characters in American films are frequently clumsy, ugly, greasy, loud, stupid, slant-eyed, stereotypical, squawking Chinese bad guys. Chinese athletics, and in particular Chinese women, certainly would not fit the images of the American people (Plymire 1999: 161).

The subject-matter of this initial discussion on the postcolonial issue of global capitalism, nationalism, class and Orientalism concerns itself with the development of sport in China and, in particular, China's relationship with the West and also with Taiwan. As a focus of analysis, Chinese sport is capable of providing a great deal of information about history and social development itself, since one of the central tenets of thought throughout this section is that sport both contributes to and is constitutive of Chinese culture. Sport does not exist in some social or historical vacuum isolated from Chinese history and social development. Since the core theme of this analysis is sport and postcolonialism in China, it is worth noting in conclusion the broad themes developed in this chapter.

Conclusion: Sport, Postcolonialism and Modern China

In this chapter, we have attempted to set out a discussion of postcolonialism in Modern China, some critiques of contemporary texts on Chinese sport and our preliminary thoughts on sport and postcolonialism in Modern China. The discussion has been organized around three propositions: (i) that there are two types of postcolonialism in the Chinese context, one of which is Chinese internal imperialism and the other Western imperialism; (ii) that contemporary Chinese sports texts have been dominated by Western cultural hegemony and its discourse; and (iii) that Chinese sport as a unique social formation within this study of postcolonialism has presented fresh perspectives on economic, political, social and cultural issues.

While postcolonialism fulfils the aims of opposing colonial representation and values from the West, it remains a debatable issue in the field. Ahmad's and Dirlik's criticisms of postcolonialism consider that postcolonial intellectuals are entirely attempting to hide their complicity in global capitalism and Western economic power, and that they ignore the issue of class. Details of these criticisms are outside the scope of our discussion here. However, it is important to recognize that postcolonialism has brought new possibilities to the analysis of sport in Modern China. In particular, after China's Open Policy in 1978, sport has become one of the most effective media of Western economic and cultural imperialism. In Chinese postcolonial discourse, sport is not only a tool of the Chinese government in upholding Chinese nationalism against Western imperialism, but also an agent of postcolonialism in Chinese cultural centrism. This process has been under way since at least 1978. Herein lies a contradiction within the problematics that are sport, postcolonialism and Modern China.

Notes

1. Interest in the West and concepts of democracy, science and modernisation were challenged by Marxism as the impact of the October Revolution of 1917 in Russia took effect. It was during this debate that the political division between the Nationalists and Communists occurred. The May Fourth Movement (1919) is often discussed in relation to the New Culture Movement that followed in Modern China.

2. TWI, IMG's television arm, is the largest independent supplier of sports programming to Chinese stations, with properties such as the English Premier League and the Wimbledon and Australian Open Tennis championships (see *Sport Business*, January 1999: 20–1).

6

'Paki Cheats!' Postcolonial Tensions in England–Pakistan Cricket

Jack Williams

Test match cricket in the 1980s and 1990s was fiercely aggressive and competitive. Captains discouraged players from fraternizing with opponents off the field. Withstanding a battery of fast bowlers required physical courage, but playing success depended as much on mental toughness. Sledging, verbal insults intended to break the concentration of opponents, became commonplace. Of England's matches, those against Pakistan were the ones marked most by animosity and suspicion. Derek Pringle, a former England player, described Pakistan as 'the side most likely to get the blood bubbling', with matches 'filled with acrimony as old prejudices surface' (*Independent,* 24 July 1996). The animosities of England–Pakistan test cricket can be seen as a result of white English society's difficulties in adjusting to the postcolonial epoch. For many Pakistanis the antagonisms surrounding test cricket reflected the racism of English society and perpetuated discourses of white supremacy that had underpinned British imperial expansion.

Cricket and White English Moral Superiority

The most unpleasant outbursts of ill feeling between England and Pakistani sides occurred on the England tour of Pakistan in 1987 and the Pakistan tour of England in 1992. On the 1987 tour of Pakistan, England players felt that Pakistani umpires were deliberately cheating by showing obvious bias in favour of the Pakistan team. After England lost the first test match by an innings – a match in which England players felt that many of them had been victims of dubious LBW decisions – the England captain Mike Gatting was reported to have said 'We knew roughly what to expect but never imagined it would be quite so blatant' and that 'The bad decisions went against us by 10–1' (*Wisden 1989*: 910; *Guardian,* 30 November 1987). In an interview published in 1990,

Raman Subba Row, chairman of the TCCB, the body responsible for English test cricket, said that 'the cheating was aided and abetted by the Pakistani officials – oh, absolutely, absolutely! There is no doubt. It was a carefully conceived plan' (Bose 1990: 23). Most English cricket journalists covering the tour shared these suspicions of Pakistani cheating.

Matters came to a head just before the end of the second day of the second test match, played at Faisalabad, when England were in a strong position. The claim of Shakoor Rana, one of the Pakistani umpires, that Gatting had been wrong to move a fielder erupted into an ugly confrontation, with Rana and Gatting appearing to be on the point of exchanging blows. Rana was reported to have called Gatting 'a f***, cheating c***' while Gatting called Rana 'a shit-awful umpire'. There was no play the next day, as Rana refused to take the field until Gatting apologized to him. This was the first instance in test cricket of a day's play being lost because an umpire refused to take the field. The England players threatened to strike in support of Gatting. The match restarted on the following day after the TCCB ordered Gatting to apologize to Rana. It was suspected that the British government had urged the TCCB to ensure that the match recommenced. Gatting's apology, written on a scrap of paper, was only of the most cursory nature. The British press took Gatting's side. Mike Selvey of *The Guardian* wrote that 'Gatting was grossly wronged . . . First he was insulted by an untrustworthy umpire and then let down by the TCCB.' Martin Johnson of *The Independent* described ordering Gatting to apologize as 'pathetic, even by the Test and County Cricket Board's own remarkable standards . . . When firm action was called for – and few here doubt that it should have been cancellation of the tour – they sold their team and management down the river.' *The Sun* proclaimed that 'What the country wants . . . is TOTAL support from the Government' and complained that 'the spineless bunch on the Test County Cricket Board would betray our team'. The headline of a *Daily Mirror* article about Gatting being forced to apologize read 'NO BALLS' (*Guardian,* 22 December 1987; Green 1997 116–17; *Sun,* 12 December 1987; *Daily Mirror,* 12 December 1987).

In 1992 a confrontation between the English umpire Roy Palmer and Pakistani players during the Old Trafford test match was condemned by sections of the English sports media as almost as bad as that between Gatting and Shakoor Rana. Palmer had cautioned the Pakistani bowler Aqib Javed for bowling too many short-pitched deliveries at the England tail-end batsman Devon Malcolm. At the end of the over the Pakistani players complained that Palmer had thrown Aqib Javed's sweater to him in an offensive manner. The Pakistani players then surrounded Palmer in an aggressive, gesticulating manner. During a limited overs international match at Lord's in late August the umpires changed the ball during the England innings. The match referee refused to say why the ball had been changed; but in an article printed in *The Daily Mirror* with the massive headline 'HOW PAKISTAN CHEAT AT CRICKET' the England batsman Allan Lamb alleged that Pakistani players had tampered with the ball. He claimed that throughout the summer England players had suspected that the Pakistan fast bowlers had achieved reverse swing, a form of bowling that had undermined the England batting, by illegally scouring one side of the ball with their nails, or possibly something like a bottle top (26 August 1992). Lamb's comments led to two libel trials – the first between Lamb and the retired Pakistan fast bowler Sarfraz Nawaz and the second between the former Pakistan captain Imran Khan and Lamb and Ian Botham. At the first trial, Don Oslear, the third umpire, revealed that the umpires had changed the ball in the Lord's match because they believed that it had been tampered with. The two test series of 1987 and 1992 seemed to confirm expectations of England cricketers and journalists that cheating was endemic in Pakistan cricket. Many seemed to share the view of the former England player and cricket broadcaster Tom Graveney, who said in 1987 that when 'you go to the sub-continent you know that two things will happen. You will suffer Delhi belly – and you will get done by the umpires . . . Claims of cheating by Pakistani players are nothing new. They have been doing it since 1951 when I first toured there . . . it has got worse and worse'(*Daily Mirror,* 10 December 1987).

There is evidence of cheating by Pakistani teams and umpires. In his sympathetic study of the Pakistan fast bowlers Wasim Akram and Waqar Younis published just before the 1992 tour, the English author John Crace wrote that 'All Pakistan umpires unofficially admit that Imran has been the one captain who has never asked them to help him out' and that on one occasion Pakistani umpires had walked into the Pakistani dressing-room to ask Imran for their instructions (Crace 1992: 15–16). As Imran Khan wrote a foreword to this book, it seems that this incident had taken place. Two Pakistani umpires resigned in 1980. One claimed that the Umpires' Association was not sufficiently independent of the Pakistan Board, and the other mentioned attempts to persuade him to take a 'nationalist line' when umpiring (*Cricketer International,* October 1987: 18–19). In 1989 the Pakistani cricket journalist Nasir Abbas Mirza wrote that test matches in Pakistan were won not so much on the field as by 'clandestine planning in the offices'. Pakistani umpires, he alleged, were at the mercy of the BCCP officials and had 'no choice but to acquiesce in the unreasonable demands of the Board and the captain, which . . . may vary from asking for an LBW to outright victory'. (*Cricketer International,* June 1989: 21). Following the Pakistan-New Zealand test series of 1990–91, Mudasser Nazar, the Pakistan B team coach, was reported to have said that the practice of illegally roughing up balls had to stop (Crace 1992: 86). At the Sarfraz Nawaz–Allan Lamb trial in 1993 the England player Christopher Cowdrey produced video recordings showing 53 instances of Pakistani ball tampering (*Times,* 19 November 1993; Oslear and Bannister 1996: 96). At the end of 1987 statistics showed that batsmen of teams touring Pakistan were more likely to be given out LBW by Pakistani umpires than were Pakistan batsmen, though the disparity between the number of LBW decisions in favour of and against the Indian team made by Indian umpires was even greater.

Evidence of cheating by Pakistani teams does not necessarily mean that Pakistani teams cheated more often than other teams or cheated as often as was imagined by many in English cricket. In 1987 the remarks of Haseeb Ahsan, manager of the Pakistan touring team, that cheating 'had become a technique for all cricket teams, that they must pressurize the umpire to the extent that they get one or two wrong decisions in favour of the bowler', were taken in England as proof that Pakistan teams had a policy of cheating; but his further comments that 'everybody is doing it. It has now become absolutely necessary in professional cricket today' (Gatting and Patmore 1988: 179) could be regarded as a more or less accurate description of how test cricket was played. Probably English expectations that Pakistan teams and umpires would cheat caused mistakes and misunderstandings to be seen as cheating. In Derek Pringle's view 'a dodgy decision or two . . . gets passed from one dressing room generation to the next, snowballing in significance until the original germ . . . becomes mutated to the broad swathes of prejudice such as "PAKI CHEAT!" so beloved of headline-makers, and now sadly part of the lingua franca wherever English is spoken' (*Independent,* 24 July 1996).

Underlying convictions about Pakistani cheating was the belief that English cricket was morally superior to Pakistani cricket, that Pakistanis were not living up to the standards that the white English had observed in cricket. Edward Said has emphasized that discourses that emphasized the alterity of Asia and that assumed that European culture was morally superior to that of Asians were crucial in creating the justifications for European imperialism. Assumptions of cheating by Pakistani cricketers and umpires can be seen as continuing these discourses of white English moral superiority. They indicate that while Pakistan had been granted independence from Britain, the tendency of the former colonizers to see alterity as inferiority remained strong.

Assumptions of English superiority were reflected in the dislike of touring Pakistan. Tours to Pakistan seem to have been more arduous than those to other test-playing countries. The heat, food, and stomach upsets and the Islamic prohibition of alcohol were seen as hardships. Political riots interrupted matches on six of England's first eight tours to Pakistan. At most venues

England parties were accommodated in five-star hotels, though matches in the more remote parts of Pakistan could be a trial. Ian Botham does not seem to have been alone among England players in describing Pakistan as 'the kind of place to send your mother-in-law for a month, all expenses paid' (Botham 1995: 211). The reaction of England teams to touring Pakistan reflected an inability to see Pakistan in other than English terms. The cricket journalist and administrator Tony Lewis, who had captained the England tour to Pakistan in 1972–73, wrote about the persistence of a 'blind belief that what the English professional does is always right', of England teams becoming locked into 'a fortress mentality' and that 'orderly English professionals as soon as they are overseas . . . perform like overheated sergeants of the old Empire, loose [sic] patience and start a slanging match between "them" and "us"' (*Sunday Telegraph,* 19 July, 30 August 1992). In Derek Pringle's experience, few England players 'ever attempted to embrace or understand the culture they were plonked in the middle of, preferring instead to cocoon themselves with videotapes and familiar comestibles' (*Independent,* 24 July 1996). While international sportsmen may believe that they require a certain level of comfort in order to perform to the best of their ability, England cricketers showed little understanding of Pakistan's economic problems as an underdeveloped country or of how the poverty and culture of Pakistan resulted in part from British imperialism.

Animosity towards Pakistani cricket can also be related to white English resentment about the global movements of people characteristic of postcoloniality. Racial abuse from spectators at England–Pakistan test matches reflected white hostility to those of Pakistani descent living in England. At Trent Bridge in 1987 racist chanting and Pakistani spectators' identification with the Pakistani team led to fighting with England supporters, and the throat of one Pakistani supporter was slashed (Licudi and Raja 1997: 40). At the Headingley test in 1992 a pig's head was thrown into the part of the ground where Pakistani supporters were congregated. At the England–Pakistan test match at Headingley in 1996 *Asian Times,* an English-language newspaper published in England for Asian readers, reported that racist chants were 'prevalent and unabated' and led to fighting (22 August 1996). In *The Observer* Chris Searle wrote of white spectators shouting 'Stab the Paki' and of 'racist overtones right over the length and breadth of the Western Terrace . . . loud, clear and squalid' as if 'the pus of four centuries of Empire was pulsing out' (18 August 1996). The behaviour of Pakistan spectators was not always blameless. Pakistani spectators did respond to insults and may have provoked trouble on occasions. In 1992 Pakistan spectators caused a charity match between an Indian XI and a Pakistan XI at Crystal Palace to be abandoned when it looked as if India would win (*Times,* 29 July 1992). Pakistan supporters attacked the cars of Ian Botham and Mike

Gatting. The commitment of Pakistani supporters for the Pakistan team was seen, and even condemned, as a lack of commitment to English society and an example of their alterity. In 1987 an editorial in *Wisden Cricket Monthly,* one of the two leading cricket magazines published in England, claimed that at a limited overs international at Edgbaston 'hordes of Pakistan "supporters" came not merely to watch the cricket but to identify – with a fanatical frenzy and to the embarrassment of Imran and his players – with "their team"' (July 1987:3). In 1990 Norman Tebbit, former chairman of the Conservative Party, wondered whether Asians living in England could pass his 'cricket test'. He asked 'Which side do they cheer for? Were they still harking back to where they came from or where they were?' (*Times,* 21 April 1990). Although Prime Minister Thatcher quickly dissociated herself from these comments, their expression by a politician as prominent as Tebbit suggests that many whites still assumed that being British involved accepting all the values surrounding traditional white notions of Britishness. Such an attitude implied unease with the multiculturalism of Britain as a postcolonial society.

The British press, and particularly the tabloid newspapers, often reported the England–Pakistan confrontations of 1987 and 1992 in a joky but insulting style that stereotyped and caricatured Pakistanis. In 1987 *The Sun* had a headline 'PAK YER BAGS', and in 1992 'PAK OFF THE CHEATS FOR FIVE YEARS'. Haseeb Ahsan was described as the 'Crackpot of Karachi'. Readers were offered the chance to win a '*Sun* Fun Dartboard – Stick One on the Cheat of Pakistan!' which had an image of Shakoor Rana on it so that 'you can hit him right between the eyes'. In 1992 Colin Milburn, a former England player, called Javed Miandad, the Pakistan captain, in a *Sun* article 'the Colonel Gadaffi of cricket' (10, 16, 21 December 1987, 22 July 1992). In 1992 the *Daily Mirror* described the Pakistan team as 'Javed's Brat Pack' and captain Javed Miandad as a 'wild man with a face you might spot crouched behind rocks in an ambush along the Khyber . . . Friends say he is a wow at creating curries. Unfortunately these aspects of his character are rarely glimpsed on the field – except for his taste for stirring.' A *Mirror* sports columnist wrote of Pakistanis 'being even hotter on apologies than they are on vindaloos' (8 July 1992). Stereotypical, unflattering views were also found in broadsheet newspapers. In a *Sunday Telegraph* article that led to a libel case that was settled out of court, Simon Heffer wrote that the Pakistan cricket board had a corrupt view of the game and that fair play was probably only seen on Pakistan cricket grounds when they were used for public floggings (12 July 1992). In *The Guardian* Mike Selvey described Haseeb Ahsan and Javed Miandad 'as "thick" as in thieves' (22 December 1987).

The Pakistani Perspective

By Pakistanis the widespread belief in English cricket that cheating was endemic in Pakistan cricket was resented and viewed as a perpetuation of the assumptions of white supremacy that had upheld the Empire. Many felt that whenever England lost to Pakistan the immediate response was to accuse Pakistan of cheating. In 1987 it was argued in *Dawn,* the English-language newspaper published in Karachi, that English cricket assumed 'that there is no way an English team can be beaten fair and square. They are invincible. If, perchance, they should lose (which is pretty frequently these days), it is always because they have been robbed. When they are abroad, it is easy to explain their failure on umpiring' (13 November 1987). In 1994 when Imran Khan had revealed that on one occasion he had used a bottle top to scour a cricket ball, an article in *Eastern Eye,* an English-language Asian newspaper published in England, argued that

> The issue is no longer about ball-doctoring or cheating. . .There is no sense of justice or honour in the British press's crusade to ride the world of 'Paki cheats' . . . There is only one over-riding and uncontrollable emotion that is fuelling this relentless attack – Jealousy.
> The only crime that Pakistan's cricketers are guilty of is that of being simply better than England . . .
> The whole sorry saga highlights the fact that England cannot accept that teams from the Sub-Continent are better than them (17 May 1994).

Even some white cricket observers in England argued that English accusations of Pakistani cheating stemmed from beliefs that Pakistan could beat England only by cheating. Simon Barnes wrote in *The Times* that 'the English prefer to reduce the greatest bowlers in the world to gullygully men: sleight-of-hand conjurors, wily oriental gentlemen. England were not defeated, England were *tricked*' (29 August 1992).

White English assumptions of superiority were seen as judging Pakistan cricket by double standards. Pakistani umpires were dismissed as cheats, while English umpires were regarded as the best in the world. Wrong decisions made by English umpires that favoured England were seen as simple human errors. England representatives at the ICC opposed the Pakistan calls in the late 1980s for umpires from neutral countries. The England representatives argued that no sponsor had been found to pay for neutral umpires; but they also believed that, as English umpires were the best in the world, neutral umpires were not needed at test matches in England. In 1985, John Woodcock's editorial in *Wisden Cricketers' Almanack,* a publication so prestigious that it could be considered part of the English cricket establishment, argued that if neutral umpires were introduced into test cricket, 'England would never play under the best umpires which are their own, and that would hardly be satisfactory. They could meet at Lord's with an Indian at one end and a Pakistani at the other' (*Wisden 1985*: 54). In the *Pakistan Times* Farooq Mazhar wrote that the English treated calls for neutral umpires as 'an insult to their men in white' (27 November 1987).

Many Pakistanis felt that the England party and journalists had exaggerated any bias on the part of Pakistani umpires. Some argued that so many England batsmen had been given out in the first test in 1987 because they could not distinguish between Qadir's googly and his flipper. In the *Pakistan Times* Abdul Haye wrote that no Pakistan captain had ever behaved in such an 'uncouth manner' towards an umpire as Gatting had done to Shakoor Rana, and that no Pakistan team had ever 'squealed like Gatting and his men' (15 December 1987). Pakistan players believed that some English umpires cheated. Imran Khan thought that English umpires were consistently better than Pakistani umpires, but that not all were 'good' (Crace 1992: 15). The English cricket journalist Matthew Engel wrote in 1992 that Pakistan cricketers had become 'terminally convinced, rightly or wrongly, that English umpires are against them. It may be that there is an element of self-fulfilling prophesy in their attitude' (*Dawn*, 11 July 1992). In 1996 he claimed that 'there really is a culture of anti-Pakistani feeling among English umpires. The best of them will hide it well, and try hard not to let it influence their judgements, even subconsciously. But many believe that the Pakistanis have, more than anyone else, broken the laws about ball-tampering; that many of their players appeal aggressively and argumentatively; and that successive captains have allowed these habits to foster' (*Dawn Magazine*, 7 August 1996).

In 1982 Pakistani players felt that English umpiring mistakes had prevented them from winning the series against England. Haseeb Ahsan was reported to have said that during the Pakistan tour of England in 1987 'English umpires had tried to demoralise the Pakistani team and rob them of their credit due' (*Dawn*, 29 November 1987). On the 1992 tour of England the Pakistan manager Intikhab complained that 'When we are fielding, the umpire has been looking at the ball very frequently . . . When England are fielding, it's not happening. There's no consistency. That's unfair' (*Guardian*, 31 August 1992). Mistakes by the English umpires Mervyn Kitchen and Ken Palmer were seen as vital factors in England's winning the fourth test at Headingley in 1992, a test England had to win to retain any chance of winning the series. In a Pakistan cricket magazine Salim Malik, the Pakistan vice-captain, described the English umpiring as having 'crossed . . . all limits. The umpires were determined to engineer a win for England. For this they were prepared to go any distance . . .

This was my third tour of England but I have never seen so much cheating there before. I have no hesitation in saying that a planned cheating programme was executed to frustrate us' (quoted in *Eastern Eye,* 27 October 1992). The Indian test match batsman Sunil Gavaskar claimed that England had 'sneaked' a win with the umpires' help (*Daily Telegraph,* 24 August 1992). Even some English cricket observers felt that mistakes by the English umpires had helped England to win. Geoffrey Boycott thought that Gooch should have been given out three times in his second innings, and that Miandad was right to feel cheated (*Sun,* 28 July 1992). In *The Guardian* Mike Selvey wrote that it was wide of the mark to suggest that the umpires had been 'intentionally biased – all right, cheats', but wondered about the 'furore that would have ensued had this match been played in Karachi and the roles reversed (*Guardian,* 28 July 1992). Scyld Berry found:

a smell during the fourth Test I had never detected before in a Test in England. There was something in addition to the inevitable, unconscious, bias which umpires have towards home teams and in particular home captains. Tight-lipped and highly formal, the umpiring at Headingley generated the impression that, come what may, judgements were not going to be delivered in Pakistan's favour until England were safely established in both their innings (quoted in Licudi and Raja 1997: 48).

Pakistanis saw the accusations of ball tampering in 1992 as further examples of English cricket's double standards. County sides had allowed bowlers to gouge balls. In 1992 Surrey were fined £1,000 for ball tampering in a match where Waqar had played for Surrey, but had also been warned about ball tampering in matches in 1990 and 1991 in which Waqar had not played. Don Oslear suspected that in 1993 Lancashire and Surrey had tampered with balls when Wasim and Waqar were playing for them (Oslear and Bannister 1996: 86–8). Other forms of ball tampering, though against the rules of cricket, had long been practised in English cricket. In *The Times* Simon Barnes wrote 'everybody knows that ball-doctoring is as much a part of English cricket as the tea interval' (29 August 1992). The former England fast bowler Fred Trueman said that bowlers 'have been messing up the ball as along as I've been around, and from what I hear, a lot longer' (*Daily Mirror,* 31 August 1992). Derek Pringle admitted to having used lip salve to keep the shine on a ball, and claimed that polishing cricket balls with illicit substances and lifting the seam were 'accepted by both professional players and the umpires'. Geoffrey Boycott compared ball tampering with speeding by motorists: irresistible, and what everybody did at some time. He saw ball tampering as 'technically a breach of the rule but cheating – no it's too emotive a word' (*Independent,* 27 July, 1 August 1996).

Pakistani players and cricket followers noted that ball tampering by England players did not provoke outcries of cheating on a scale similar to those lodged against Pakistani teams. On the England tour of India in 1976–77 laboratory tests proved that England players had smeared Vaseline on the ball to help their bowlers. Bishen Bedi, the Indian captain, claimed that the England team 'got the fullest backing from its establishment' over these 'unfair means' (*Wisden Cricket Monthly,* May 1988: 11). When England in a test match against the West Indies in 1991 became the only team to have had a ball changed because of illegal tampering, this had passed largely unnoticed (Illingworth and Bannister 1996: 85), though the Pakistani touring party in 1992 were aware that John Holder, the England umpire responsible for having the ball changed, was not a member of the umpiring panel in 1992. When Michael Atherton was allowed to retain the England captaincy after being noticed by a television camera rubbing dirt on a ball and then misleading the match referee about this, *Eastern Eye* carried a front-page picture of Atherton rubbing dirt on the ball with the headline 'GOTCHA!' Its writer, Nadeem Khan, pointed out that: 'This is the moment that every Asian cricket fan has been waiting for . . . For far too long the issue of cheating has been confined to jibes at Pakistan . . . WHO ARE THE CHEATS NOW?' (2 August 1992). Although retired England players called for Atherton to be stripped of the captaincy, this incident was treated as an isolated episode and not as part of a general tendency to cheat in English cricket.

Pakistani Cricket and Decolonization

For Pakistanis success in international cricket has been an assertion of Pakistan national identity, part of the attainment of decolonization. The Pakistan cricket journalist Omar Kureishi has said that 'Only two things really bind this country together. One is war and the other is cricket' (Marqusee 1997: 91). Governments may have interfered with cricket in Pakistan to bolster their domestic popularity, but this also suggests that they saw success in test cricket as a source of national prestige. The depth of support for the Pakistani team among those of Pakistani descent in England shows how cricket has been a focus of Pakistani national identity. Denigrating Pakistani cricket is seen as an insult to Pakistani nationhood.

Debates about decolonization and postcoloniality have stressed that granting formal political independence has often been only a partial dismantling of empire. As Said has shown, imperial domination can persist in other forms. The privileged position of English cricket in the administration of international cricket can be seen as an example of how the power of the former colonizer survived the abandonment of direct political rule. In 1994 Kenan Malik wrote in *The Independent* that the map of the world 'may no longer be coloured pink, but the spirit of Empire lives on in the game'. He added that the former Conservative minister and editor of the *Telegraph* William Deedes had observed that when 'we gave up the Empire and the white man's burden, we passed much of the load on to our cricketers' (*Independent,* 26 July 1994). Until 1993 England and Australia could veto proposals of the International Cricket Council and the president of the MCC, still a private members' club, nominated the chairman on the ICC and the MCC provided the administration of the ICC. Even after 1993 the headquarters of the ICC remained at Lord's, the ground of the MCC.

Details of the ICC's internal politics are scarce. Only the briefest of statements are issued to the media after meetings. Sketchy evidence suggests that friction was common between the England and Pakistan representatives in the 1980s and 1990s. England's privileged position was seen as a vestige of imperialism. A. H. Kardar, the first captain of the Pakistan test team and president of Pakistan's Board of Control from 1972 until 1977, was reputed to have tried to break 'the post-imperial dominance of Lord's'; but it also thought that his tendency to be 'dictatorial and quickly angered' may have 'ruffled the feathers' of the England cricket establishment (*Wisden 1997*: 1404; *Dawn Magazine,* 7 August 1996). How far the abandonment of their veto by England and Australia was due to pressure from Pakistani is unclear; but Shahid Rafi, a Pakistani delegate to the ICC, claimed in 1992 that Pakistan had initiated discussion of the England–Australia veto, which he described as 'undemocratic and [it] creates a gap between the two and the six' (*Dawn,* 4 July 1992). At the ICC Pakistan were the first to call for neutral umpires at test matches, a policy that the TCCB opposed. In the 1980s cricketing relations with South Africa were a continuing cause of friction between the England representatives and those from Pakistan, the West Indies, India and Sri Lanka. After the 'rebel' tour of South Africa by England cricketers in 1982, Pakistan and India threatened to abandon their planned tours of England unless the rebels were banned from test cricket. Much bitterness surrounded an ICC meeting in 1993. England delegates had expected that an earlier decision for the 1996 World Cup to be held in England would be confirmed, but they were outmanoeuvred by those from India, Pakistan and Sri Lanka, who, by promising a larger proportion of the profits to the associate members, ensured that the next World Cup would be played in the sub-continent, with that of 1999 taking place in England. Alan Smith, an England delegate, said of the meeting that: 'There was no talk of anything like cricket. It was, by a long way, the worst meeting I have ever attended' (*Wisden 1994*: 26). In the opinion of the Indian-born journalist Mihir Bose the England delegates had assumed that the meeting would be 'yet another old boys' gathering with the associate members continuing to be treated "much as the Soviet Union used to treat its Eastern European satellites"' (*Wisden 1997*: 21). Arif Ali Abassi, a Pakistan cricket administrator, spoke of England's representatives having 'the Raj hangover . . . They cannot accept the colonials beating them at their own game . . . The future of the game is shifting to the sub-continent' (Marqusee 1997: 82).

England delegates to the ICC were usually tight-lipped about the attempts of representatives from Pakistan and other Asian countries to have a larger say in the running of international cricket; but cricket journalists argued that Pakistan was trying to extend its influence at England's expense. In 1981 Robin Marlar wrote that the worst aspect to the debate over granting Sri Lanka test status, a move that carried full membership of the ICC and that Pakistan supported, was:

> the racial element, no more buried and equally dangerous as the iceberg underwater. With Sri Lanka a Full Member, the predominantly white members might be outvoted four to three and thus thrown back on the interest vested in the foundation members [the England– Australian veto], an interest which is politically bankrupt in a world which counts votes and pulls down privilege (*Cricketer International,* August 1981: 12).

A *Wisden Cricket Monthly* editorial in 1986 asked whether there was a 'Lahore/ Karachi aim to centre world cricket power there' (February 1986: 3). In 1987 the former England captain Raymond Illingworth saw the Gatting–Shakoor Rana issue as part of:

> an international plot to deprive this country of its influence in world cricket – a political power game.
>
> Cricketwise, Pakistan has always been iffy, and Pakistanis, in the main, difficult. Now they're becoming downright Bolshie. Given a chance they would trample all over us . . .
>
> Out there I heard and read repeatedly of campaigns to take the International Cricket Conference to the sub-continent and to blazes with England . . .
>
> We have spread the game and made allowances for eccentricities in other countries. But we have been weak . . .
>
> It's time we showed we won't tolerate being messed about (*Daily Mirror,* 10 December 1987).

In 1989 E. M. Wellings wrote in *Wisden Cricket Monthly* that at the ICC: 'Collectively the coloured group has bedevilled the game. It is time for others to form a common front in defence of it.' For him the ICC was 'that shoddy body' that had been running 'further and further off the rails for many years' and he suggested that England and Australia break away (July 1989: 27). India was seen as the prime mover of the decision for the 1995–96 World Cup to be staged in Asia; but Pakistan cricket officials were condemned for supporting this. Richard Hutton, editor of *The Cricketer International*, wrote of the 'axis in the Indian subcontinent, whose emissaries are suddenly able to summon a solidarity little in evidence in their other dealings with each other' (March 1993: 2).

The increased influence of India and Pakistan in the administration of international cricket from the mid-1990s has taken cricket to new heights of commercialization. The expansion in the number of limited-overs one-day international matches from 66 in 1990 to 153 in 1999, many being played in countries where little or no first-class cricket has been played, generated vast television revenue. Bangladesh was admitted to test cricket in 2000. The Indian businessman Jagmohan Dalmiya, who became president of the ICC in 1997, is usually regarded as having masterminded this burgeoning commercialization of international cricket, but Pakistan and Sri Lanka are generally believed to have supported his policies.

This Asian-led commercialization of international cricket was much criticized in England. In the late 1990s cricket journalists in England implied, though it was never stated quite so boldly, that cricket had become mired in sleaze during Dalmiya's presidency of the ICC. It was argued that the increased numbers of limited overs competitions, particularly in localities with little tradition of cricket playing and where match results meant little, had led players to accept illicit payments from bookmakers in India and Pakistan for match information or for fixing matches. The former England player Vic Marks thought that 'it is crazy that countless one-day games with no inherent meaning take place worldwide each year' (*Observer*, 7 May 2000). Rob Steen wrote that reducing the 'plethora' of limited overs competitions, which attracted brimming crowds in Dubai, Dhaka and Nairobi, but had 'no meaning beyond themselves' meant that 'caring about failure can be tricky' (*Financial Times*, 14 April 2000). *The Guardian* sports columnist Frank Keating wrote that Dalmiya could not 'escape the sober charge of complicity in the fatuous devaluation of cricket as a whole. You desperately yearn for the days only a decade ago when the ICC was an almost unheard of adjunct of dear old MCC and its buffers . . . who would hold amiable meetings over a couple of pink gins about the value of leg-byes.' Since then the 1995–96 World Cup had been taken to Asia, 'Doubtless to the joy of bookmakers. The game – and for sure the certainty of its morals and ethics and innate goodness – has never been the same' (*Guardian*, 4 May 2000). In the 1990s it was assumed that bribery and corruption in international cricket stemmed from the scale of betting on cricket in Asia, and particularly in India. Pakistani players were the first to be accused of accepting bribes; but this did not attract great waves of outrage from English cricket on a scale similar to those concerning Pakistani umpiring or ball tampering. In part this may have been because assumptions of Pakistani cheating in cricket had become so ingrained that another form of cheating was no longer considered newsworthy; but it could also have been linked to the fact that match fixing was not usually thought to have occurred in matches involving England. *The Cricketer International, Wisden Cricket Monthly* and the *Wisden* annual discussed match fixing and bribery, but press coverage reached a massive scale only in 2000 with the allegations that the white South African captain Hansie Cronje had accepted bribes to fix matches. The Cronje revelations provoked great comment in the broadsheet press on how Dalmiya's presidency of the ICC had created conditions that allowed corruption to flourish.

Defining the postcolonial as other than the epoch following imperialism has been notoriously difficult, and indeed, as Childs and Williams have shown in their discussion of oppositional and complicit postcolonialism, the term can have contradictory meanings (1997: 19); but much postcolonial discourse has emphasized the condition of hybridity. Hybridity has been celebrated as the means whereby those who were colonized have drawn upon indigenous and imperial culture to create a hybrid culture with the synergy to be superior to its antecedent cultures. In a Pakistan context cricket can be seen as an expression of hybridity. Introduced to the sub-continent by the white imperialists and embedded in discourses that linked its sportsmanship with white English assumptions of their moral fitness to exercise imperial power, cricket was taken up by the colonized and in Pakistan was seen as essential to decolonization and in the formation of national identity. The reservations of English cricket surrounding the Asian drive to exploit the commercial possibilities of international cricket indicate how far cricket administrators in India and Pakistan have ascribed new and different values to the game.

This Asian drive for the greater commercialization of international cricket can be seen as part of the late-twentieth-century globalization of sport and of globalization in general. While it can be argued that globalization is a decentred *mélange* to which many cultures are contributing, Ritzer has made a strong case for seeing globalization as the spread of Westernization and of Americanization in particular (Ritzer 1998: Chapter 7). Fast food, credit cards and jeans, very much the icons of globalization, are American cultural artefacts, and while the internet can be regarded as a resource for a decentralized global economy, the American corporation Microsoft dominates computer software. The enhanced commercialization of international cricket has been stimulated largely by the revenue to be gained from satellite television and sponsorship, and can be seen as an imitation of the American model of sports presentation, with sports events packaged to maximize their televisual appeal. The expansion of limited overs international cricket owes much to how it meets the requirements of television. As with other forms of globalization, the heightened commercialization of international cricket, though Asian-led, can be described as Western cultural imperialism, though ironically, while British governments have encouraged the economic deregulation and easing of restrictions on the international flow of capital, so often regarded as vital features of globalization, cricket in England has been reluctant to embrace the Asian-led commercialization of international cricket. In the 1980s and 1990s cricket had been a cultural space where the Pakistani desire for decolonisation had clashed with the residual white English assumptions of moral superiority which had validated imperial power, but paradoxically Asian leadership in international cricket has resulted in cricket becoming a force for Western cultural imperialism, even though this was a form of cultural imperialism with which English cricket had felt uneasy. The tensions of England/Pakistan cricket in the late twentieth century do much to highlight the complexities and contradictions of the postcolonial condition.

7

'When Gold is Fired It Shines': Sport, the Imagination and the Body in Colonial and Postcolonial India

James Mills and Paul Dimeo

Introduction

The body has been an important analytical tool in recent years in studies of South Asian history and culture. Two main sources lay behind this focus. On the one hand the work of Edward Said emphasized the place of cultural constructions of the body in the manufacture of the ideology of Western superiority and non-Western inferiority that was so important in legitimating the colonialism of Europe, and indeed has continued to feature in the collective denigration of imagined groups such as Arabs and Muslims. By representing in literature, art, journalism, and so on the physical manifestation of individuals deemed to belong to such groups as somehow 'different', 'corrupted' and 'unpredictable' when compared with the 'normal' bodies of those from the West, the control of those featured as 'normal' over those seen as 'different' was justified and made to seem part of a natural order (Said 1986, 1989).

Foucault, of course, was the second source of the focus on the corporal as an analytical tool in South Asian Studies. He argued that the body became central to the operations of the modern state from the end of the eighteenth century onwards. Modern systems of production and government control demanded that individuals be able to submit their bodies to regular and repeated work organized around timetables, deadlines and the techniques of mass production. Watching, recording, regulating and anticipating the functioning body of the individual therefore became of the highest importance to modern states. Consequently a range of institutions and technologies was devised to ensure large populations of strong and regulated bodies ready for work and for duty;

and Foucault implicates such phenomena as modern medicine, the factory system, modern prisons and penal techniques and psychiatry in this web of disciplinary techniques (Foucault 1989).

The body as discursive site and as subject of disciplinary power then were the two, separate but related, sources of the recent focus on the body in South Asian Studies. The range of studies that focus on the body in medicine in India (Arnold 1993), in psychiatry in India (Mills 2000), in prisons and convict systems in the region (Anderson 2000; Sen 2000), in constructions of masculinity and femininity in South Asia (Sinha 1995) and in representations of race, caste and communal identity there (Bates 1995) all originate in the insights of Said and Foucault. However, they tend to share the outlook that, whatever the merits of Said and Foucalt's conclusions, according to their own evidence when it comes to South Asia their observations are useful and stimulating, but not necessarily applicable.

Despite the relative lack of research on sport in South Asia (see Mills and Dimeo 2001) there is a number of studies of certain games and ritualized physical activities in South Asia and among the South Asian diaspora (see Dimeo 2000). The body is rarely the focus of any of these, but a number of them do provide useful insights into the importance of the body in the experience of sport in the region and into the place of sport in conceptions of the Indian body. The broad conclusion that can be drawn from these pieces is that in order to understand the development of sports in India[1] it is necessary to understand the way in which these activities relate and intertwine with existing concepts of the body in the cultures of the country and to examine the way in which the often intense corporal experiences of sports extend other social and cultural experiences and identities.

This chapter will consider existing studies of sport in South Asia and the insights that they provide into the relationship between sporting activities and the body in colonial and postcolonial South Asia. After this introductory historiogrpahy, it will then use the body as an analytical tool in approaching the early history of football in South Asia. It will demonstrate that football there acted for the colonizers both as an idiom and as a technology for imagining and transforming the Indian body. However, and perhaps more importantly, it will show that the game also became implicated in Indian attempts to resist these colonial corporal politics.

The Body and the Historiography of Indian Sport

Of the work that does exist, the most important study of indigenous sports and games is that by Joseph Alter. He published *The Wrestler's Body* in 1992 as an anthropological approach to *Bharatiya kushti* or Indian wrestling in north

India, an activity that is a fusion of Hindu sporting traditions dating back to the eleventh century and Persian martial skills introduced by the Mogul armies after the sixteenth century. He argues that any attempt to understand the meaning of the sport for its participants or for the supporters and patrons of individual wrestlers or of particular *akharas* (Indian gymnasiums) must place the body of the wrestler at the centre of the analysis. For the individual, the commitment to the rigours of a wrestler's life signals a personal search for the answers to the philosophical questions 'Who am I, and what am I put on this earth for?' The answers to these questions come from physical discipline and from the subjection of the body to challenging regimes. This was explicitly explained by K. P Singh, one of the most prolific writers on Indian wrestling, who insisted that:

> When you seek to develop your character, develop it in such a way that it becomes a treasure trove of magnetic power. Do not expect that the riches of life will fall at your feet. You must search for the true meaning of life. Whether through enterprise or through the rigid practice of *vyayam* [exercise], the goal is to plant the seed of human magnetism in this flesh and bone body. When milk is boiled, cream develops, and when gold is fired it shines (cited in Alter 1992: 258).

For the society around the wrestler however, it was the achievement of moral status through physical training of the body that gave the wrestler a position as 'an icon of the individual self'. Wrestling as a means not simply of strengthening the body but also of consolidating the virtue of the individual meant that the practice of the sport could come to have meaning for groups in the wider society. Alter points to the convergence of wrestling ideology and the Hindu nationalist politics of the militant *Rashtriya Swayamsevak Sangh* (RSS) political activists in India. The RSS have used wrestling displays to inspire young recruits and have sponsored wrestling tournaments in order use the occasions to link their extremist agendas with the traditional virtues of those trained in *Bharatiya kushti*.

Indeed, an example from another source shows just how potent the body of the Indian wrestler can be in the politics of modern India. Paul Brass (2001) located wrestlers at the heart of communal riots in Aligarh in 1979. A prominent local wrestler was stabbed to death in the city by an unknown assailant, and his body was paraded by Hindu militants through the streets of the various neighbourhoods as a means of gathering support for their planned attacks on the Muslims of the city. This incident sparked violence between the two religious communities in Aligarh that resulted in deaths on both sides. It seems that the body of the Hindu sportsman, and perhaps significantly the dead body of the Hindu sportsman, became an emblem through which meanings related to religious nationalism could be mobilized.

Despite these intriguing glimpses of indigenous sports in Indian society, most of the studies of sport in South Asia have however taken as their focus the games introduced by the British during the period of their colonial rule. Tony Mangan's work on the 'games ethic' in colonial contexts rarely attempts coherent theoretical analysis; but it does offer a number of examples that provide insights into the centrality of sports in the British efforts to control and transform Indian bodies. The depiction of the Indian body as weak and inferior in comparison to the strong and superior body of the European and the subsequent effort to discipline Indian bodies to 'improve' them was at the heart of the politics of colonialism. Mangan's case studies show that sport was self-consciously employed in British educational institutions for Indians as part of the programme to 'discipline their bodies in the manliness and hardihood of the English public schoolboy' (Sir J. Pelie, cited in Mangan 1998: 133).

In citing the example of Cecil Earle Tyndale-Biscoe, who was a headmaster at Srinigar in Kashmir, Mangan reveals that local physical culture among the elites of the region emphasized that muscular development was seen as undesirable. The muscular body was a symbol of the peasantry, who had to develop brawn for the toils of agricultural labour. Such a body was therefore emblematic of being low-born and from peasant stock, whereas a body that was slim and lacked muscle demonstrated that the individual in question was of elite status. His limbs physically manifested the fact that he had no need to resort to manual labour. It was the slim physique that lacked muscular development that was the ideal body shape for the leaders of local society in Kashmir.

Sports were introduced by Tyndale-Biscoe to transform the bodies of the local boys, as they needed to be strengthened to make them suited for roles that the British wanted Indians to play. His games-playing schoolboys became the agents of a range of social programmes that Tyndale-Biscoe imposed on the local community. During cholera epidemics staff and pupils would fill in cesspools and clean streets and compounds of filth; in summer hospital patients were treated to outings on the local lake; in winter the pupils provided fuel for the poor; all year they saved lives from fire and water, and even rescued animals that they felt had been mistreated.

In order to meet these new demands on their bodies imposed by the colonial schoolmaster the boys were subjected to rowing, boxing, cricket, various athletic exercises and football, and they thereby, as Tyndale-Biscoe observed, 'made a beginning in making that low-caste stuff commonly called muscle' (cited in Mangan 1998: 183). Indeed, he was not simply concerned through sport to transform the capacities of Indian physiques, as the activities that he introduced also demanded changes in the adornment of his pupil's bodies. Gold nose-rings and ear-rings, worn as markers of privilege and of caste status, were quickly removed when boxing was forced on the students, as impacts on the jewellery caused nasty injuries. The traditional dress of the *pheron*, a long woollen garment pulled over the head and worn down to the ground, was similarly discarded over time by boys wearied by the extra burden of exercising in such robes. The English uniform of trousers and shirts was soon adopted. Thus Tyndale-Biscoe transformed both the Indian body and its decoration through the medium of imposing sporting activity on his pupils. Though Mangan does not articulate it, here is an important example of sport playing a central role in what Appadurai (1993: 335) has called in colonial India the broader 'project of reform [that] involved cleaning up the sleazy, flabby, frail, feminine, obsequious bodies of natives into clean, virile, muscular, moral, and loyal bodies that could be moved into the subjectivities proper to colonialism'.

Because Mangan is apt to celebrate these 'many victories [of] Western moral imperialism' (1998: 181) (the book is after all dedicated to 'gentle and benign imperialists') he tends not focus on or explain the ferocity of the resistance to the measures of men like Tyndale-Biscoe. Hindu religion forbids contact with leather, as it is a product of the cow, which is believed to be the most sacred of animals. Mangan does mention the refusal of boys to play football at first, because kicking the ball involved physical pollution: 'take it away, take it away . . . we may not touch it, it is leather'. He also shows that in order to force the boys to kick the ball Tyndale-Biscoe herded them into an enclosed yard and armed his staff with sticks, and through the application of direct violence to their bodies coerced them into contact with the leather. Indeed, he notes that one boy, struck on the face by the defiling article, was subsequently turned out by his family, who refused to allow him in the house because he was polluted. It seems from Mangan's account that the boys destroyed over fifty footballs in their attempt to resist contact with the leather.

However, in Mangan's analysis this is a 'delightful illustration of the introduction of soccer' (1998: 184). A more balanced reflection on this incident would of course realize that it is doubtful that anyone but Tyndale-Biscoe and Mangan would agree with this. The rejected son, his appalled family and his frightened peers would between them have experienced physical force and corporal pollution and had all done as much as they could to resist the colonial schoolmaster's demands on their bodies, which were imposed with corporal violence. Such a story is replete with significance as to the place of the corporal in the development of Western sports in colonial India. Mangan's examples show, though he fails to realize it, that the body was not simply the target of colonial designs, but it was also the site of indigenous resistance to those designs, and was the point at which colonial objectives and sporting endeavours were refused or negotiated.

Michael Anton Budd (1997) recognizes this in his focus on 'physical culture' movements in the nineteenth century and the incorporation of their rhetoric into Indian resistance movements. He argues that these movements, aimed at developing fit and strong bodies through exercise and gymnastic practice, had their origins in modernity and the development of modern consumerism in the West. However, he explains that aspects of these regimes quickly appeared in the programmes of Indian nationalist writers such as Sarala Debi and Swami Vivekananda. Budd argues that this was not a result of Indians simply bowing to colonial coercion, which appears to be the implied conclusion advanced by Mangan in his failure to explore Indian reactions to Tyndale-Biscoe. Nor was this apparent interest in Western fitness techniques evidence of a desire on the part of the colonized to ape the colonizer.[2] Budd concludes that elements of the Western 'physical culture' movements aimed at the body were selected in order to rejuvenate indigenous traditions of corporal discipline, and were chosen to bolster resistance to British rule. This was possible because 'physical culture' techniques were not seen as culturally specific: 'Like other implements of colonial rule such as military equipment and transportation technology, it [physical culture] was not considered inherently or uniquely Western, but as separate from its user, and capable of serving any master' (1997: 85).

Studies of cricket by Richard Cashman (1980) and Ramachandra Guha (1998) similarly argue that the Indian body was a key site for negotiating with Western sports through Indian culture and politics. Cashman argues that cricket was not simply accepted by Indians because the English willed it. It was the case instead that cricket became so popular in India because it perfectly suited existing cultural beliefs about pollution through bodily contact:

> In earlier times cricket was an acceptable game partly because it was non-violent in the sense that it did not involve blood-letting and bodily contact which could cause not only injury but defilement. This was particularly true in the late nineteenth century when Indian society was governed by rules which regulated human contact and which ordained that indiscriminate mixing was socially dangerous (1980: 138).

Guha's example in Bombay of the emergence of Palwankar Baloo bears much of this out. Baloo was a member of the Chamaar caste, a community of leather-workers that ranks at the lower ends of the Hindu social system. The label commonly attached to groups at this end of the Hindu system, that of 'Un-touchable', hints at the fear of pollution through physical contact with such groups on the part of the Indian upper castes. While it was the high-caste

Brahmins that dominated the game in Western India, Baloo learnt the game as a servant at the British cricket club in Poona. Indeed, such was his talent that the elites of the Indian club, the Deccan Gymkhana, were obliged to include him in their team to lead the bowling (Guha 1998: 170–3). On the field this was not a problem, as the game of cricket did not, as Cashman has suggested, involve the possibility of direct bodily contact with the 'Untouchable'. But off the field, the physical barriers between the elites and Palwankar Baloo were hastily re-erected and rigidly reinforced, as Guha illustrates: 'The Brahmins played with Baloo on the cricket field but would not dine with him off it. In fact, during the game's ritual 'tea interval' he was made to stand outside the pavilion, at a distance from his team-mates, and served tea in a disposable cup' (1998: 170).

Indeed, writers on the postcolonial history of cricket have similarly pointed to the body in order to explain the emergence of the game as India's abiding sporting passion. It has been argued that 'logically after independence, football should have become India's number one sport. It . . . certainly permeated greater layers of Indian society, even down to the semi-rural areas' (Bose 1986: 35). Cricket, however, now dominates the Indian sporting calendar. Arjun Appadurai has concluded that this has nothing to do with an enduring nostalgia for the Raj, but rather is entirely implicated in 'bodily competition and virile nationalism' (1996: 25). Indian men learnt to play cricket at school or from friends on the parks at the same time as the successes of the national team were becoming an important means of expressing Indian independence both to the former colonizer and to the wider world. The regular playing of the game for Indian men, especially as youths when the body was young and healthy, means that for these males, even in later life when they are no longer active as players, 'the pleasure of viewing cricket for the Indian male, as with virtually no other sport, is rooted in the pleasure of playing or imagining playing cricket' (1996: 44). That the game is charged with nationalist meaning adds an extra dimension to the 'erotic pleasure of watching cricket', as the game comes to link 'gender, the nation, fantasy and bodily excitement' (1996: 44). Appadurai argues that cricket has become so important to the Indian male because it is one of the chief means by which he physically experiences important aspects of his identity such as his 'maleness' and his 'Indian-ness'.

Overall, then, writers on sport in South Asia have provided examples that emphasize that the analysis of the body is important for understanding the history of sports in India, while a focus on sports is a useful way of examining the politics of the body and the ways in which certain regimes have imagined and sought to shape bodies in South Asia. Indian cultures often included sports such as wrestling, where the objective was to reform the body through physical discipline in order to remould the 'mind' or 'soul'. In the colonial period, the British used sports to focus on the Indian body in order to transform it into types considered more suitable or desirable by the colonizers. However, Indian bodies were also sites for resisting these intentions, and indeed for mediating and negotiating them. Understanding why Indians took on European sports requires an analysis of local corporal politics and understandings, rather than simply an overview of colonial designs.

Football, the British and the Politics of Indian Bodies

The body is central to understanding the introduction of football into colonial India by the British and its subsequent spread and development; but an analysis of football texts is also important for the wider project of understanding the broader colonial designs for Indian bodies. In looking at football in this context it is possible to draw three conclusions. First of all, football was one of the means through which the British sought to control and transform Indian bodies into units suitable for colonial projects both in educational and military institutions. Secondly, the imagery of the game was an idiom in which the British attempted to construct discourses about Indian bodies that implicated them in the ideologies of colonial rule. And finally, the footballer's body was one of the sites where Indians contested these colonial discourses about their physiques.

Although football was often used as a means of excluding Indians from European circles and of emphasizing the social (and physical) distance between the two communities that was considered desirable by the British, there were many within the colonial establishment that wished to encourage football among certain Indian groups.[3] The reasons for the desire of many British to have Indians play the game lies in a range of discourses about 'race' and about 'orientalism' that coloured British thinking about India after the uprising of 1857. By the nineteenth century the British had become fascinated by 'race', and tried to classify and categorize Indians on the basis of perceived 'racial' qualities. A healthy 'race', it was claimed, was characterized by bodily vigour and strength, so that it was capable of defending itself through warfare but also capable of self-sacrifice for weaker allies. Accordingly, the strong and independent nation was constucted as one that had the 'male' qualities of physical power and prowess, while a colonized people was largely portrayed as weak and effeminate and in need of the benevolent protection of a 'male' civilization.

Bengalis were represented by the British as an example of just such a weak and effeminate people, and they were dismissed by the colonizers as possessing 'the intellect of a Greek and the grit of a rabbit' (Rosselli 1980: 121). The image of the effeminate *babu* became a dominant feature of colonial life and a general slur upon all Bengalis. *Babu* was a term of derision specifically relating to the

English-educated Bengali middle-class male who was employed in the service of the empire as an administrative or professional worker. The *babu* was widely reviled as physically weak and morally suspect for collaborating with British interests (Sinha 1995).

The origins of this colonially-constructed image of the weak Bengali are instructive, as they point to the wider cultural and social changes within which football emerged and that made football politically meaningful. The 1857 mutiny of Indian soldiers serving the British originated among Bengali officers; and thereafter soldiers from the region were viewed as unreliable. Indeed, recruitment policy after 1857 deliberately excluded Bengalis, and chose to focus on recruiting soldiers from parts of India that had remained loyal to the British in 1857. The association of men from these regions with military service and of Bengalis with treachery and exclusion from the Army led to a series of images being constructed of the martial and non-martial races of India. 'Martial' races, such as the Punjabis and Gurkhas, were constructed as essentially 'different' from the effeminate, enervated race of Bengalis (see MacMunn 1933; Fox 1985; Dimeo 1999). As Stanley Wolpert has claimed:

> The British soon [after the Mutiny] developed their spurious theories about 'martial races' and 'nonmartial races', based for the most part upon their experience with 'loyal' and 'disloyal' troops during the mutiny. Not only were there 'martial races', but also – and here Hinduism supported British prejudice – 'martial castes', least of which was the Bengali or Maharashtrian brahman, whose rebel leaders had fought so bitterly [in the Mutiny] (1997: 241–2).

Indeed, fitness for football in particular and sport in general were important idioms through which these representations of 'different' Indian bodies were constructed. One observer, for example, decided that 'by his legs you shall know the Bengali. The leg of a free man is straight or a little bandy, so that he can stand on it solidly . . . The Bengali's leg is either skin and bones; the same size all the way down, with knocking knobs for knees, or else it is very fat and globular, also turning in at the knees, with round thighs like a woman's. The Bengali's leg is the leg of a slave' (G. W. Steevens, cited in Chowdury-Sengupta 1995: 298). The contrast can be drawn with one proud officer's assessment of the Indian troops that he was recruiting and his explanation for the suitability of their bodies for war. Of the Gurkhas, he recorded the opinion that 'physique, compact and sturdy build, powerful muscular development, keen sight, acute hearing, and hereditary education as a sportsman, eminently capacitate him for the duties of a light infantry soldier' (Vansittart 1915: 60). The honing of the body through sporting activities was a factor that recommended the Nepali for service in the imperial armies in the eyes of this British soldier.

Indeed, football itself was used as an idiom in which to construct distinctions between the various martial races. An article in the *Illustrated Sporting and Dramatic News* in September 1909 described regimental football as follows. 'Practically all the men from the various Panjab [Punjabi] regiments in Burma who play in these tournaments are of two classes, Sikhs and Panjabi Musulmans [Muslims] and of these two the numbers are about equal, with perhaps a slight preponderance of Musulmans, who are more of a football build than the long and snaky Sikh . . . The Gurkhas approach more nearly to the proper type of footballers, and are powerful, sturdy, not too big, and strong on their feet, but they are decidedly slow at running, which defect neutralises their other great advantages.' The body, as constructed in the imagery of football, was the site for the British construction of different Indian body types.

These constructions had a profound effect on social relations in Bengal. Sir George Campbell, Lieutenant-Governor of Bengal in the 1870s, believed 'that if the educated Bengalees, instead of giving way to intellectual vanity, set themselves to rival Europeans in qualities depending on physical and moral tone, they are capable of very great things' (1893: 267). Consequently the following stipulations were made for those Bengalis who applied for posts in the Native Civil Service:

> By every candidate a certificate of character must be produced, as also a medical certificate of fitness for employ in any portion of Bengal. Candidates for appointments of over Rs. 100 a month must show that they can ride at least 12 miles at a rapid pace; candidates for inferior posts must have similar qualification or be able to walk 12 miles within 3 1/2 hours without difficulty or prostration. Good character, health, and physical energy [are] thus secured (Campbell 1893: 266).

Through such statements and mechanisms the British transmitted to the Bengali elites the idea that they were considered physically inferior. However, in sports, the British offered Indians a means of developing themselves physically. Indeed, many among the British saw it as part of their imperial duty to help Indians to 'improve' themselves, and deliberately set about encouraging Bengali men to engage in games. Many Indians quickly realized that physical prowess was necessary for success in the colonial order. The lesson learnt was that an ability to demonstrate to the British that Bengalis did possess physical vigour was necessary both to get ahead in colonial India and to gain the respect of the imperial power. While there were British officials and civilians encouraging Indians to play football then, there were also many Bengalis who realized the value and importance of taking advantage of these opportunities to play the colonizers' games. The most obvious place where British 'improvement' met with ambitious young Indians was in the Anglo-Indian schools and colleges.

Middle-class Bengalis had been educated in British-run Anglo-Indian colleges modelled on the British public schools of the nineteenth century, where sport was central to the curriculum. Sir George Campbell, for example, emphasized the importance of sport in the syllabus of the College of Engineering in Calcutta:

> I spared nothing to make that college complete, but the Bengalis seemed infinitely to prefer literature, law, and politics to anything that required some physical as well as mental exertion. At the same time I am bound to say that when I introduced gymnastics, riding, and physical training in the colleges, they heartily accepted these things, and seemed quite ready to emulate Europeans in that respect (Campbell 1893: 273–4).

Campbell was clear in his intentions. Sport was as valuable for education, for the making of able men, as was scholarly activity. His implication that Bengalis embraced these benefits indicates his belief in both the superiority of British ways and in his strategy for Bengali improvement. It was a strategy that the students apparently accepted wholeheartedly. Although Campbell makes no mention of football *per se*, another Briton resident in Calcutta in 1885 did spot its importance.

> Many educated Natives, in Bengal specially, have for years past felt the reproach which attaches to their want of courage and corporal activity and have earnestly set themselves to remedy these defects: hence on all sides we find efforts to follow the example of Europeans among native students. Football and cricket are becoming popular, and gymnasia introduced[4] (Trust and Fear Not 1885: 18).

Another example of similar colonial attitudes towards sports comes from the Lieutenant-Governor of Bengal in 1891, Sir Charles Elliot, who proposed measures to assist in the improvement of the Bengali 'race' through physical culture:

> In 1891–92 it was particularly noticed on every hand that there was a great increase of the zeal with which the national English games, especially football, were played. On tour Sir C. Elliot constantly watched the performances of the boys with great interest . . . He looked forward to great improvement in the physique of Bengalis in the course of one or two generations from this source . . . (Buckland 1976: 117–18).

Football was considered a source of improvement necessary for the bodies of the Bengali 'race'. The game, however, was also important in the Army, for ensuring the enduring capacity of 'martial' Indian bodies for war. One officer serving with a Punjabi regiment in Burma noticed that 'there is always some sort of game going on every afternoon, and everybody gets an opportunity of playing'. He explained that 'the great thing about our football is that it gets the men and ourselves out, and gives us good exercise and something to take an interest in', emphasizing that the games 'were not serious efforts, but merely means of improving the physique, general activity, and resourcefulness of the boys' (*Illustrated Sporting and Dramatic News*, September 1909).

The Indian soldier's body in football was however also used by the British to construct discourses about the need for the control of a 'civilized' nation over India. Michael Anton Budd has spoken of the 'denigration of the physically robust and militarily indispensable Irish as both 'savage' and weak by virtue of a lack of self-control' (1997: 92). Where the body of the colonized was physically acceptable it was denigrated by the inscription into it in discourse by the colonizer of an inherent but invisible weakness, that of indiscipline. One officer wrote of his footballing soldiers that 'the recruit, when he first emerges from his jungle or village, has rather less control over his legs than a new-born camel'. Another authored this account of the Indian soldiers' use of their own bodies when allowed free rein:

> I tried to introduce football. It amused the players highly, but no great skill at the game resulted. The players would not keep their places, but preferred getting in a jumbled mass, in which they pushed and kicked one another indiscriminately. This 'scrum' like mass never approached the goalposts, but generally wandered off the confines of the field, where abounded a plentiful growth of prickly cacti . . . the game generally ended with the ball being punctured by a thorn (Perry 1921: 108–9).

Here the Indian body and its response to football is used as a metaphor for creating a sense of the uncontrolled nature of the unschooled Indian physique. At one point these soldiers have been included in the discourse of the martial race – so no one disputes the idea that their bodies are acceptable to the colonial project in terms of strength and vigour. Yet the implied need for the British officer is present in the observations that in the game they 'pushed and kicked one another indiscriminately', and had less control of their legs than an infant animal. Even where an Indian body was martial and fit, the discourse underlying this football snapshot is of an Indian body that is still imperfect, as it has within it the flaws of being impulsive and lacking self-control. The political answer contained within this set of discourses to this 'natural' shortcoming is control by a 'higher' race, one that is physically perfect, as it is both strong and disciplined: that is, the British colonizer.

In short, then, football was an idiom in which ideas about the different types of Indian bodies were constructed and in which evidence of the flawed nature of Indian bodies was manufactured. These ideas were central to the British ideological project of legitimating their rule, as they claimed physical superiority over Indians and also to have the key to improving these problem physiques. This superiority and this ability to 'improve' the subjected were the theoretical justifications for colonial rule. Football, however, was not simply an idiom; it was also one of the techniques that was used as a technology of corporal transformation and control. In the schools and colleges the game was intended to correct the supposedly feeble body of the Bengali *babu*. In the Army football was a means of maintaining the vigour of the martial race soldiers while disciplining their supposedly 'impulsive' bodies, for, as Lord Roberts said while presenting the Durand Cup in 1892, 'the same qualities, discipline and combination, were equally necessary in good soldiers and football players' (*The Englishman*, 5 October 1892). Football was implicated in the strategies of colonialism both as a discourse and as a technology of power.

But it is of course fundamental to a consideration of football in India to look at the question of how Indians responded to all this representation of their bodies and how they acted in response to the techniques of transformation of which football formed a part. One example will demonstrate the complexities of approaching this issue in the case of football. In 1911 the Bengali football club, Mohun Bagan, saw off St Xavier's (3–0), Rangers (1–0), the Rifle Brigade (1–0), and the 1st Middlesex Regiment (1–1, 3–0), on their way to the IFA Shield final in Calcutta. The club was recognized as having a serious chance of being the first Indian club to win the most important football tournament in colonial India. With the Bengalis described as having 'simply walked over the military defence' in the semi-final, the scene was set for an exciting final against the British East Yorkshire Regiment (Mookerjee 1989). The final had brought a crowd estimated at between 60,000 and 100,000 that had travelled to the ground from as far afield as Patna, Assam and the outlying regions of Bengal. The spectators travelled by specially arranged trains, steamers and trams to see the game. A temporary telephone was installed at the nearby Calcutta Football Club ground to transmit reports throughout Bengal. Mookerjee sums up the feelings of the day thus: 'Soccer fever had engulfed Calcutta. The IFA Shield final pushed everything else to the background. Hope, once kindled, whatever the odds against be, refuses to be snuffed' (1989: 150). In an exciting match, the Indians came from a goal down to score twice in the last five minutes: 'wild excitement burst out amongst the Indian spectators . . . When the referee blew the long whistle, shirts, hats, handkerchieves, sticks and umbrellas started flying in the air' (Mookerjee 1989: 151).

This was a moment to be savoured, a victory that unified Bengalis of different religions against their colonial rulers (Nandy 1990: 318). It was also a moment when the axioms of colonial discourses on the body were dramatically reversed, a point that Indian newspapers were quick to explain. The ironic reconstruction of these discourses in the Indian media in the wake of this victory dramatically demonstrates the fact that Bengalis resented representation as physically inferior and saw football as a means of challenging such a construction:

> Indians can hold their own against Englishmen in every walk of art and science, in every learned profession, and in the higher grades of the public service . . . It only remained for Indians to beat Englishmen in that peculiarly English sport, the football. It fills every Indian with joy to learn of the victory of the Mohun Bagan team over English soldiers in the Challenge Shield competition. It fills every Indian with joy and pride to know that rice-eating, malaria-ridden, barefooted Bengalis have got the better of beef-eating, Herculean, booted John Bull in the peculiarly English sport. Never before was there witnessed such universal demonstration of joy, men and women alike sharing it and demonstrating it by showering of flowers, embraces, shouts, whoops, screams and even dances (*Nayak* 30 July 1911).

Such a quotation is all the more telling when contrasted with an article from the same newspaper that was published just prior to the Mohun Bagan match:

> We English-educated Babus are like dolls dancing on the palms of Englishmen. The education which makes Babus of us, and gives us our food whether we are in service or in some profession, is established by the English. Our . . . political efforts and aspirations are all kinds of gifts of the English people . . . English education and the superficial imitation of English habits and manners have made us perfectly worthless, a miserable mixture of Anglicism and *swadeshism* (*Nayak* 14 June 1911).

The body, then, was central to Indian conceptions of their subjection, and the frustration at corporal colonization, both in fact and in discourse, is dramatically expressed in a doll metaphor. Little wonder, then, that the football victory of Mohun Bagan was celebrated in a triumphant corporal idiom that satirizes the reversed axiom.

However, the complexity of choosing the Indian footballer's body as a site for discursive resistance is more complex still. As has been stated, the 1911 victory was a moment of nationalist triumph when one of the ideological underpinnings of colonialism, the belief in innate British superiority and in Indian physical frailty, was dramatically and publicly undone. Yet in celebrating the undoing of these stereotypes there was an acceptance of the British moral system introduced through the Anglo-Indian colleges and the Army, in which only success in sport and the demonstration of physical prowess could signal strength and self-reliance. Contained in the celebration in corporal metaphor of the victory was an acceptance of the colonial culture that dictated that the body was the correct site for judging a people and its destiny. The football final and the Indian victory was at one and the same time both a victory for the bodies of the Bengali team and the people that they represented, and yet also an acceptance and legitimation of the discourses of strength and self-discipline that underlay the body politics introduced by the British Raj.

Conclusion

We question ourselves, why with such glorious tradition, with such heritage, and with such immense resources of talented footballers, we are lagging behind those elites of soccer, who did not even exist when we lived and thrived on the game of soccer. It is because of defective management, or socio-economic conditions coupled with genetic imperfection of Indian footballers concerning physical fitness, or because of the indifferent attitude of the Government that we are yet lagging behind a good number of the soccer playing countries, even in Asia (Indian FA 1993: 1).

This chapter has considered the place of the body in analyses of sport in South Asia. It has demonstrated that while the body is rarely the focus of analysis, there are useful references to the corporal site in a number of articles on sport in the region. It then attempted to adopt the body as a focus in examining the early origins of football in South Asia. Throughout, the chapter has drawn on the twin themes evident in other academic attempts to place the body at the centre of analysis of a range of institutions and other social phenomena. These themes, drawn to varying degrees from the work of Said and Foucault, are discourse and power.

What the chapter has demonstrated is that corporal politics are central to any attempt to understand sport in South Asia, and that conversely sport has been significant in the corporal politics of the region. To understand the meaning of Indian physical activities to their local societies, and indeed to begin to explore the reasons why certain Western sports were adopted by the cultures of the region, it is necessary to understand concepts of the body and their linkages to the often changing power relations in those societies and regions. At the same time, sport has been an important set of discourses and techniques for effecting challenge and change in concepts of the body and in the corporal politics of Indian society.

In the case of football, it was demonstrated that the game provided an idiom for the discursive construction of the inferiority of the Indian body and the superiority of the European body that was so important to legitimizing colonial rule. Football presented a set of images that could be manipulated by the British to represent certain Indians as inherently weak and by representing those Indians who were deemed to be strong as corporally indisciplined. These representations were then opposed to the model of the British colonizer, which was constructed in the discourse as both strong and disciplined. Football also provided a reason for active British intervention in India, as it was deemed to be one of the technologies through which the colonizer could improve the colonized, through which 'he' could invigorate the weak body and organize the indisciplined one. In short, sport in general, and football in particular, are both idioms for discursive construction and technologies of disciplinary power.

Importantly, however, the chapter also pointed to football as an idiom in which local resistance to colonial discourses and interventions took place. The ironic evocation of the 'beef-eating John Bull' and the 'rice-eating Bengali' in the wake of the 1911 Mohun Bagan cup final victory demonstrates that Indians thought of colonialism in corporal terms and used football at certain moments to challenge British representations of them as inferior. The complexities of choosing the footballer's body as a site for such discursive challenges are, however, highlighted by the extract at the start of this conclusion. Thinking of football failure in terms of essentialized Indian bodies was of course a British trick that has been detected and dissected here. For Indians to still be thinking in these terms almost fifty years after independence suggests that the body, football and the politics of colonialism remain inextricably linked in post-colonial South Asia today.

Notes

1. The focus of most academic attention on sport in South Asia to date has been on India, and there remains a dearth of serious studies of sporting activities and experiences in Pakistan, Bangladesh and Sri Lanka. For rare exceptions see A. McKay (2001) and P. Parkes (1997).
2. Richard Holt (1989: 218) has advanced this argument in concluding that 'the native elite mostly rejected their own culture and tried to win the respect of the Raj through sport'. For a critique of this conclusion see Mills (2001).
3. For more on the use of football to draw 'race' lines see P. Dimeo (2001).
4. This paper was written anonymously; however, Sinha (1995: 82) suggests the author was Henry Harrison, Chairman of the Corporation of Calcutta.

8

'Theatre of Dreams:' Mimicry and Difference in Cape Flats Township Football

Grant Farred

> Some people think that football is a matter of life and death . . . I can assure them that it is much more important than that. (Bill Shankly, Former Manager of Liverpool FC).

The 'most damaging blow against apartheid', the English editor and author Anthony Sampson (1987: 155) suggests, was the 'sports boycott'. In view of the pivotal role that decades of sustained internal opposition, economic sanctions, and diplomatic pressure played in securing a democratic South Africa, it is difficult to regard Sampson's claims as anything other than an exaggeration. Culturally, some might validly argue, the boycott by artists, actors, writers, and musicians was more important than the sports one. The refusal to 'play Sun City', as the guitarist Stevie van Zandt described the musicians' prohibition on performing at the homeland venue, was hugely influential in alerting audiences about the conditions of life in South Africa – in some cases, in fact, artists educated their audiences about apartheid. There can be little doubt that the 'Sun City' boycott impacted on a more numerous and international audience than those affected by or interested in the cancellation of a rugby or cricket tour to the country.

However, the argument advanced by Sampson, an anti-apartheid white liberal with a long-standing interest in black culture (he was the editor of *Drum* magazine, a major mouthpiece for the first generation of urban black South African writers), cannot be summarily dismissed. South Africa is, as its Trade and Industry Minister Alec Erwin might argue, too 'sports-mad' a society for an easy rebuttal. In an earlier incarnation Erwin was a trade unionist, so he was well placed to evaluate the role of sport from a position quite unlike that of Sampson: 'Not all societies that have gone through liberation struggles have had in sport such a central political place as we had in South Africa' (Erwin 1989: 44). Allowing for the awkwardness of Erwin's phrasing and the predictable difference in emphasis, with the ex-trade unionist clearly in favour of the sports boycott and the *Drum* editor more taciturn about his position on the subject, the Minister and Sampson both acknowledge its centrality in the anti-apartheid struggle. It is not surprising, then, given the substance of Sampson's and Erwin's arguments, that barely had Nelson Mandela been released from prison in February 1990 than white athletics administrators began to clamour (successfully) for the termination of the sports boycott. Plans were made, almost immediately, for a South African cricket team to visit India, for an Olympic squad to participate in the 1992 Barcelona Games, and for rugby tours to and from the country to commence. It is also no coincidence that all these teams were dominated by white personnel. White South Africans were especially, but by no means exclusively, all too eager to take the sting out of, to slightly amend Sampson's phrase, that 'most damaging of anti-apartheid blows'.

However, much in the manner of the apartheid era, some sports were treated more equally than others. Certain codes of sport were better positioned for admission (or re-admission, depending on your point of view) to the international arena; these sports were better organized because they had greater financial resources – better facilities, ready access to the media, and stronger links to international bodies, despite the boycott. Like every other feature of apartheid society, sport bore the imprint of segregated life – often in politically salient ways. Sport, and sports journalism, was not only raced but classed and ethnicized. The main codes, rugby, cricket, and football, were all assigned places overdetermined by the cultural stratifications upon which apartheid was based – football formed the broad base of the cultural pyramid and rugby and cricket combined to make up the apex.

The most popular sport in the world, football occupies a politically loaded place within the South African cultural psyche. Historically the sport of the nineteenth-century British working-class (adopted soon after by the French and then the other European proletariats), local football was considered a second-rate code by the apartheid regime and the white press. The Afrikaner government's dismissive attitude toward football served simultaneously as measure of its anti-British sentiments and as a marker of the ambivalent cultural and political relationship it had with its own, English-speaking white population. Historically opposed to the local "English" since the early moments of European colonialism, Afrikaners nevertheless favoured rugby and cricket, those gentlemanly codes so beloved on the playing-fields of Eton and Harrow; although they had a long tradition of espousing a Manichaean white South African politics, Afrikaners versus English-speakers, from the early 1960s the

National Party (NP) government increasingly (though not without considerable reservations and misgivings) began to court the 'English' vote. Most importantly, however, football largely was shunned by white South Africans because it was *the* sport of the disenfranchised black masses. In the coloured, black, and indian (of South Asian descent) communities, rugby and cricket constituted minority cultural practices: football was the code most practised and revered. It represented disenfranchised South Africa's cultural 'theatre of dreams', to borrow the endearing nickname Manchester United Football Club's fans have given their team's Old Trafford stadium.

Football was a marker of the ethnic, historical, and ideological distinctions within the white South African community. Afrikaners read football's pre-eminence amongst the oppressed as the most culturally explicit evidence of black, coloured, and indian 'anglicization'. Because of its popularity amongst the disenfranchised, football gave public voice to these communities' propensity to value English cultural practices and artefacts above those that the regime held dear – in a word, football was favoured, not rugby. (The 'anglicization' of South African society was manifested, of course, only secondarily in the disenfranchised communities. It was a process that spoke more volubly of a British colonial heritage that had deep roots amongst the country's white English-speakers.) The investment in metropolitan football, in both the disenfranchised and the enfranchised ranks, was facilitated by the extent of the media coverage it received in local English-language newspapers such as *The Cape Times* and *The Cape Argus*. England's professional leagues constituted a staple interest for white, English-speaking South African sports journalism, a practice that soon impacted on the cultural outlook of the disenfranchised. The widespread circulation of English-language newspapers in the disenfranchised communities facilitated (we might even say encouraged, in the Althusserian sense) the interpellation of oppressed South Africans into metropolitan culture. Since local football (of both the professional and the amateur variety) was implicitly denigrated through the media's determined under-reporting of it, metropolitan football assumed a disproportionate public import.

The regular, if not extensive, reports about the exploits of Liverpool, Manchester United, Leeds, Chelsea, Tottenham Hotspur, Arsenal, and Nottingham Forest Football Clubs made them, in the absence of a local equivalent, hugely significant. These English clubs became double-edged symbols of sporting accomplishment for coloured South Africans: these metropolitan institutions became football clubs that could be adored but never emulated, creating a cultural desire that was palpable but unfulfillable. Players in the townships of Hanover Park or Mannenberg could admire a goalscorer such as Liverpool's Kenny Dalglish or a goalkeeper such as Spurs' Pat Jennings, little boys could tackle like Leeds' Billy Bremner or dribble like Forest's John Robertson, but apartheid ghettoized their cultural horizon. They could pretend, not unlike countless thousands of youths in England, Scotland, and Ireland, to be performing for Liverpool in their after-school pick-up games; but they could never hope (unlike their metropolitan counterparts) actually to play for an English League club. 'Liverpool' was both *a priori* and always already a dream, not so much a sign of the distance between metropole and periphery but an indicator of the deliberate circumscription of apartheid society.

However, while apartheid reduced the disenfranchised's 'theatre of dreams' to the microcosmic ghetto, the relationship between English and South African township football frequently exceeded and complicated those boundaries. Restricting itself to the final two decades of the apartheid era, this chapter will examine the unique cultural links between the working-class coloured community of the Western Cape and English football clubs. Through a discussion of this mimicry, both in terms of the possibilities it offers and the complex ways in which it is 'surpassed', this chapter will engage with the significance of the coloured working-class's singular support for metropolitan cultural institutions. This coloured constituency is different not only from white South Africans, but also from its black and indian counterparts, and from its own middle-class. The coloured township–English metropolis link is, furthermore, a cultural affiliation that has a long history, and one that has endured into the post-apartheid moment. In fact, we might even say that this relationship has thriven in the past decade, an age in which satellite link-ups have now made several English games available every week on MNET, the lone South African 'cable' station.

However, this chapter has been circumscribed to the period between 1970 and 1990 because of the era's cultural and historical significance. After some fifteen years of almost relentless struggle against the NP government (beginning with the Soweto uprising of 1976), the end of this era marks apartheid's terminal point – perhaps best remembered simply as 'February 1990', the historic moment when Nelson Mandela was released and the black liberation movements were unbanned. As an inaugural moment, 1970 stands less as an absolute historical marker than as a metonym: a sign of deracination, an uneven and lengthy process by which the Group Areas Act had effectively uprooted several disenfranchised communities and forced them into barely completed townships and suburbs. The Act was a cornerstone of apartheid legislation, because it racialized the nation's geography, dividing the country into four distinct living 'Areas' – for whites, indians, coloureds, and blacks. The best urban, suburban, and rural areas were, needless to say, reserved for whites; members of any of the other races were uprooted in order to accommodate whites and to ensure the 'racial purity' of each 'Area'. Paradoxically, one of the consequences of the Group Areas Act was that it inadvertently facilitated (some might even suggest that it initiated) the process of community (re)construction for the coloured working-class through the cultural appropriation of metropolitan football clubs. Forcibly relocated from urban (and suburban) areas they had occupied for generations to the outlying Cape Flats, the new residents of the coloured townships formed football clubs that borrowed the names of English professional clubs.

Teams from the Cape Flats townships, which from '1970' became the new home of the coloured working-class, used their metropolitan counterparts as a template from which they could produce their own football identity. In the process, township teams displayed both familiarity with the metropolitan club and a complicated cultural agency – one where the tendency to replicate the English club coexisted with the latent (or not-so-latent) desire for an independent football identity. For the most part, township clubs not only adopted the name but imitated the style of the metropolitan institution – the several Cape Flats teams called 'Chelsea' or 'Leeds' acknowledged their debt to Chelsea of London or Leeds of Yorkshire by playing the game the way the English clubs did in that faraway league. For all the similarities, the identification between the township and the professional clubs is, however, misleading in one crucial way: the superficial mimicry, significant as it is, undermines or appears to undermine the agency of the local football community. However, the choice of names and football aesthetics (to call a club Chelsea rather than Spurs, to play like Leeds rather than West Bromwich Albion), the adaptation of the metropolis to the township, articulates a complex and often disguised agency; it marks a negotiation between idealizing the metropolis and appropriating the cultural values that speak most directly to and of conditions in the townships, and the football aspirations of their inhabitants.

Township football mimicry, the process by which township clubs produce a cultural identity that self-consciously idealizes, imitates, and appropriates the metropolitan original, is remarkable for at least two reasons. Firstly, in an era in which the print media dominated sports reporting (an informational monopoly only effectively challenged in the last few years by the advent of satellite television), working-class coloured teams constructed themselves as 'Leeds' or 'Chelsea' out of a largely 'imagined' and truly imaginative sense of who and what the 'original' was. They read about 'their' teams (English clubs with whom they experienced a real affinity and whose wins and losses were of great consequence to them) in the *Cape Times* and the *Cape Argus*, and then 'read' themselves off of those metropolitan clubs. The township residents translated imaginatively from the English city of Manchester to the Cape Flats township of Mannenberg, creating a vibrant, mobile football imaginary out of the "stationary" words (and the few accompanying pictures) on the page. Not only did the *Cape Times* transport the township residents to England, but the Cape Flats fans transported metropolitan football matches back to Mannenberg and Hanover Park – they 'replayed' those matches, domestically, in their collective and individual imaginaries, and in their animated conversations about the latest performances of Liverpool, Arsenal, and Spurs.

Secondly, as Homi Bhabha has so convincingly argued, mimicry is also invariably about difference – 'in order to be effective, mimicry must continually produce its slippage, its excess, its difference' (Bhabha 1994: 86). The condition of apartheid, the remove of geography, the distinction between metropolitan professional institutions and amateur township ones, questions of race, and even the very process of cultural translation, are all, as this chapter will show, not only obvious but crucial (and even problematic) markers of the 'difference' between London's and Heideveld's 'Chelseas'. Mimicry is also, as Bhabha makes clear, about the potential of the imitator to 'exceed' the original object or identity. Therefore, as much as township clubs sought to become like their metropolitan templates, there were Cape Flats teams that 'exceeded' imitation. Mostly, however, mimicry is an uneven, hybrid process, one that comprises different modes (and degrees) of imitation and innovation. Negotiating between their own sense of footballing style and that of their metropolitan models, clubs such as Leeds of Hanover Park and Heideveld sometimes struggled (with greater or lesser commitment) to overcome their status as 'cultural derivatives'; for some township clubs, the English model sufficed, and they amended their identities only minimally; others, however, attempted to transform, with varying degrees of success, themselves into local 'originals'.

While this chapter focuses extensively on the ways in which amateur township clubs imitated professional English ones, it concludes with an all too cursory reflection on a working-class Cape Flats institution that throws into question the very process of cultural imitation. Everton Amateur Football Club (AFC) of Heideveld, a highly successful team from a township on the eastern fringes of the Cape Flats, represents an instructive instance of an 'original'. Everton AFC is a local club that did considerably more than distance itself from Everton FC of Liverpool, England: unlike township clubs such as Leeds and Chelsea, who successfully mimic (in the superficial sense of the term) and achieve an aesthetic symmetry with their metropolitan counterparts, Everton AFC marks the unmooring of the township from the metropolis. The Heideveld club articulates both a distinct agency and a cultural reinscription of Cape Flats football. Everton AFC established itself as not only 'different' from Chelsea AFC but as, arguably, the fulfillment of township football's potential for cultural autonomy – achieved, it is important to note, without denying the initial value of mimicry.

It's a Cape Flats Thing, Try to Understand

> Now on the Flats the frozen trees
> dedicate their broken histories.
>
> Donald Parenzee, 'Uprooted'.

Unlike white, English-speaking South Africans, who supported metropolitan football clubs without the intention of replicating them, working-class coloureds engaged in a deeper cultural imitation. White mimicry was, if you will, of a shallower and an occasional variety – enfranchised South Africans maintain a sharp distinction between English football institutions and their own domestic clubs. They support Manchester United, but they do not attempt to 'become' a local version of the English club – they do not call their sides, as coloured township teams do, 'Leeds' or 'Chelsea'. White clubs are more blandly named, taking their identity from local geography rather metropolitan football inspiration. (Paradoxically, they are in this way following the English tradition of naming – 'Liverpool' takes its name from the city, as do 'Leeds', 'Sheffield Wednesday', 'Sheffield United', and so on. This is the norm in English football; clubs such as Arsenal, from north London, are the exception, being originally named after the Woolwich Arsenal munitions factory in South London, where the club was originally founded.) The white club from the Cape Town suburb of Wynberg is called 'Wynberg Amateur Football Club' (AFC), and Green Point's team is known as 'Green Point United AFC' More frequently, white links to the metropolis are disguised, borrowing nicknames and sometimes the design of the English side's uniform. Wynberg AFC, for example, are also known as the 'Magpies', after the English side Newcastle United, and their outfit is an imitation of the metropolitan team's black and white stripes.

White South Africans' highly mediated articulation of their metropolitan affiliations is remarkably similar to that of (predominantly English-speaking) coloured middle-class. Like their working-class counterparts, the coloured middle-class supported English clubs passionately, but they stopped short of outright mimicry[1]. They took their inspiration from the metropolis (a club such as Battswood, from the coloured section of Wynberg, adopted with tremendous success Liverpool's disciplined passing game as the football model for their team); but the coloured middle-class named their clubs after local institutions such as schools (Battswood Teachers' Training College), churches (St John's, St Raphael's, St Luke's), or, in one instance, directly from the local Young

Men's Association (YMO). The smaller and more generally middle-class indian community also followed this pattern. They rooted keenly for Spurs or Manchester United, but their clubs were (like their middle-class coloured and white South African counterparts) more likely to be named after local geography than after English football institutions. (Leeds and Chelsea, however, have a certain following in this community as well.)

Writing about English football after the First World War, Arthur Hopcraft (1978: 42) evokes many of the same sentiments expressed by Cape Flats residents when they learned the results of metropolitan matches in the 1970s. By 'association with the [metropolitan] team', he writes, 'positive identity could be claimed by muscle and in goals. To win was personal success, to lose another clout from life.' Hopcraft's grasp of the depth of fan identification, the vicarious accomplishment of making tackles and scoring goals ('by muscle and in goals'), can easily stand as metaphor for the relationship between metropolitan player and a fan from the periphery. The English writer's poetic tendency ('another clout from life') reveals a passion – if not a discourse – that would be not at all out of place in the coloured township of Hanover Park, where Liverpool results may not be quite a 'matter or life and death', but are certainly of huge consequence. However, this kind of psychic affiliation with the metropolis would not be as understandable in the black townships of the Western Cape. In Langa and Guguletu, the latter quite literally just across the road from the coloured township of Mannenberg, a different tradition held sway, one that we might accurately label a hybrid of the postcolonial and the 'Africanist'. Black township footballers cherished a set of cultural practices rooted in local communities and those Third World nations that had thrown off the shackles of colonialism. Here, perhaps more than in the coloured townships, it was a country such as Brazil that was admired for the flair, spectacularity, and individual brilliance of its footballers. The Brazilian icon Pele was a hero, metonymically put, in both Mannenberg and Guguletu. But for the most part, mimicry reflected a very different visage in the black townships: Pele rather than Dalglish, the Mozambican-born Eusebio (who represented Portugal in the 1966 World Cup) rather than Nottingham Forest's John Robertson. (As a regional minority, Western Cape blacks also identified with professional football clubs from the north of the country, black clubs such as Orlando Pirates and Kaizer Chiefs – based in Soweto, the nation's 'black capital'. They adopted these cultural models, sometimes calling their clubs 'Young Pirates' or 'Young Chiefs'.)

As important as the ideological distinctions are that separate working-class coloureds from their own middle-class and from black, indian, and white South Africans, it is equally difficult to account for these differences. The racially slippery distinctness (because it verges so closely on indistinctness, the racially elusive that expresses itself culturally and politically) of coloured identity has assumed, predictably, a special pertinence in the post-apartheid era. The coloured affinity (which goes beyond the working-class) with the English metropolis has persisted – at the expense, some would argue, of a deeper interpellation into (and more unproblematic affiliation with) the 'new' nation. Nowhere is the resilience and vibrancy of those links more evident than in, ironically, South Africa's 1998 World Cup hero Benni McCarthy – a national icon. A product of Hanover Park, McCarthy's greatest ambition was, as he told a reporter shortly after returning from France, to play for Manchester United. (This from a player on the books of the Dutch champions Ajax, a club infinitely more successful than the English team in European competition.) McCarthy's cultural and athletic desire is telling, both because it speaks so volubly of the coloured working-class's continued ideological investment in English football, and, more importantly, because it marks the difference between apartheid and post-apartheid potentialities. It was during the (extended) moment of apartheid, before the township hero McCarthy could dream of scoring goals at Old Trafford, that the local became a substitute for and an imitation of the metropolis. McCarthy is thus culturally salient, not so much as a player (talented though he is), but as a political sign. The Hanover Park native stands as the representative *par excellence* of the possibilities of enfranchisement, the coloured township footballer who has been issued the historic licence legitimately to imagine – and perhaps even realize – a cultural scenario about which his predecessors from the Cape Flats could only dream. His Manchester United is an entire political epoch removed from the 'Liverpool' (that conflation of admiration for the metropolitan institution with the township's capacity for footballing emulation) of the apartheid township. McCarthy's dream is, as it were, the literalization, if not the realization, of 'Liverpool' as cultural metaphor.

A metaphor that, as it turns out, requires a quite literal translation – from English into Afrikaans. Like the majority of working-class coloureds from the Cape Flats, McCarthy speaks Afrikaans rather than English as a home language. In the coloured community, language is a marker of class – as McCarthy's imperfect command of the language demonstrates. English is the language of the educated and financially successful and stable middle-class; Afrikaans, often a hybrid version of it, is the *lingua franca* of the working-class. (English-speaking township dwellers are not only in the minority, they understand that their mother tongue is read as an indicator of social aspiration – it articulates either a desire for or a history of a more elevated class position. To speak English is, in crucial ways, to situate oneself outside the dominant experience of the coloured working-class. McCarthy's recent acquisition of the language coincides not only with the public demands of his newfound fame, but also with his family's relocation to a middle-class suburb. But the choice of English was also, for some families, an anti-NP gesture that transcended class lines.)

The predominantly Afrikaans-speaking township residents are, paradoxically, culturally linked to the two 'antagonistic' white ethnic communities – to the 'Anglos' by sport, and to the Afrikaners by language. Through their investment in English football township residents are thus engaged in dual cultural translations: they convert (and adapt) the metropolitan practice into the terms of the periphery through a language that has no vocabulary, or empathy, for football. Working-class footballers have to translate English culture into township Afrikaans, a process that involves changes in pronunciation (of English names), understanding culture as geography (England as a collection of physical sites, as well as cites), and, most importantly, a telling instance of the hybridization of the Afrikaans language – a hybridization that is not unusual in township life.[2] In discussing football and their English heroes, the inadequacy of the footballers' mother tongue and their limited formal education produce 'football-speak', a language where sentences in English follow phrases in Afrikaans – or vice versa. ('Ek is 'n Liverpool fan' translates as 'I am a Liverpool fan', to cite a simple example.) The technicalities of the sport, however, are almost always described in English, so that the metropolitan cultural practice serves a pedagogical purpose – people learn to speak a specific kind of English because of their interest in the game, not because of the desire for upward social mobility. English football makes language (a second language, in this case) a matter of culture, not class aspiration.

However, the most ironic aspect of the Cape Flats' cultural identification is that the English clubs so admired by the coloured working-class were themselves proponents of racism. It is only since the mid- to late-1980s that black players, born and bred in England, became a significant force in the game. Up to that point, black players such as West Ham's Clyde Best (a fixture in the East London team in the late 1960s) and Forest's Viv Anderson (a key member of the late-1970s championship side) were notable exceptions in a lily-white league. The exceptional team in this regard was the West Bromwich Albion side of the late 1970s. Albion contained an array of black talent, with the gifted left-winger Laurie Cunningham, the redoubtable striker Cyrille Regis, and the combative midfielder Remi Moses (later one of the first black players to join Manchester United), all regulars in an outfit that played attractive football. (But Albion's moment of fame was too brief, and their success insufficient to win them fans away from Liverpool and Spurs. Racial identification could not, as it were, counteract the tradition of support that these other, predominantly white, clubs enjoyed in the coloured community.) The issue of race and racism thus complicates the township–'Liverpool' cultural nexus. How could disenfranchised

South Africans, so keenly aware of the racism in their own society, overlook metropolitan racism? Surely they could not have been unaware of it? How could they, as oppressed black subjects, idealize sports institutions to which they bore no physical resemblance? Was racism displaced racism eviscerated? Were the likes of Liverpool and Arsenal not simply offering an English version of sports apartheid? Was apartheid so heinous a system that it ameliorated all other forms of racial discrimination, especially one mediated (and palliated) by a passion for football? Or was Bill Shankly, read through the lens of Karl Marx, unerringly correct in his assessment of the sport's societal significance? Is football not only 'more important than life and death', but in fact so powerful an 'opiate' that it invalidates (metropolitan) racism?

Because of the township's powerful 'imaginary' bond to the metropolis, the Cape Flats were able to ameliorate the racism inherent in the English game. It is, moreover, because English football represents a certain politics of relief that the racism that should render 'Chelsea' and 'Arsenal' abhorrent to disenfranchised South Africans instead makes them not only palatable but desirable.[3] As oppressed members of a highly racialized and stratified society, they were well versed in both the obviousness and the nuances of race politics. (English football racism was familiar, but it was not immediate in the way that apartheid affected disenfranchised lives – geography muted the impact; passion rendered it largely insignificant.) Cape Flats football is, by virtue of history, an always already politicized space. From its roots as by-product of Group Areas social engineering, to the tensions with middle-class coloured clubs, to the intra-township team rivalries that mar(k) and sustain the practice, Cape Flats football has been intensely political. It is for this reason that identification with individual English players or clubs offers itself as a unique ideological space that serves a dual function. It is, firstly, an athletic arena where narrow political debate is ruled offside, and where metropolitan racism is (either tacitly or explicitly) acknowledged but is never allowed to dominate the debate. Colloquially put, it is a cultural territory where passion rules, where arguments about support for Liverpool as opposed to Manchester United are the norm, where there can be endless debate about the merits and demerits of metropolitan stars such Dalglish, Bryan Robson, or Paul 'Gazza' Gascoigne. The symbolic and emotional affiliation with English football provides a relief from the constrictions of disenfranchised South African life: it allows for the heightening of the unadulterated joys of football without the political invocations that are inextricably bound up in it as township practice. Discussions about Liverpool's last performance, or speculation about Manchester's chances of winning the league title, regulate the political realities that so indelibly mark township life.

It is in this way that the preoccupation with English football not only represents a temporary 'escape' from the condition of township life, but fulfils a second political role – this time a more local one. Through their discussions about and their investments in the affairs of Liverpool or Arsenal, footballers from the various teams in the township league are able to converse and make community across local divides – Manchester United fans play for both 'Chelsea AFC' and 'Leeds AFC'. This complicated conception of community is important in a township environment where clubs are often fierce expressions of local – based on different sections of the township (and sometimes even gang-based), pride, identity, and loyalty. Intra-community tensions are mediated through metropolitan affiliations, because this 'de-personalizes' (and in so doing, defuses) local disagreements. Disputes about the attacking merits of Spurs or the defensive shortcomings of Nottingham Forest offer a release for cultural (and political) tensions that would otherwise find no ready outlet. It is precisely the depth of the attachment to metropolitan clubs, rendered effective by its lack of immediacy, that enables them to ameliorate local antagonisms. The township league thus derives an 'overarching' cohesion from afar, a sense of community produced (incidentally) out of a shared affinity with the English institutions they idealize.

Scoring from the Cultural Rebound

> The people who came to support were basically working-class people . . . It sounds a bit corny but Liverpool really is the club of the people.
>
> Kenny Dalglish (1996: 57), Former Liverpool player and manager.

There is a story about Liverpool FC in the 1970s that is culturally illuminating even though it is, in all probability, little more than apocryphal. The poster in a Liverpool churchyard read: 'Jesus Saves'. Beneath it some wag, undoubtedly a Liverpool FC fanatic, scribbled: 'And John Toshack scores from the rebound'. Such was the passion that Liverpool FC aroused in the mid-1970s, when the team boasted talents such as Steve Heighway, Kevin Keegan, and Toshack, that one person's Saviour was merely the foil for another person's goalscorer. Located on the river Mersey in the English county of Lancashire, Liverpool is among the poorest cities in Europe. The 'working class' Kenny Dalglish describes when he got there in 1977 was increasingly seeing its ranks depleted – as the docks stood more and more idle and the number of factories dwindled, so the number of the unemployed swelled. The elevation of football to the status of religion was thus easily made. Jesus may offer to save your soul, but Toshack, or Dalglish, or Ian Rush, or the current teenage prodigy Michael Owen are far more likely to save your Saturday afternoon at the club's Anfield Road stadium. Or, as

Arthur Hopcraft might have it, an Owen goal might spare you 'another clout from life' on Merseyside.

However, John Toshack's spectacular feats were crucial not only to the economically depressed inhabitants of Merseyside. His accomplishments resonated loudly on the 'sandy wastes of the Cape Flats' (Rive 1981: 12). John Toshack's ability to score from a goalkeeper's errant save transformed him into a cultural lodestar, a metonym for the coloured community's uniquely symbiotic relationship to metropolitan England: Toshack could stand at once as the individual hero, the Liverpool goalscorer, and the composite representative of all the English clubs and their (individual) stars. Toshack is only in the most nominal sense of the term a cultural import. He is, more accurately, a measure of the depth of the coloured working class's integration into English football culture and a marker of the metropolis's cultural transportability: Toshack is the metropolitan star made 'native' in the periphery, claimed as hero because his successes and failures impact people's daily lives in the coloured townships.

As complete as the identification with and admiration for Toshack footballing brilliance is, it also marks a point of cultural disjuncture. Like all metaphors, 'Toshack' is a sign of approximation and therefore an indicator of incompleteness and aporias. Ingenious as the act of transporting the Liverpool player from Merseyside to the township of Mannenberg is, key components of metropolitan history do not make it to the other end of the cultural trade route. In South Africa, the journalism on English football is a limited genre, compensating for depth with a mild sensationalism. It is a mode of sports reporting that, not unusually, concentrates on results, moments of individual brilliance and failure, occasional fortuitousness, and a cursory survey of a team's strengths and weaknesses. An 'imported' journalism, it is shorn of the nuances familiar to a metropolitan audience – it rarely reflects upon the histories of class and religious caste so indelibly woven into the fabric of English football. It does not, for example, explain Arsenal's long affiliation with the Church of England or Newcastle's affinity with Catholicism; nor does this brand of journalism explore Manchester United's wealth, relative to, say, Southampton's shallow coffers – teams that compete in the same league, but who live in very different economic universes. This is not to exaggerate the religious implications of an Arsenal–Newcastle game or to suggest that a Manchester–Southampton encounter is nothing but low-level English class warfare. Rather, these unspoken 'conflicts' serve as a reminder of what is lost in the process of cultural translation – a number of subtle tensions are overlooked, vital components of histories are omitted, and the political aspects of football narratives are undermined. Transported to the Cape Flats, 'Liverpool' is thus, for all its ideological import, a metaphor focused on cultural identity.

Of course, the lack of political familiarity with the class histories of English football clubs does not mean that the politics of class is not a significant component of township sport. Despite their lack of familiarity with the politics of class so central to Dalglish's description of Liverpool fans, township footballers still grasp his Merseyside populism. Township communities know, even if it is articulated more through inflection and suggestion than through informed critique, as much about the politics of Liverpool as they do about the city's football club. Footballers in Hanover Park understand the conditions of life in the metropolitan city because of the politics inherent in the sport. From its earliest roots in the newly urbanized British and French proletariat of the Industrial Revolution, football has always been, as it continues to be, grounded primarily in working-class communities. 'The core values of the game as a professional sport, aggression, physical emphasis, and regional identity, meshed', according to Chas Critcher (1979: 161), 'with other elements of that . . . working-class culture, elements carried within its network of small-scale organizations and supportive mechanisms'. These values were key to the formation of professional football in Manchester and Liverpool (key cities in the process of nineteenth-century industrialization) and, moreover, are still manifest in these English institutions. Their 'working-class' roots make them understandable, if not always intellectually 'knowable', to communities on the Cape Flats.

Geographically bounded by the apartheid law, the 'regional emphasis' of township football was especially strong – supplementing, and sometimes exceeding, the 'physical' elements so central to the sport as township practice. Cape Flats clubs were also 'supportive mechanisms', social institutions where sections of a township gathered not only to play or organize for football, but to construct a social identity that made them distinct in the township. In Hanover Park, for example, Lansur United AFC supporters and players congregated at the 'club house' (a wood-and-iron construction in the chairman's backyard) regularly for matters that were purely social – to play card games or darts, to drink, or just simply to enjoy the company of those with whom they shared a cultural identity. It was for this reason that, like their English counterparts, township residents were, on a microcosmic level (specific areas in a township as opposed to inter- or intra-city rivalries) fiercely loyal. A loyalty, it should be said, commensurate with (and within) the circumscription of the Group Areas Act, which rendered the townships, more individually than collectively, 'organic' cultural units; football was a practice that gave fundamental shape to life in places such as Hanover Park or Heideveld. As a city and a coloured 'area', Liverpool and Hanover Park are both communities that used football – in different degrees, of course – as cultural means to exceed their status as merely sites of labour for capital. Football enables the construction of an identity that transforms the 'recreational' into the highly politicized practice. For Liverpool FC and its fans it is battle between the privileged South of England and the hard-bitten, industrial North, while on the Cape Flats, of course, players also give a unique political substance to their 'working-class' status. They are not only the South African equivalent of the Liverpool working-class; theirs is social oppression compounded by the realities of disenfrachisement. In the coloured townships (much as in a predominantly black Liverpool neighborhood such as Toxteth), class is overwritten, or complicated, by race – even, of course, as metropolitan racism is refracted through (and overlooked because of) the passion of cultural affiliation.

English football's greatest cultural impact registers itself in a complex fashion: a negotiation between the metropolis's ability to make its own names resonate on the Cape Flats and the capacity of township residents to appropriate those names for their own use. Not so much in the names of their stadiums; Liverpool's Anfield Road; and Leeds's Elland Road are recognizable venues, but they are ultimately sites impossible to replicate in a community where football grounds are shared by a dozen or so clubs and where the very notion of property ownership is alien; people who live in rented 'council' houses can dream but not actually conceive of having a football field belong exclusively to them. The names of English-based players (they are as likely to be Scottish or Irish as they are to be English), on the other hand, are loaded with meaning. Liverpool's Dalglish and John Barnes, Manchester's Bryan Robson or Gordon MacQueen, or Spurs' 'Gazza' set the mythical standard for township players – the intent is to 'play like Barnes' or 'Gazza'. These are appellations adopted or given as nicknames, indicating admiration for both the metropolitan star and the local one. Most importantly, in a society where apartheid limits their ambitions and restricts their horizons, metropolitan names enable township footballers to express their talents through metaphor – township players become, if only for a single moment or a solitary game, the very embodiment of the athletic excellence they so admire and covet. (It is through this tendency, the capacity for idealization, that township football becomes a metaphor for a more general sports condition: expressing what is culturally valuable and admirable through our desire to emulate it. Supporting Liverpool is only a mimetic step away from wanting to play like Liverpool's Paul Ince.) In that brief instance, scoring a brilliant goal or making an incisive pass, local footballers go from wanting to be 'Gazza' to making like 'Gazza'. On this occasion township footballers offer their community, and themselves, a glimpse of what their talents, fully expressed, might look like, how their amateur dreams might be elevated in the stadiums at Elland Road or Anfield Road. This is mimetic desire fulfilled: the rare occasion when the township and the metropolis conjoin, when the Cape Flats amateur and the English professional can be conflated. In that singular (but not necessarily single), exceptional moment apartheid's restrictions are brilliantly overcome (as geography is transcended) and the Saturday or Sunday afternoon encounter is transformed from cultural metaphor into physical (albeit transient) reality.

In his explication of the Scottish football fan's support for the country's national team, Stuart Cosgrove offers a reading that both reflects and differs from the kind of projection, identification, idealization, and displacement (of a thwarted football career) found amongst coloureds on the Cape Flats. Scottish fans, Cosgrove writes, 'are motivated by a dream, a dream that is past, present, and future . . . a dream that relates directly to the nation and its progress. The dream is one of Denis Law's bicycle kicks, it's Slim Jim Baxter making the ball talk, it's pulling on a navy jersey and it's King Kenny scoring through the English keeper's legs.' (The Scottish fan's 'dream' is made all the sweeter by the accomplishments of Denis Law and Dalglish, Scotsmen who succeeded in the English league with Manchester United and Liverpool, respectively.) For the coloured player or fan from the Cape Flats, apartheid South Africa was too divided a country to evoke any discourse of the 'nation', even as they struggled alongside other disenfranchised communities to effect that political construct; for this community the 'past and the present' have been a seamless continuum of oppression and marginalization. The identification with English football is, then, a profoundly anti-National(ist Party) gesture by township residents – a measure of their disenfranchisement and their distance from the regime, an all too brief triumph over the devastation of the Group Areas Act.

While the Cape Flats fans, like their Scottish counterparts, appreciated brilliant ball skills and deft goalscoring, coloured passion and political antagonism did not have a ready cultural outlet, a stage on which it could express itself. Coloureds had no opportunity to do football battle against whites as Scotland did in its annual battle with England, its 'Auld Enemy'; for these disenfranchised South Africans there was no satisfaction in the shape of witnessing Dalglish inflict the ultimate humiliation – a football practice called 'nutmegging', 'scoring through the English keeper's legs'. However, township communities have developed their own, highly local, versions of adversarial football passion. The football grounds at Bonteheuwel were home to countless tough battles between Sea Point Swifts and Bluegum Wizards, Hanover Park hosted several exciting 'derby' games between Lansur United and Surwood United, and at Heideveld fans witnessed many a rousing contest between Everton and Chelsea. The scale of the contest was greatly reduced, but both the intensity – the passion of Cosgrove's Scottish fan was matched on the Cape Flats even if the terms of the game were markedly different – and some of the identities were instantly recognizable.

What's In A Metropolitan Name?

The name carries within itself the movement of a history that it arrests

Judith Butler, *Excitable Speech*.

Most of the Cape Flats clubs who adopted names such as 'Leeds' or 'Chelsea' were formed in the late 1960s and early 1970s. Displaced to townships that were being constructed while they were moving in by the Group Areas Act, deracinated coloureds found themselves in a cultural vacuum. When the residents of embryonic communities such as Heideveld and Hanover Park formed the first township football clubs, they did so with few resources. Located as they were in this interregnum, between the vivid memories of settled communities on the fringes of downtown Cape Town and the uncertainties of their new life on the Cape Flats, they reached outside their immediate geographical confines for cultural identity. In this moment of historical crisis and trauma (what Parenzee calls 'broken histories'), the newly established townships of the Cape Flats resorted to that which they, in the most complex sense of the term, 'knew'. Deeply acculturated in the ways of the metropolis, they accessed England, an ideological space that represented for them communal stability and geographical fixedness, socio-political securities so gravely lacking in their own experience. Amidst the multiple structural and psychic dislocations wrought by apartheid deracination, English football clubs became a symbol of community (and cultural) resilience. The very names of English clubs carried within them, in those early days when 'community' was spoken of in the past tense (signifying the pre-Group Areas moment), the possibility of cultural and political survival.

These imported names spoke of the commitment to a history that they wanted to create and perpetuate because their other past had been so violently 'broken' and decimated. Metropolitan clubs such as Liverpool, Leeds, and Chelsea had not always thrived, but they had survived – all of them had overcome the disruption of the world wars, the chaos of internal crises, and the ignominy and humiliation of relegation to lower leagues. English football clubs became pivotal talismans, life-saving and community-building institutions of the cultural variety for the unsettled – and struggling to adjust – residents of the Cape Flats. Without knowing it, apartheid's perniciousness transformed English football clubs into models of hope, of footballing prowess, of community creation and maintenance, and of social cooperation. 'Liverpool' facilitated, in a small but culturally crucial way, the production of a community – and communal life in the township – in the face of apartheid hostility. The Group Areas Act was, after all, little more than a (racist) commitment to destroying organic social units – 'Liverpool' and 'Leeds' offered themselves as an unexpected counter to the potentially debilitating effects of deracination.

However, much as the township 'politics of adoption' was a response to apartheid's 'politics of disruption', the choice of 'Arsenal' and 'Chelsea' as a cultural identity was also motivated by a more visceral and considered sense of footballing affinity. Township clubs assumed English identities because they, or at least some of the key founding members, admired the individual qualities, the 'character', if you will, of these metropolitan institutions. The two most popular English clubs were Leeds and Chelsea, teams with contrasting styles, but both of which appealed, for vastly differing reasons, to township communities. Leeds's outstanding features were their tough tackling, their solid defence, and their uncompromising style, appropriate for a Yorkshire city that valued hardness, resilience, and a no-nonsense approach to life and the game of football. The late-1960s, early-1970s Leeds side, a very successful team, boasted a series of 'hard men' such as 'Big Jack' Charlton, Norman Hunter, and their redoubtable skipper, the combative Scotsman Billy Bremner. (Their strikers, Allan Clarke and Mick Jones, scored goals through grit and graft, only rarely through guile.) Leeds's salient features translated well on the Cape Flats, where survival required the very qualities Leeds of Yorkshire embodied so fully in their football. In his essay 'Football and Working-class Fans', John Clarke (1978) captures the spirit of Leeds and the working-class ethos it so unabashedly proclaimed: 'The worker, as breadwinner, could not afford to wilt under this pressure [of the factory], any more than the footballer could afford to give in to physical challenges on the field. Both in football, and in male working-class life, this idea of toughness sanctioned certain types of violence as normal'. The kind of 'toughness' that Leeds prided itself on was, as Clarke points out, always laden with the potential for 'violence' – the kind of combative *machismo* that the Yorkshire club almost single-handedly transformed into a style of playing football.

Leeds's was an approach that found a willing constituency on the Cape Flats, where township life required no small amount of 'toughness' to get by. The Leeds United AFC of Heideveld and Hanover Park, to mention but two township derivatives, imitated the style of their English progenitors with astonishing success – to say nothing of the countless clubs that adopted the philosophy but not the name. With the occasional exception, the local Leeds players eschewed the dribbling and ball artistry so beloved of other township clubs. For them, football was a game to be played directly – they relished the 'physical challenges' so innate to the Yorkshire team's (and their) game, and dared other teams to beat them with fancy footwork and ball control. Leeds of the Cape Flats played the game according to a simple philosophy: the ball was cleared long and hard out of defence, their midfielders were bruising in the tackle, and their forwards aggressive in their quest for goals. In a cultural word, this was Jack Charlton, Billy Bremner, and Allan Clarke come to township life. It was not that these local clubs could not pass the ball around the park, or 'play football', as Leeds FC fans would have had it; it was, rather, that they believed that they were playing football the Leeds way, a style accurately suited to the conditions under which they lived.

On the other hand, Chelsea of London were a study in contrast. Defence was not their strong suit, because this was a club that prized slick ball control, deft footwork, and goals carved out of long, twisting dribbles – goals that left defenders helpless in the wake of Charlie George and Peter Osgood's silky moves, or those moments when Alan Hudson stole goals out of nothing with a quick shimmy and a shake of his hips. In the absence of Leeds's stout defence there was the breathtaking goalkeeping of Peter Bonetti, a man nicknamed 'The Cat' because of his swift reflexes. (There was, however, one Chelsea defender who did relish protecting his 'keeper, the 'hard man' Ron 'Chopper' Harris. A central defender, he earned his sobriquet because of his habit and ability of felling opponents ruthlessly as readily as he would tackle them fairly.) This was how Chelsea of Heideveld, of Bridgetown, and of the working-class neighbourhood of Lansdowne played. They moved the ball adroitly with swift, incisive passes; their teams were a collection of talented individuals who might not always play as a unit, but always promised to enthrall the fan and mesmerize their opponents with flashes of skill. Unlike Yorkshire's Leeds, Chelsea of London did not win many trophies; but they played football with an abandon that enabled their township imitators to overcome both the restrictions of apartheid and the sometimes stifling confines of the working-class. Like their metropolitan namesake, township Chelsea(s) encouraged their players to aspire to the spectacular. They always tried to play, to use a phrase coined in August 1998 by the Newcastle manager Ruud Gullit, 'sexy football' – Chelsea played to please the connoisseur of deft, intricate passing and long-range shooting, with defenders who loved to go forward and attack even as they left themselves open to a quick counter by their opponents. They played a stylish game, preferring the ball at their feet, and always shirking the excessively physical challenges that were Leeds's very essence. You went to watch Chelsea for pleasure and excitement, not necessarily because you expected them to win. As Gullit, who himself played for and managed Chelsea, remarked: 'I'd rather lose 5–4 than draw'. Gullit was not only describing a scoreline, he was summarizing a football club's entire philosophy.

Like their namesake, township Chelsea(s) relied on the individual brilliance of their goalkeepers to keep them in the game. Indeed, Chelsea of Heideveld produced, in Charlie Jongbloed, one of the two best goalkeepers ever to play football in the Western Cape. The local keeper too bore the appellation of 'The Cat', and his long and illustrious career was studded with many an unbelievable save. After a while, however, the township 'Cat' tired of being a one-man defence, and he moved on to the club's neighbours, Everton, a team that (much more than their English 'forebears') played brilliant football – without ever, like Chelsea local and metropolitan, shirking their defensive responsibilities.

Everton AFC of Heideveld, a club with a valid claim to being the most successful township team in the history of Cape Flats football, demonstrates an important development in the working-class game. It is precisely because English models dominate the style of football, express a desire for a cultural identity, and articulate a series of relationships with the metropolis, that Everton AFC is such a salient township club. This is the team that shows how the process of cultural mimicry can be disrupted through redefinition: Everton of Heideveld demonstrate how idealization is transformed through township agency, how a metropolitan name can be hollowed out and reinvested with an autonomous identity; Everton shows how cultural appropriation can lead to a radical transmutation that renders the original model almost unrecognizable, the shared name the only remaining trace of the metropolis. Unlike England's Leeds and Chelsea, Everton of Merseyside (they are Liverpool FC's neighbours) were not a club to inspire identification. With good reason, many of their English opponents would add. Solid without being tough, with hints of stylishness without a full commitment to it, they are an institution marked by stolidness – moderate success, a club without any dramatic failures.

Loosely affiliated with the Anglican Church in Heideveld (much as the metropolitan club had early links to the Church of England, as well as to the Catholic Church), the local Everton adopted the blue and white strip of their Merseyside progenitors. However, from their origins in 1969 they have been a club committed to flair. Everton AFC's defenders, such as Errol Caswell, Colin Solomons, and John 'Piggy' Richards, passed the ball as adroitly as their midfield – an area of the park where Elroy Stokoe, Patrick Jooste, and Norman Philips were truly brilliant. Philips was articulate and incisive in his distribution, gifted in his ability to break down defences; Jooste was an authoritative and commanding presence in the midfield, coupled with a lethal shot. Up front, Gerald Hartzenberg's speed and trickery, 'Tickies' Caswell's (Errol's brother) neat flicks and powerful shot, and Gary Arendse's ability to head the ball further than most players can kick it wreaked havoc with many a defence. The Heideveld team played their football with a relish that was at once disciplined and full of bravado. Everton AFC combined the township predilection for ball skills with the English insistence on 'keeping your defensive shape'. But the Heideveld club did not interpret this phrase in the prevailing English terms, which is to say playing dourly, taking no risks, and putting a premium on not conceding goals. For them it was attack with responsible flair – threaten the opposing goal without leaving your own vulnerable.

The Heideveld club marks the point at which the metropolitan model recedes and township autonomy, not an outright rejection or complete disavowal of Everton FC, becomes salient. As the Cape Flats amateurs produced their own distinct footballing style, they transformed 'Everton' into an 'independent' township name, and evacuated Everton of Merseyside from their identity – Everton AFC represents the transmutation of metropolitan idealization into township originality. The amateur club's 'declaration of cultural independence' demonstrates how, in Judith Butler's terms, the 'history of the metropolitan name' can be 'arrested'; it evinces how it is not only possible to 'arrest' the metropolitan name but to create an entirely new and different history in the process of doing so. Metropolitan identification is not evacuated by a preferred local playing style, but that style does mark the (partial) invalidation and transformation of the imported name. On the playing-fields of the Cape Flats, 'Everton' evoked only one identity – the local one, because Everton AFC played a brand of football that was not only different from that of their English namesake, but one that was more highly regarded than the metropolitan model. The Cape Flats amateurs succeeded in wresting 'Everton' from the county of Lancashire, unmooring it culturally, and then re-inventing it. Everton AFC made Everton FC a Merseyside institution that was not so much unrecognizable as 'undesirable' – Heideveld boys wanted to play like 'their' Everton, not the English model.

Everton AFC is, however, an exceptional township club. For almost three decades now they have been tremendously successful. They have a solid organizational structure (their founder member Job Petersen has been there since the beginning, as chair, manager, and coach, a longevity rare in most township clubs), a tradition of winning (at the very highest level, boasting honours such as the Maggott Trophy and the Virginia Premier League), and a long line of talented players (several of whom have won the highest honours available to them). Of all the township clubs that have taken on English clubs' names, Everton alone have been able to convert the initial moment of cultural mimesis into a subsequent expression of cultural autonomy. They have established themselves as different from both their progenitor and their 'fellow-mimics'. Amongst the (understandable) proliferation of 'Chelseas' and 'Leeds' on the Cape Flats, 'Everton AFC' registers uniquely; they can barely even be called, not to put too fine a point on it, mimics – or 'idealizers' – in name. The Heideveld club is a symbol for township possibility, a marker of 'difference', if you

143

will. But it is their very exceptionalism that proves the mimetic rule: an autonomous cultural identity is extremely difficult to establish, and footballing independence is hard to craft after the metropolitan name has been adopted. Everton AFC is unique in that it is a club that has been able to resist the 'burden of naming'; or, differently put, they have been to effect a spectacular liberation from their 'cultural arrest'. Unlike other township clubs, they have not become local versions of their English progenitors; but Everton AFC does show how loaded a metropolitan name is, how it carries within it a series of practices, a style, a complete ideology of football. Football is, if you will, not only 'more serious than life', it is, if you assume the name of 'Leeds' or 'Chelsea', itself a way of sporting life. But so is Everton, that point where the township disarticulates the metropolis. The English city of Liverpool may have been where the process started, but it is in Everton AFC that the township expresses itself as an indigenous, unique, and autonomous cultural identity. The Heideveld club is what happens when Cape Flats teams translate themselves into and ground themselves in the (insistently) local. Everton AFC, in liquidating Everton FC, marks the juncture where the township declares the metropolis redundant for its cultural purposes. The amateur club may contain within its ranks Liverpool FC fans, but they are undoubtedly Everton AFC players.

Notes

1. There are rare exceptions to the middle-class practice of not naming their clubs after English institutions, of which the suburb of Lansdowne's Wolverhampton Wanderers (named after a struggling club from the English Midlands) and Factreton's Manchester United may be the most prominent examples.

2. The kind of hybridization that football encourages is not unusual in township life, because township residents are frequently involved in translation of the cultural, political, and ideological variety. It has produced a language locally known as 'Kaaps', which is to say one indigenous to the Western Cape – it is a language that was used in print, amidst considerable controversy, in the 1970s by the coloured poet and playwright Adam Small, and has subsequently gained much wider political acceptance. 'Kaaps', however, is a unique blend of English and Afrikaans, and it has its origins in the townships. From there it has gravitated out toward the middle-class coloured suburbs, but that is still a discursive form indelibly marked by its class roots, and therefore frowned upon.

3. It is not just that black players were systematically excluded from the game, but that the opposing fans barracked black members of the other team. When

Liverpool played against their neighbours, the Everton fans would wave cardboard bananas whenever the Jamaican-born English international John Barnes touched the ball. He was, they implied, a monkey, fit only for swinging from trees and eating fruit in the jungle, certainly not a suitable opponent for their all-white team. It took a considerable amount of time before black players' own clubs came, in any substantive way, to their protection. Black players too, as Paul Gilroy discusses in *Small Acts* in an essay comparing the boxer Frank Bruno to the footballer John Barnes, have rarely publicly engaged the issue of racism – West Ham's Ian Wright has arguably been the black player most prepared to take up the issue of racism, both on and off the football pitch.

9

The Postcolonial and the Level Playing-field in the 1998 World Cup

Bea Vidacs

The postcolonial has been looked at variously by various authors. Kwame Anthony Appiah (1991) has asked the question whether the post- in 'post-colonial' was the same as the 'post'- in 'postmodern'. His answer was yes, in the sense that both terms signified a negation of a previous authority. Other than negation, however, the two concepts are not of the same order and do not speak to the same complex of issues. The denial in postmodernism stems from an existential *angst* that, in Western societies, is much more esoteric than real, whereas the experiences that dictate negation in the postcolonial context are much more experiential than theoretical. The ambiguity becomes clear if we compare Patrick Chabal's (1996) discussion of the postcolonial, which largely focuses on the Western causes and locus of the postcolonial, and that of Achille Mbembe (1992), a Cameroonian scholar, whose work was one of the inspir-ations for the volume in which Chabal's analysis appeared. Mbembe's notion of the postcolonial specifically claims to apply to Africa and does not concern itself with the West, except to use some Western theorists to explain African realities. Thus in Mbembe's discussion the postcolonial is not used to charact-erize a rejection of modernity, nor is it a critique or negation of the colonial as modern or otherwise, but rather it is a scathing critique of the postcolonial state (in the temporal sense of that which follows the colonial), which locks itself and the population that is forced to co-exist with it into what Mbembe has labelled a zombification, a mutual inability to get out of an impasse, and the collusion of all parties in maintaining this impasse. Mbembe of course is fully aware of the continuing effects of the colonial on these practices (cf. Mbembe 1986), but his concern is to try to understand the nature of the postcolony and to see by what means the postcolonial state (including ruler and ruled) continues to stay the way it is. What may lead authors to conflate the two concepts, apart from their superficial similarities, is that under both conditions there is a de-centring of authority, and most importantly there is a disappearance of certainties – the taken for granted can no longer be taken for granted. Authority of all kinds is undermined. Yet I would argue that 'postmodern' and 'postcolonial' are talking of two very different things. Most significantly, the absurdity of the existence of most Africans is something that most Europeans or Americans would find hard to fathom. Rather than being theoretical, the absurdity is lived on an everyday level by Africans. (The fact that much of postmodern theory grows out of literary theory helps reinforce the idea that the two concepts can be conflated together, since many 'postmodern' writers hail from former colonial countries, and they are taken to be representatives of the Third World itself, while of course their sensibilities are equally shaped by their particular and particularizing and yet universalizing blend of the Third World and the First World – their experiences in the West shape their perception of their beginnings as well.) At the same time it also needs to be pointed out that Mbembe's concept of the baroque nature of power in the postcolony (characterized by excess, ridicule, obscenity) is not really unique to the Third World as a location. A number of his critics have pointed out that he is really talking about power *tout court*, not just power in the Third World, and this view is reinforced by the fact that he is using examples from communist-era Eastern Europe to characterize his conception of power (cf. Trouillot 1992).

Thus there are at least three senses in which the postcolonial can be used. First, in the temporal sense, as in what happens after the end of the colonial (which arguably has never happened; but whatever did happen has changed the flavour if not the structure of power). Second, in the sense of the lived experience of peoples living in this hypothetically post-colonial colonial world. In this second sense there is a certain kind of absurdity of existence, which unlike the absurdity of the existence of people in the West (except for the very marginalized, whose perceptions of and relation to power will probably bear more resemblance to those of Third World peoples) is felt in the daily lives, on the skin, in the belly, of the people who have to live it. These lives have aptly been characterized by Mbembe and Roitman as being woven 'in incoherence, uncertainty, instability and discontinuity' (1995: 325). And finally, the postcolonial can also be used in the sense of the effects of the appearance of Third World peoples (immigrants, including intellectuals) in the West, whose new visibility and empowerment (their voices are more audible than ever before, despite the prejudices and discrimination they may face) undermine the certainties of the West. I would argue that it is in this sense that postcolonialism is postmodern, though it has been hotly debated in postcolonial studies whether the veritable industry of postcolonial theory and writing is not leading to a co-optation by the West of the Third World (Bhabha 1994; Ghosh 1998).

I wish to concentrate on the second of these senses of the postcolonial, the postcolonial condition as it is experienced by Cameroonians. Having studied football in Cameroon during more than 19 months I had ample occasion to experience, along with the football teams I worked with and the people I came into contact with, the absurdities and the total incalculability of life in Cameroon. Translated to the world of football, this incalculability includes the constant postponement of the beginning of the championship, or, even worse, the re-beginning of the championship. This will frustrate any attempt to work efficiently (in addition to bringing financial ruin) by maintaining the team's form during the recess. It is difficult to hold training sessions during what is supposed to last just a week but is continually extended for weeks on end, with constant rumours going on about the imminent re-beginning of the championship. It also includes the incalculability of the rains falling and of the team that has the better boots winning the otherwise already lost match, because the hitherto leading team's players have started sliding about uncontrollably in the mud.

Under these circumstances those who participate in football can be seen and see themselves in a heroic light. They perceive themselves as wanting to create something: something concrete, something real, a better future, a good team, that everyone will remember and that will be the talk of the town. Coaches very often claim that they do not train football players, but Men, in the 'old-fashioned' defiant and bathos-filled sense of Kipling's *If*. If they knew the poem they would subscribe to its basic tenets, no matter how anachronistic these virtues seem to us in the West. Thus as an ideal, at least on the level of desires and will, in Cameroon football represents not just modernity, but rather an antithesis of the zombification, inertia, and impasse of the postcolonial condition, described so vividly by Mbembe and others. In practice the general state of Cameroon constantly frustrates this desire, and one could subscribe to Mbembe's thesis and recognize the zombification he talks about in football, mirroring the general state of affairs of the country.

Christian Bromberger (1995) has argued that football as a world-view provides a way for people to create a narrative through which they can make sense of their lives. Certainly, football also functions in this sense in Cameroon, though given Cameroon's post colonial position in the world and the postcolonial condition in which it finds itself the narratives that Cameroonians create and the meanings that they draw from them are likely to differ from those told by the people of Turin, Naples and Marseilles studied by Bromberger. Bromberger stresses the connection between what he calls 'democratic societies' and the evolution of football. He points out that the attraction of football and other sports is largely to be found in their evocation of the 'fundamental values of democratic societies', i.e. the meritocracy in football. 'The stadium then is the *par excellence* place where the democratic imaginary, celebrating the equality of chances, universal competition, personal merit, concretizes itself' (1995: 197). Of course, Bromberger contrasts this vision of modern sports with the Aztec game of *tlatchli*, arguing that in the Aztec case the fixed nature of social statuses precluded any competition in the modern sense of the word, that is, that winning or losing did not matter, as it does in modern sports. It is clear from his counter-example that what he really wishes to confront is 'pre-modern' and modern, rather than 'democratic' and non-democratic. At the same time he seems to imply that modernity and democracy (the equality of chances) are the same. While there is truth in the idea that modern (post-feudal) society has opened up the fixity of statuses compared to earlier times, it is far from obvious that we can unambiguously equate modernity and the equality of chances. Even in the Western world this often proves to be an illusion, and I would say that it is doubly so in the postcolonial world. Cameroon is anything but democratic, but it would be fallacious to argue that it is not modern.

The modernity question is one that deserves a little detour. To quote Robert Thornton (1996: 137):

> Because of their different relations to power, Modernism and postmodernism have quite different meanings and values in the Third World. Despite the fragmentation of modernism in the West, the aporias of reason, the politics of pastiche, the crisis of authenticity and the pervasive presence of simulacra, the Third World appears to be embracing modernism and modernization as never before. . . . For the most part, this appears to be true of African élites as well [as of Asian élites, which he discusses first], who are not only still modernizing but seem to be set to continue their commitment to modernization well into the future. The post-modern anxieties of the post-industrial West seem irrelevant to them.

I would only add to this that the embracing of modernity is not limited to élites, but rather represents a hope of a better future to most people, even if this wish to join the modern crowd is often expressed in a consumerism of wanting to have a hold on the external emblematic features of modernity (cf. Gandoulou 1989). That it also goes deeper than that can be seen in the comment that I heard from a woman, of not much education, living in a small village, who – rejecting someone's designation of a man as being important for having been to Paris – exclaimed 'Paris! What is Paris? You have to work there just as much as you have to work here, if you work hard in the village, you have everything.' She added as an afterthought: 'all we lack is development: we need electricity, a paved road, and drinking water'. Thus when modernity means the hope of the fulfilment of such basic needs, rejecting modernity is impossible. Though on the level of infrastructure Africa is behind Europe, it cannot be argued that

Africans are not modern. What they do is to straddle the modern (and even the postmodern) and the traditional, sometimes subverting the one with the other. (For example, DeBoeck (1996) shows the ability of both traditional chiefs and the 'modern' Mobutu government mutually to subvert each other). This modernity is represented by Europe (and North America), and the attitude of Africans to Europeans or whites is highly ambiguous. Cameroonians are aware of their colonial past and neo-colonial present, and see many of the ills of the postcolonial period as emanating from their continuing (unequal) relationship to Europe. Thus the attitude is part distrust, verging on hate, and part admiration and a wish to emulate, in order to obtain the emblematic values of Europe. Coupled with this is a wish to be recognized by the larger world as actors in their own right and on an equal footing.

Part of this quest for recognition is to be found in football. To return to Bromberger, he argues that the meritocracy evident in football (that is to say its modernity, which he identifies with democracy) can be derailed by the intervention of chance events: thus the better team does not always win. In his view this is what creates the tension of the game, because it symbolizes and humanizes the vagaries of life. This is no doubt true in Cameroon as well; but there is another dimension to the question. The ideal of the level playing-field is very seductive, both in the sense of a space where it is possible to do something, to have achievements that are real, as opposed to Mbembe's simulacra, and also in the more conventional sense of 'the better team wins', regardless of external realities, i.e. the relative socio-economic and political strength, the symbolic (and the real) capital of the participants. Thus football can be seen as providing an opportunity to invert the actual power relationships reigning in the world. This is a moralizing concept in both of its senses. In the first sense it is a negation of the postcolonial condition: instead of despair and inability to act, it affirms the possibility and efficacy of action. In the second sense it is also a moralizing concept, where virtue (superior ability) is and will be rewarded, and the revenge of the underdog becomes possible, thus providing an opportunity for justice to be done, not just in sport, or in football, but in the larger context of the world. The meaning of the level playing-field is fraught with contradictions, which is precisely what, I would argue, provides much of the tension and sense of excitement of the game. The main contradiction is of course that by positing the 'level playing-field' in the second sense it is claimed (consciously or unconsciously) that the game is outside the framework of the everyday, real relations of power, while at the same time the significance and meaning of the game, or of a particular match, or competition, derives precisely from the fact that it is reinserted into this larger framework and gains its significance and meaning from the outside world.

The 1998 World Cup was much awaited by Cameroonians in a large measure due to the factors outlined above. As the World Cup took place in France, it was seen by many as an opportunity for Cameroon to take revenge on France for all the indignities that the colonial past and the continuing neo-colonial presence (from economic dominance to France's perceived maintenance of Cameroon's largely unpopular political regime in power) thrusts upon them. As is well known, Cameroon did not go beyond the first round; thus it never got the opportunity to beat France. The match that seemingly decided Cameroon's fate was that between Cameroon and Chile.

It was a dramatic match with dramatic consequences. It took place on 23 June in the afternoon. In order to advance to the second round, Cameroon absolutely had to win, whereas for Chile even a draw was enough to advance. Chile opened the score around the 30th minute; towards the end of the first half a Cameroonian goal was disallowed as offside. In the second half one of the Cameroonian defenders got a red card, and Cameroon continued the game at a numerical disadvantage. Despite this, with beautiful and determined play the Cameroonians started to dominate and eventually managed to equalize. Then François Omam Biyick, the captain of the team, positioned a little behind two Chileans, scored a goal, which was disallowed by the Hungarian referee for no reason that anyone could see.

I watched the match in a bar in Yaoundé, and there was palpable shock in the room. People could not believe their eyes. They shouted their scandal, and someone yelled 'It's impossible, the whites don't want blacks to win.' A woman behind me asked in disbelief: 'So, whites do such tricks?' They kept repeating 'It was a good clear goal!' In the meanwhile another Cameroonian player was sent off, and eventually the match ended on the score of 1–1, and thus the Indomitable Lions were eliminated.

Immediately following the match there were riots in Yaoundé (the political capital) and Douala (the economic capital), where the public – for the most part the young and disenfranchised of these two cities – attacked all whites who happened to be around. Being Hungarian, like the referee, I had an additional reason to be concerned for my safety; but in fact I saw nothing of the riots as after the match I took refuge first in a restaurant and later at a friend's house.[1] Apparently, what had happened was that spontaneously from some of the popular areas of town young people, carrying placards saying things like 'Enough is enough' and 'Whites go home' and chanting anti-white and anti-FIFA slogans, had filed down to some central areas of the city trying to find whites to beat up, and in several instances had managed to do so. Ironically, many of these whites happened to be people who were completely unaware of what had happened. The rioters surrounded one of Yaoundé's supermarkets, where many whites are known to shop, and had a face-off with the police who were protecting it. Elsewhere in town some whites were pulled out of their cars and roughed up, while some windshields got broken. The police dispersed the crowd with tear-gas, and by evening the hostilities were over. According to an Anglophone news report:

> The pandemonium was brought to a halt when the delegate general for National Security, Bell Luc René, suddenly appeared. He called his boys to order then moved towards the demonstrators who were already constituting groups and pleaded. 'Your cause is genuine and your point has been made' (*The Herald*, No. 624, 24–25 June 1998: 2).

Apparently elsewhere too, the police mostly pleaded with the population to stop. One can imagine how difficult it was for the police themselves to contain their own emotions.

All the headlines of Cameroon's newspapers the following day dealt with the match and the racism involved. To quote some of the titles: 'The cretin'; 'Dracula devours the Lions' ('Two goals cynically refused, and two red cards. Dracula has freed himself to drink the blood of the Lions'. *La Nouvelle Expression*, 380: 6, 24 June 1998). (Incidentally, the reference to Dracula also shows that Cameroonians are far less removed from the Western imaginary than we might think). They were unanimous, regardless of political leaning, that what had happened in the match was a blatant example of racism. This confirmed what had been the opinion of many people all along, that whites were in cahoots to frustrate Africans. Even prior to this match, throughout the World Cup the distribution of red cards, as well as other decisions of the referees, seemed to people to be biased against Third World peoples in general, and against Africans in particular. (Although in other contexts Cameroonians are apt to identify Brazil as a Third World country, in discussions of this aspect of the competition Brazil was identified as one of the 'great football countries', and thus assimilated to the powers that be.) In this context the riots seemed justified, and there was practically no condemnation in the newspapers of the violence unleashed on the capital and on Douala, as it was seen by everyone as a natural response of frustration to what was seen as inadmissible partiality on the part of the referee.

This perception of bias was further reinforced by the fact that the same evening there were two other matches, one between Morocco and Scotland and another one between Brazil and Norway. They were played simultaneously to avoid fixing the results to benefit one of the teams in passing to the second round. Brazil was already qualified, but if Norway managed to beat Brazil it would advance instead of Morocco. Morocco beat their opponents 3–0, but at the last minute the referee of the Norway–Brazil match awarded a penalty kick to Norway, which the Norwegians translated into a goal, and so won the match. The penalty did not seem justified, raising charges that it was awarded in order to ensure that Morocco would not pass to the second round. This event coupled with Cameroon's questionable elimination made people's suspicions of racism perfectly plausible to everyone.

The following day I spent most of the morning in a '*teleboutique*'.[2] As I entered the shop, the first sentence I heard from the young woman running the store was: 'We are going to kill whites here!' At almost the same moment, a young man who was setting up his CD-stand, which was also inside the boutique, said to me 'Don't be afraid, Madame.' Amidst these contradictory statements I sat down to wait my turn to make a long-distance phone-call to Douala. I spent more than an hour waiting, and got a wide array of commentary on the match, and people's interpretations of what had happened. During most of the discussion I was ignored (perhaps studiously); but some people (people kept coming and going during the whole time) even engaged me in conversation.

Primarily the discussion consisted of reliving the match and the disbelief and hurt that everybody experienced during and after. A lot of what was going on was venting, in general against whites, the injustice that had befallen Cameroon. The young woman kept repeating that whites were going to be killed. Another young woman added that 'It is not even the referee, but FIFA. But what is FIFA? Is God white? The whites cheat. They are afraid of us, so they resort to such tricks.'

The young CD vendor said that if he were the government he would declare the return of the Lions a holiday. Behind this statement was a sentiment that kept being repeated for the next few days, which was actually how the match got etched into Cameroonian memories: in the eyes of Cameroonians the Lions had won the match. The return of the Lions is declared a holiday when they win or do extremely well, as for example in 1990, or when they qualified for the participation in the 1994 World Cup;[3] thus making the day a holiday would symbolically 'correct' the result on the football pitch.

The pure hate that emanated from people against whites was quite amazing to experience. The most striking example was that strangers on the street, who normally refer to me and address me as '*la Blanche*' (white female) when they want to call my attention to themselves, suddenly would be looking at me appraisingly and say with considerable disgust '*le Blanc*' (generic white [male]). This 'de-gendering' and essentializing indicates more eloquently than anything else the depth of people's bitterness over what happened in the Cameroon–Chile match, and it demonstrates how such discourses are constructed. I, along with all whites, became the enemy, reduced to one aspect of my identity, the colour of my skin. Race and gender are two of the most obvious markers of any person's biological identity, and taking away one of these, as these people were doing, meant that the battle lines could be drawn more sharply, white against black, black against white, just as people perceived them to have been drawn on the football pitch. Add to this the fact that women are not considered to be seriously concerned with football, and that therefore leaving me my identity as a female would have provided an opportunity to side-step the issue and see me as negligible from the point of view of the 'war' that was being declared.

Within a few days the sentiment got translated into jokes, some of them also indicating that recognition or non-recognition of my gender status constituted an important dividing line in deciding whether I was perceived as the enemy or not. Two days after the match I was in one of Yaoundé's textile markets with a friend, and we overheard two teenagers producing the following exchange: 'Is this the white who killed us?'; 'No, this is a woman!'

The discourse to which the Cameroon–Chile match gave rise in Cameroon is remarkable for its consistency and centredness. It was an essentializing discourse, which, as is shown in the above example, removed all possibility of ambiguity and alternative interpretation. To a great extent the government set the stage for it. Thus it was the Minister for Youth and Sports who had first started to talk about the injustice and racism of whites already at the stage of Cameroon's second match against Italy, when Raymond Kalla had received a red card. In an interview on Cameroon Radio he recalled the 1982 World Cup in Spain, where Roger Milla's goal against Peru was disallowed, and attributed the decision to the racism of the referee (cf. *La Nouvelle Expression*, 24 June 1998, 380: 8). CRTV later proceeded to re-broadcast that segment of the match. The riots were a spontaneous expression of people's frustrations. The newspaper coverage produced a seamless totalizing discourse on white racism, and a conspiracy theory according to which FIFA wished to eliminate all Third World teams from the competition. This theory was buttressed by evidence from earlier matches of the World Cup.

Dissent within this discourse was almost impossible, which is surprising in the sense that Cameroonians on other occasions have been quick to lay the blame on the government or on other factors within Cameroonian society (cf. Nkwi and Vidacs 1997; Vidacs 1998), even if we accept Mbembe's thesis that ultimately there is a certain kind of collusion in these expressions of dissent. (His point is that while critical of the state and of power, people get sucked into the excesses of the state, and thereby both are neutralized.) In this case, however, in finding an external enemy the government and the people could find a common ground, and in the totalizing anti-FIFA, anti-white and anti-European discourse the fragmentation of the postcolonial is temporarily hidden, and the wink (which Werbner (1996), paraphrasing Clifford Geertz, has called *par excellence* the gesture of the postcolony) is lost. Mbembe's collusion is there, in that everybody forgets what they know about the insufficiencies of the preparation for the competition and the pervasive ills of Cameroonian football. An important feature of this essentializing and totalizing discourse is to be found in a decontextualization of the match in different ways. Cameroon's World Cup participation is reduced to this one match – the other matches Cameroon played are of no relevance, and the effects of the local (insufficient preparation, lack-lustre performance in the African Nations Cup, late appointment of the head coach) on the performance of the team are forgotten. At the same time, of course, the match is also recontextualized within the historical framework of earlier World Cup injustices and in the framework of global power relationships (which is also historically conditioned).

There were some attempts to reframe the match, but they were drowned out. The following discussion of the grounds on which some people tried to put this particular match into the larger context in a certain way falsifies the tenor of the debate, because by devoting equal time to it I will give an exaggerated sense of its importance. Nonetheless, it merits our attention because it highlights the nature of the postcolonial condition both inside and outside football in Cameroon. The main voice of criticism was that of Joseph-Antoine Bell, the outspoken former goalkeeper of the Lions, who tried to frame the debate within the context of Cameroonian football. Bell's main points were a flat denial that there was a conspiracy against Third World peoples: he claimed that Cameroonian players were just not as good as their opponents, and that crying racism was a way to hide the inefficiency and corruption of the Cameroonian football establishment, and of Cameroon in general. He also called attention to the fact that if Cameroon had won its first match against Austria, the 'misjudgement' of the referee would not have mattered against Chile. He also criticized some of the tactical choices of the coach, Claude LeRoy.

Many Cameroonians were of the opinion that Bell was being unpatriotic, and an apologist for FIFA. One opposition paper dubbed him the 'spokesperson of FIFA', primarily trying to safeguard his position as a commentator on Radio France Internationale, and accused him of being bitter since he had made an unsuccessful bid for the position of President of the Cameroonian Football Federation (Fécafoot), in 1996. Others accused him simply of unpatriotic conduct. Among my friends there were people who simply stated that they could not agree with Bell, even though many of them had supported him in earlier times.

Some letters to the editor in the opposition paper, *Le Messager*, tried to defend Bell. One letter-writer started with the provocative and ironic title 'Let's kill Joseph-Antoine Bell'. Among other things, he wrote:

> For some, the majority of Cameroonians, only the results count; for others, above all for Joseph-Antoine Bell, the way in which they are achieved is just as important. . . . He goes against the tide. Here in Cameroon a market share obtained by corruption, an election won by the stuffing of the urns, a profit realized by the exploitation of the people [*les salariés*] are proof of patriotism. It is sad, really sad to see the journalist who takes '*gombo*' [bribe], the policeman who sells the road, the teacher who sells exam papers, the minister who gives away an enterprise for a symbolic franc after having received a tip, to declare that Joseph-Antoine Bell is not a patriot . . .' [The writer concludes by saying:] Henceforth it is clear that Bell is our bad conscience. While the entire Republic is praising the Indomitable Lions he is still pointing accusatory fingers. . . . Let's kill Joseph-Antoine Bell, so that we can finally have peace in carrying out our dirty little affairs (*Le Messager*, 19 July 1998).

This impassioned defence of Bell shows that there are some Cameroonians who see the problem of football in the larger context of the problems of the country; and there were a few other such voices too. Above all Pius Njawe, the then-imprisoned journalist and owner of *Le Messager*, one of the main opposition papers, in his editorial also called attention to the lack of preparation and other problems; but in the same issue there were also two scathing articles decrying the racism of the World Cup. Mongo Beti, one of Cameroon's most famous intellectuals, also raised similar objections. Unlike Bell, these commentators agreed with the popular interpretation that these events were part of white racism, but contextualized the problem similarly to Bell. However, on the whole these voices were drowned out, and the average Cameroonian could not but see the issue in the totalizing framework described above.

Let's return to the concept of the level playing-field. The perceptions of a level playing-field, which as I argued in my introduction lie at the heart of the game, were the ones that were upset in the 1998 World Cup. The whole edifice of the notion that the better team of the moment wins collapsed, thus upsetting a certainty that is one of the few that still hold in the otherwise uncertain lives of Cameroonians. This is connected to the positive aspects of the ambiguous stereotypes held of whites, in the sense that it could be argued that, lacking in local certainties, Cameroonians, like other Africans, ambiguously turn to (or rather create) outside models (of the 'great nations') to make some kind of sense of their own lives. (Liisa H. Malkki (1995) makes a similar point about the faith Hutu refugees place in the ability of Western powers and agencies to set right what went wrong in their country.) The ideals that are attributed to football do not quite function in Cameroon. One letter writer even made the point that it is illusory to think that refereeing is going to be impartial on the world scale when such 'errors' are well known to happen in Cameroon all the time. However, as a reference point these ideals are very important, and by positing the level playing-field, people also posit that somewhere, if not at home then outside Cameroon, there is fairness and justice. The 'ideal' world of football has shown itself to be lacking in fairness. Reality (the socio-economic power structure on a global scale) reasserted itself with a vengeance; and I would argue that this smashing of the illusion of the level playing-field (and the concomitant postponement of the revenge of the underdog) was what created the bitterness, disbelief and despair.

Notes

1. Until this match I took pleasure in telling people that I was Hungarian. Following it I found it prudent to say when asked that I came from the United States (an equally true statement). My personal friends, aware of my nationality, could easily make the distinction between me and the referee, and if anything were amused by the irony of the situation I found myself in, while at the same time remaining sympathetic. All of them expressed concern, one going so far as to come and visit me two days later, saying that he had been worried about me, as he had not seen me the previous day.

2. These are little stores where there are a couple of telephone booths, and often one can also find a photocopying machine, or a computer where there is someone who does word-processing. It is an ingenious way of overcoming the lack of infrastructure. People can make and receive phone-calls, receive messages and keep 'phone dates'.

3. This was the time when the public holiday declared by the head of state coincided with the day of a general strike called for by the opposition to commemorate the anniversary of the 'stolen elections' of 1992, thereby subverting it completely (cf. Ntonfo 1994: 214).

10

Sport, Nationality and Postcolonialism in Ireland

Alan Bairner

Introduction: Sport, Nations and National Identities

Analysis of the relationship between national identity and sport has tended until relatively recently to focus almost exclusively on what might be called official nationalisms. That is to say, commentators were concerned primarily with how nation states have harnessed sport to their own interests. Far less attention was traditionally paid to the links between sport and those nationalisms that were and remain involved in undermining the status quo in general and specifically the hegemonic position of existing nation-states. Since the beginning of the 1990s, however, this situation has begun to change, and major works dealing in whole or in part with the use of sport by submerged nations to promote their ambitions have begun to appear (Bairner 1996a, 2001; Hargreaves 1992, 2000; Kidd 1992). Yet, ironically, it would seem that academic interest in sport in Ireland has always been more concerned with sport's counter-hegemonic potential than with the relationship between sport and official nationalism (Mandle 1987). Thus, Gaelic games above all have been assessed primarily in terms of their capacity to support a nationalist project aimed initially at ending British rule in Ireland and, since the 1920s, at creating a unitary 32-county Irish Republic. This emphasis has been challenged to a certain degree by Cronin (1999), whose more recent work has revealed the extent to which sport, and in particular soccer, has become implicated in the construction of what one might regard as an official 26-county Irish nationalism, which is at ease with the partition of Ireland and, therefore, with the six counties of Northern Ireland remaining under British jurisdiction. Against this, however, I have argued that 'it is difficult to speak of a fundamental transformation of Irish national identity while the issue of unfinished business continues to loom large in political nationalist opinion as well as within sections of the country's major sporting organization, the Gaelic Athletic Association' (Bairner 1996a: 327). That said, it is equally important to recognize that there is no such thing as a single Irish national identity. Nor can one even talk legitimately of two national identities on the island of Ireland – one Irish, the other British. Rather we must be mindful of multiple versions of Irishness and Britishness, most of which can be traced back to the peculiar relationship been Ireland and Britain, which has been characterized by many, but by no means all, as, historically, colonial and, subsequently, postcolonial (Howe 2000). This chapter explores the relevance of the concepts of colonialism and postcolonialism to Ireland using examples drawn from the world of sport. Specific attention is paid to Northern Ireland, because of its importance to nationalist and anti-colonialist historiography and iconography. However, the whole of Ireland is also considered in terms of sport's involvement in strategies of accommodation and resistance to British influence.

Ireland and Postcolonialism

According to Murray, 'the term "postcolonial" itself seems, at times, to encompass material and methods that are extremely diverse, with a potential to obscure the use of the word in a constructive manner' (S. Murray 1997: 2). It is one thing to state that the modern world order is postcolonial. But, as Moore-Gilbert comments, 'such has been the elasticity of the concept "postcolonial" that in recent years some commentators have begun to express anxiety that there may be a danger of it imploding as an analytic construct with any real cutting edge' (Moore-Gilbert 1997: 11). Certainly its value in discussing Irish cultural politics is necessarily restricted. For example, it is interesting but also somewhat surprising to find an Irish writer claiming that 'the question of national identity is more difficult and ambiguous on the periphery of the British Empire than at its English centre' (ní Fhlathúin 1997: 67). Arguably Ireland, which is particularly close to the Empire's 'English centre', and according to some interpretations was historically part of that centre, has actually encountered more intense difficulties with issues of national identity than most former component parts of the British Empire. Certainly the Irish experience of imperialism, colonialism and postcoloniality and of the relationship between these categories has been both complex and unusual, not least because Ireland's precise relationship to the Empire is so difficult to classify. The Irish example confirms the truth of Murray's assertion that the postcolonial order is 'one characterized by fluidity and hybridity, a cultural criss-crossing, what has been referred to as the "in-between"' (Murray 1997: 4) It has even been argued that Ireland was itself both 'imperial' *and* 'colonial' (Jeffery 1996). For Quayson (2000), the study of postcolonialism should include any country that has ever had an experience of colonialism. This would include the United States as well as South Africa, Canada and Australia – none of which would feature prominently in most studies of the postcolonial condition. It would also include Ireland, which is often included in studies of the postcolonial but is less commonly to be found in the ranks of the imperialist powers. Yet, as Kibberd (1997: 97) argues, 'only a rudimentary thinker would deny that the Irish experience is at once post-colonial and post-imperial'.

According to Quayson (2000: 2), postcolonialism 'is as much about conditions under imperialism and colonialism proper as about conditions coming after the historical end of colonialism'. One reason for this is the fact that there may exist important continuities that connect the two periods. Arguably this is especially apparent in the case of popular culture in general and sport in particular, in so far as the games that people play can acquire a quasi-neutral status that allows them to be embraced just as enthusiastically in one epoch as another. With specific reference to sport, I have suggested elsewhere that there are three main factors that determine Ireland's relationship with Britain and the subsequent difficulties created in terms of the politics of national identity (Bairner 1996b). First, there is the physical proximity of the two countries and, in particular, the historically close links between their respective ruling elites. Second, there is the ongoing presence of a sizeable group of people, resident for the most part in the north-east corner of Ireland, who regard themselves as British. In this example at least, as O'Dowd (1990: 46) observes, 'the "motherland" is not a faraway country but a neighbouring island with which there have been centuries-long exchanges of population'. Third, contrary to these other phenomena, Ireland was home to its own distinctive sporting culture before the imperial project was carried through. Similarities between Ireland and Scotland can be drawn in this regard; but it is difficult, if not impossible, to find other exact parallels. This sporting culture provided the Irish with fertile terrain upon which to wage cultural wars. Given the close links between Britain and Ireland, however, to speak of Ireland unequivocally as a postcolonial society is scarcely appropriate. The history of Gaelic games, on the other hand, might lead to a rather different conclusion.

Gaelic Games and Irish National Identity

Writing about the relevance of music to the construction and reproduction of Irish national identities, McCarthy (1999: 108) argues that 'in the history of any country, the transition from colonialism to independent nationhood is a traumatic one' and there is an eagerness to establish 'an identity that would define a national community and set it apart from other nations'. Just as an Irish music movement played its part in helping to establish a certain image of Irishness, for well over a hundred years, Gaelic games in Ireland have contributed to the maintenance of a distinctive national identity. As a result, they can be regarded as having been integral not only to anti-imperialist strategies but also to the construction of postcolonial Irish society. However, they are by no means the only sporting vehicles for the reproduction of Irish nationalist identities. Although British games such as rugby union have played an undeniably important role in the construction of a unionist identity, specifically in the north-east corner of Ireland, they are also contributory factors in terms of the development of Irish sporting nationalism. More universal games, most notably association football, have facilitated inter-community competition, which in turn has been of considerable importance in ensuring a continuing division between 'them' and 'us', specifically in Northern Ireland. The point is, however, that in certain circumstances both the 'them' and the 'us' play precisely the same games. Thus concepts such as 'imperialism' and 'post-colonialism' at once appear to lose a certain amount of their explanatory power. Indeed, as with all matters relating to identity formation, the situation has always been and remains more complex than a superficial application of fashionable theoretical perspectives might lead one to believe.

As we shall see, despite being organized on an all-Ireland basis, the GAA has increasingly looked like a rather different organization depending upon the side of the border from which one has viewed its activities. Equally ironic is the fact that the 32-county organization of 'British' sports has created a situation in which northern unionists play for and support 'Irish' teams, whatever their reservations may be about closer political or even economic links between the two parts of Ireland. Less surprisingly soccer, which is organized in Ireland along boundaries established by partition and which possesses a world-wide capacity to heighten passions and, from time to time, to provoke violence, has persisted in providing a sporting arena for the acting out of ethno-sectarian divisions.

Those who study the relationship between sport and politics commonly ask what sport can do to help heal divisions. Rather than focusing primarily on that question, however, this chapter begins by simply considering certain episodes in the world of Northern Irish sport that have taken place since the signing of the Good Friday agreement and that can be shown to have political relevance particularly in terms of what they tell us about popular attitudes towards the peace process. Overall, like many other events in Northern Irish social and cultural life, some offer grounds for optimism and others indicate that the divisions that ensured the persistence of conflict for almost thirty years are still as deep as ever.

The three episodes chosen for this purpose are the debate about the GAA's Rule 21, which, until it was rescinded in November 2001, excluded British security forces personnel from membership, the heated discussion as to whether or not Donegal Celtic, a soccer team based in nationalist West Belfast, should have fulfilled a fixture in 1998 against the RUC and, finally, the European Championship victory in early 1999 by Ulster's rugby union players and the accompanying claims that their stirring deeds had united the people of a traditionally divided society. In addition, there is a brief commentary on the relationship between sport and the ongoing peace process in Northern Ireland, followed by some concluding remarks on the relevance of postcolonial theory to the social significance of sport in contemporary Ireland.

The Rule 21 Debate

Of the many contentious issues that surround the GAA, none is more likely to generate heated debate than Rule 21, which has traditionally denied membership of the association to British security forces personnel. According to Cronin (1996), the refusal over many years to rescind Rule 21 is evidence that the GAA has been locked in a traditionalist world-view that is totally at odds with the new Ireland. He argues that 'by refusing to drop rule 21 and clinging onto a self perceived and self important role which the GAA believes it has at the heart of Irish nationalism, the Association is placing itself at odds with direction taken by the broad nationalist community, its political leaders, and the views of many ordinary GAA members' (Cronin 1996: 18–19). This argument, however, is far easier to sustain if one views the role of the GAA from a southern, and perhaps a postcolonial, perspective rather than one that takes into account the very different circumstances that prevail in the north of Ireland and that would be regarded by many nationalists as remaining colonial. Indeed, these rival perspectives have been reflected in the internal debate about Rule 21. For nationalists in the north, there are still compelling arguments for rejecting those coercive institutions of governance that are most closely linked to the imperialist project – the type of response to colonialism that Albert Memmi (1990: 85) describes as 'withdrawing physically' from the conditions of colonial life.

The rule has been discussed within GAA circles for many years. During a meeting of the central council on 29 May 1998, a decision was deferred until after the introduction of a new policing service for Northern Ireland. There can be little doubt that the prevailing attitude in the south supported moves towards the removal of Rule 21. Writing in the *Irish Times*, Kevin Myers (1998) offered a particularly strident expression of this view, declaiming that, whilst the GAA persists with its ban on the RUC and the Royal Irish Regiment (RIR), 'there is no ban on the authors of the Omagh holocaust, no ban on the "Real IRA", no ban on kneecappers, no ban on those [who] have buried a widowed mother by moonlight while her orphan children waited vainly and alone for months for her safe return, no ban on those who hold still the secrets of a dozen secret graves or more, no ban on those who have bombed Northern Ireland senseless'. Moreover, even in the north there is a view, as expressed in the main nationalist daily paper, the *Irish News*, just over a week after the referendum on the Good Friday Agreement, that 'every aspect of rule 21 is contrary to the spirit of the initiative endorsed by 85 per cent of the Irish population ten days ago' (*Irish News*, 1 June 1998). Similarly, a prominent northern Catholic clergyman, Fr. Denis Faul, speaking in advance of the 1998 special congress of the central council, was quoted as saying that 'the world would view any ban in sport at the present time in a very unfavourable light, and such an organisation as the GAA must give very good example' (Farrell and Mooney 1998).

In GAA circles in the north, however, the official line taken by county boards, almost certainly as a response to popular sentiment, was for the ban to continue until such time as security arrangements in the north of Ireland have been fundamentally restructured. In the Irish Republic the case for abandoning Rule 21 as part of the nationalist community's contribution towards the peace process may have appeared incontestable for all but a small republican minority. In any case, the men and women whom the ban affects are members of the security forces of a foreign state with which the Republic of Ireland, in what might be described as its postcolonial phase, has developed strong and largely harmonious diplomatic relations. For many nationalists in the north of Ireland, however, these selfsame security forces were regarded as belonging to a colonial administration. As a result, such nationalists saw the reasons for excluding members of the British army and the RUC from the GAA as being as convincing as ever. They cited examples of harassment of Gaelic players and fans by members of the RUC and British army soldiers, particularly those belonging to the locally recruited RIR. Constant reference was also made to those members of the GAA who had been killed by the security forces and also by loyalist paramilitaries, who are themselves widely regarded in republican circles as having acted in collusion with the security forces on a relatively regular basis. Furthermore, the occupation of Gaelic grounds by the security forces remained a burning issue, particularly in south Armagh, where the highly successful Crossmaglen Rangers club has been seriously affected in this way (Bairner and Darby 1999).

Linking the debate about Rule 21 to the question of policing, the Sinn Fein assembly member Barry McElduff stated that 'the people who are arguing for Rule 21 to be removed are missing the point within the policing debate. I cannot envisage the day when the nationalist people have any trust in the RUC'. McElduff added that 'as long as there are British forces within the six counties there will be opposition to dropping the rule' (McCusker 1998). This kind of thinking was largely responsible for the majority of Ulster counties' rejection, both in 1998 and in 2001, of the demand for the immediate removal of Rule 21 from the GAA's statutes. The issues involved were presented as ones that should be of concern to all Irish nationalists, but are of paramount concern to nationalists in the north. Responding to the pro-abolition stance of the GAA President at the time, Galway's Joe McDonagh, it was declared in the West Belfast-based *Andersonstown News* (30 May 1998) that 'we in Antrim know far more about Rule 21 and its effect than any Galway man'. In 1998, this view was sufficiently persuasive to make some southern county officials join their northern counterparts in blocking the immediate removal of the ban.

Despite all this, however, there are many GAA members, even in the north, on whose behalf the *Irish News* arguably speaks, who have felt for some time that the removal of Rule 21 would have been a timely gesture – a contribution to the peace process by a major element of Irish civil society. Indeed, when the rule was finally removed in 2001, one of the six northern counties, Down, voted for change along with all the southern counties; and even in some of the other northern counties, the majority in favour of retaining Rule 21 was considerably narrower than in the past. The fact that the retention of Rule 21 was by no means universally supported even in the six counties highlights divisions of a broader character within northern nationalism. Nevertheless, the degree to which this issue can be characterized as indicative of a north–south divide reflects deep-seated differences within Irish nationalism as a whole, many of which are closely bound up with questions concerning Ireland's relationship with colonialism and postcoloniality. The decision to remove Rule 21 was taken in response to the creation a new police service in Northern Ireland, which, it is argued, will be more representative of and acceptable to the community as a whole. The fact is, however, that Ireland remains partitioned, and the removal of Rule 21, which, in reality, has implications only in Northern Ireland, was taken for the most part by southern nationalists who appear increasingly less concerned about the estranged north.

Donegal Celtic versus RUC

Divisions within northern nationalism were also exemplified by the debate on whether or not the West Belfast soccer club, Donegal Celtic, should fulfil a fixture with the RUC during the 1998–9 season. A Steel and Sons Cup match involving the two clubs was scheduled to be played on 14 November 1998. Originally the mood in the local media, notably the *Andersonstown News*, was one of eager anticipation. Many people in the immediate area, however, immediately expressed their anger that a soccer club based there should even contemplate having dealings with the footballers representing a discredited and wholly unacceptable police force. Feelings of this sort intensified as pressure on Donegal Celtic was increasingly applied, directly by Relatives for Justice, a group representing families of people who had been killed by the RUC, and, more covertly, by the republican movement. Increasingly it was argued, even in the *Andersonstown News*, that playing the match would give offence to a substantial section of the local community. On 8 November a majority of club members who attended a special meeting to discuss the issue voted in favour of playing the match. In the following days, however, rumours of sinister visits being paid to the homes of Donegal Celtic officials and players grew and, on 12 November, the club's management, having been told by some players that they would be unable to play if the fixture were to go ahead, decided to withdraw from the competition. As Kevin Hughes (1998) commented even before the final decision had been made, 'Donegal Celtic must feel like somebody keeps deviously moving the goalposts so as to ensure they can't ever win, in a sport they probably feel should have its name changed to political football.'

Many West Belfast nationalists supported this outcome. Claiming that opposition to the match had been based on 'solid reasons', Fr. Des Wilson (1998) argued that 'it is for the elected representatives of the people to make clear whether the RUC is acceptable or not to their own people and what should be done about future policing'. However, there were also large numbers who felt that Sinn Fein had exceeded its remit in this instance, and that the rights of nationalist soccer fans in the area had been denied. Representing that point of view, the editorial of the main nationalist daily newspaper, the *Irish News*, argued that 'republicans are wrong to force a vulnerable football club to take up cudgels against the RUC on their behalf' (*Irish News*, 14 November 1998). A particularly insightful overview of the issue was provided by the socialist journalist, Eamonn McCann (1998), according to whom, 'people in West Belfast, and in other areas, not all of them nationalist, have good ground for iffyness about the RUC. But a political party which burdens a football club with "responsibility" for carrying this view is simply refusing to shoulder its own responsibilities.' Scarcely surprising was that fact that unionists and loyalists adopted an even more condemnatory tone. For example, Gary McMichael, the leader of the Ulster Democratic Party, claimed that 'the blatant intimidation that forced Donegal Celtic to withdraw from a scheduled match with the RUC highlights the fact that, not only is intolerance and sectarianism still alive and well, it is being nurtured by Republicans' (McMichael 1998).

At the purely sporting level, moreover, the whole episode highlighted the extent to which soccer (particularly in the shape of support for Glasgow Celtic) has maintained its status as the most popular sport in nationalist West Belfast despite the overtures of the GAA. This may help to provide further insight into the republican movement's attitude towards the Donegal Celtic team. Certainly amongst the purists within the GAA there is a degree of disquiet at the fact that Gaelic clubs in the area are often used for the purposes of watching English premiership soccer. As John Haughey (1998), wryly commented, 'I couldn't help but ponder on the irony that the Sinn Fein president was asking a sporting club to cancel a fixture on the same day another sports club from West Belfast were playing in a major GAA semi-final.'

What is undeniable is that, as a public relations exercise, Sinn Fein's strategy was seriously flawed. Large numbers of West Belfast residents, including many Sinn Fein voters (and soccer fans), expressed the view, usually in private, that, on this occasion at least, the party's representatives had wilfully ignored the wishes of many local people for narrow ideological reasons. Anecdotal evidence suggests that this unwanted outcome has even been recognized by the Sinn Fein President Gerry Adams himself. It was certainly imprudent at a delicate stage of the peace process for Sinn Fein to take for granted the votes of those who may have given the party a temporary mandate, but are not yet wholly convinced by the party's commitment to peaceful politics. Denying such people a football match might seem like a relatively minor misdemeanour. But any evidence of arrogance or complacency in politics is always best avoided. As one prominent republican wrote, 'in the Donegal Celtic debacle, the nationalist community turned on itself and it wasn't a pretty sight' (O Muilleoir 1998).

As regards the wider political context, the impact of the Donegal Celtic saga has been to underline the fact that northern nationalism, particularly in the urban context, has never coalesced around a single, pure conception of Irishness. Although there are many who would regard both the Irish language and support for Gaelic games as being integral to their sense of identity, for others their Irishness is reproduced despite (and in the case of following Celtic) by way of activities that are deemed to be foreign in the eyes of the purists. This is not, of course, an uncommon feature of postcolonialism. As Memmi (1990: 211) notes, with reference to the attitude of colonized people towards the imperial core, 'for many of us who rejected the face of Europe in the colony, there was no question of rejecting Europe in its entirety'. Soccer has long been used by Irish nationalists in Belfast as a vehicle for promoting communal identity and engaging in cultural resistance. It has seldom been solely a medium for assimilation or accommodation. Indeed, it should be noted that one of the main reasons why a junior club like Donegal Celtic attracts the degree of interest that it does is because West Belfast has had no senior soccer club since Belfast Celtic were forced to leave the league in 1949. The fact that this club had enjoyed enthusiastic support for over half a century is evidence that interest in the 'foreign' game in Belfast is in no way a new phenomenon occasioned by global cultural forces. Rather support for soccer in Belfast (and, indeed, in Derry city) testifies to the game's close links to urbanization and the growth of an industrial working class. Now, as in the past, therefore, Irish nationalism in sport and also in politics is considerably less cohesive and more complex than some simplistic readings might have us believe. However, there are those who would accept that point but continue to insist that Ulster unionism on the other hand is indeed characterized by cohesion and homogeneity. But, even that simple 'truth' is negated by the briefest of glimpses into the relationship between Ulster unionists and sport.

'Stand Up for the Ulstermen . . . !'

It has often been argued that the essence of Ulster unionism is essentially negative, and that it relies predominantly on feelings of anti-Irishness. However, the attitudes of unionists to rugby union suggests a more complex set of emotions. Linked to this indeed is the fact that rugby can also create problems in the minds of nationalists in Northern Ireland as well.

Organized, unlike soccer, on a 32-county basis, and with a national team that represents the whole of Ireland, the game has contributed to the construction of Irish sporting nationalism. It is a popular sport in the Irish Republic, where, far from being played and watched only by those who retain some nostalgic feelings for the former union of Great Britain and the whole of Ireland, it is a perfectly acceptable activity for Irish nationalists in the eyes of all but the most obdurate defenders of traditional Gaelic games. Because of the game's British roots, however, together with the fact that in the north of Ireland it has tended to be played for the most part only by unionists, most of them middle-class, the exploits of Ulster (and even Irish) rugby players have seldom caused excitement in northern nationalist, far less republican circles. Indeed, Ravenhill, the headquarters of Ulster rugby, has been traditionally to all intents and purposes an essentially Protestant and unionist (as well as middle-class) space. Nevertheless when Ulster played the French side Colomiers at Lansdowne Road on 31 January 1999 in the final of the European Cup, in attendance was not only Seamus Mallon, the leader of northern nationalists in the new assembly, but also his republican counterpart, Gerry Adams.

One can only speculate on the reasons why these men were at a game that, certainly in the past, would have been of little interest to the people whom they represent. In public relations terms, their absence would have been noted. In sections of the British and Irish press, however, there were suggestions of genuine support amongst northern nationalists for the Ulster team. Undeniably, such claims were greatly exaggerated, no doubt in the interests of creating a feel-good factor at a time when the peace process was facing severe difficulties. But Gaelic clubs did send messages of support to the Ulster rugby players, and

Catholics from the north did indeed travel to Lansdowne Road for the final. The presence of these Catholic fans, moreover, is indicative of a growing involvement of northern nationalists at all levels in a game that was once regarded as being alien to them. Certainly the Chief Executive of the Ulster Branch of the Irish Rugby Football Union, Michael Reid, is conscious of changing patterns of participation. 'Inspired by the wide cross section of the community that began coming to Ravenhill', writes Bruce McKendry, 'he [Reid] believes the sport has a great chance to attract and retain supporters from a whole new generation, and a whole new part of the population of Ulster . . .' (McKendry 1999: 178). Indeed, according to Reid, 'rugby is the only sport in the north which can currently attract both sections and that's something we must work on' (McKendry 1999: 179). However, the degree of nationalist involvement should not be exaggerated. The high numbers of Northern Ireland flags which were unfurled in Dublin on cup final day were clear evidence that rugby in the north is still a unionist game. As the northern nationalist middle-class has grown, however, inevitably the interest of Catholics in middle class activities, including rugby, has also increased. Thus, whilst the endeavours of the Ulster rugby players may have had scant impact on sports fans in Ardoyne or Crossmaglen, there are signs that the cultural context within which the sport is played in the north is changing. As this happens, however, sport will yet again reflect political and social cleavage. Even if substantial sections of the northern middle classes can set aside their sporting, and perhaps even their political, differences, working-class members of the rival traditions may find it less easy, or indeed desirable, to do so. As I have argued elsewhere, 'when all is said and done, a triumph for the Irish rugby team still offers as little cause for celebration on the unionist Shankill as does a victory for the Ulster rugby players or the Northern Ireland soccer team on the Falls' (Bairner, 2000: 73).

The fact is that, although rugby's presence in Ireland is the direct consequence of British colonialism, like soccer it has also been able to offer a medium for the expression of Irish sporting nationalism. Furthermore, rugby has even allowed Protestants in the north to acknowledge their own postcolonial Irishness. One wonders, however, what more can be expected from sport as regards the further settling of political differences between the Irish peoples.

Sport and the Irish Peace Process

Since George Orwell first expressed the opinion that sport can best be described as 'war minus the shooting' and probably for much longer than that, the relationship between sport and conflict has been widely discussed. By its very nature, sport tends to involve competition, which it is relatively easy to situate on a spectrum that has war at its most dangerous extreme. Sports educators actually refer to certain activities as 'invasion' games, thereby evoking overt images of conflict and conquest. There is, of course, a substantial debate as to the precise role that sport can play in its guise as a form of warfare without weapons.

On the one hand, there are those who speak in terms of catharsis. Sport provides the vehicle through which people can express and act upon feelings of suspicion and downright hatred without causing too many casualties. Sport is a substitute for war. Indeed, according to the theory of the civilizing process, first propounded by Norbert Elias and Eric Dunning (1986), sport performs a service by offering opportunities for the socially approved arousal of moderate excitement in public places in an evolving context in which social pressure has led people to exercise stricter control over their feelings and public displays of behaviour. Alternatively, studies that are specifically concerned with the relationship between sport and the formation of particular identities have been more inclined to argue that sport not only reflects those feelings that can culminate in armed conflict, but frequently exacerbates these feelings (Sugden and Bairner 1999).

While debates of this type are relevant to the role of sport in all social formations, they are particularly pertinent when one is confronted with what have become generally recognized as deeply divided societies. The description itself is a curious one, since all societies are deeply divided along at least one and probably along several fault lines. With regard to sport, all these sources of division – gender, age, social class, sexual orientation and so on – are significant. The fault lines that are most closely identified with deeply divided societies, however, are associated specifically with ethnicity, race and national identity. Furthermore, these sources of division are extremely influential as regards sport, which not only reflects ethnic, racial and national divisions in such societies, but also serves to intensify these divisions by contributing significantly to the construction and reproduction of certain identities and, by implication, to the maintenance of the gulf that exists between particular social groups. In this respect, the north of Ireland has been no different from a multitude of other divided deeply societies, postcolonial or otherwise. It is arguably unique, however, in terms of the precise configuration of relationships between imperialism and assimilation, colonialism and postcoloniality.

In the case of this particular conflict, therefore, sport reflects and contributes in certain ways to the context in which attempts to build and secure peace take place. At the same time, however, it continues to be intimately bound up with those divisions, both between and within communities, and this is what makes the ultimate prize so difficult to attain. It is evident from the rugby example that there is a constituency that now revels in its affluence and its cosmopolitanism, real or imagined. For such people, the peace process has to work, inasmuch as it will create the kind of polite society in which old-fashioned differences can be set to one side in favour of greater pluralism and respect for diversity.

Both Gaelic games and soccer, however, offer plenty of evidence, some of it cited earlier in this chapter, of the extent to which old animosities linger in certain areas and amongst certain groups of people. Some grains of comfort might be found in the fact that since the 1998–9 soccer season, Linfield, with their predominantly Protestant support, have been able to fulfil fixtures at Solitude, the home ground of Cliftonville Football Club, based in north Belfast and mainly supported by nationalists. For almost thirty years all games between the two clubs had been played at Linfield's ground, Windsor Park, or from time to time at neutral venues. It must be recognized, however, that the games have only been allowed to go ahead with severe restrictions having been imposed on the number of fans permitted to attend and against the backdrop of a major security operation. Those seeking evidence of real political change will point to the fact that the games went ahead at all. The more pessimistic observers, on the other hand, taking note of the artificial context in which they took place, will remain unconvinced that the deep-seated sectarianism that lies at the heart of the conflict in Northern Ireland and remains a major obstacle to political progress has been weakened in many areas of sport or indeed in most areas of the wider society.

The fact that the British Ministry of Defence has indicated its intention to withdraw security forces from property owned by Crossmaglen Rangers Gaelic Athletic Club has also been cited as evidence of progress and a possible factor in prompting the GAA to move more quickly towards rescinding Rule 21. Once again, however, a more realistic assessment is that this move was interpreted by many northern Gaels as being simultaneously both a cosmetic exercise and the overdue righting of a manifest wrong. As one journalist reported, 'the news was welcome across Ireland, though some within the GAA and the Crossmaglen club remained sceptical. "We've heard it all before" was a familiar refrain' (Donegan 1999). As a consequence, the eventual removal of Rule 21 was almost certainly far more dependent on policing reforms that are deemed to be acceptable to a majority of northern nationalists.

In general, it can be seen that high-profile sport in the north of Ireland is still more likely to strengthen the divisions that make peace so difficult to achieve than to help create the conditions in which a solution to the conflict can be found. Indeed, it would be asking too much to expect sport to succeed where politicians and Church leaders have manifestly failed over many years. Sport in Northern Ireland does bring people together, and can provide the basis for cross-community cooperation. It retains, however, an enormous capacity to reproduce sectarian identities. Indeed, by contrast with more settled societies where, at worst, sport can be represented as a form of 'war without weapons', in the north of Ireland it too often remains linked to the lingering threat of a return to 'war with weapons'.

The concept of postcolonialism is particularly problematic in the context of the six counties of Northern Ireland, regardless of whether one adopts a nationalist or a unionist perspective. As the examples drawn from the world of sport and discussed in this chapter indicate, for many nationalists the north is still fundamentally affected by its colonial status. This helps us to understand not only continued support for the GAA's Rule 21, but also opposition to all forms of contact, sporting or otherwise, with the British security forces. In the eyes of unionists, on the other hand, far from being a colony, Northern Ireland is an integral part of the United Kingdom, which, like the whole of Ireland prior to partition, played a significant part in the British imperial project. For them, playing rugby is a British occupation. Furthermore, to support Team Ulster in Dublin is, at least in part, to celebrate the achievements of a British team in a foreign capital. Naturally not everyone adopts one or other of these extreme positions concerning the history of Ireland's relationship with British imperialism. However, the future of sport in the north of Ireland, like the future of Northern Irish society more generally, is surely dependent upon the successful reconciliation of these two rival world-views. Sport may be able to play a small part in the struggle to bring this about, not least by providing alternative (and arguably cathartic) channels for the expression of cultural identity and difference. For the most part, however, it is likely to remain an important part of the socio-cultural terrain upon which traditional rivalries will continue to be acted out.

Conclusion: Sport, Postcolonialism and Ireland

The use of the word 'postcolonial' to describe any part of Ireland is fraught with danger. According to Conor Cruise O'Brien (1980: 27), for example, 'if we speak of Ireland today as being "post-colonial", we should recognize that the word has to be used in a double sense: "post-colonial"' in the sense of having undergone colonial domination, and also "post-colonial" in the sense of having taken part in colonial domination over others.' The point is a fair one. Nevertheless, there is a tendency in some quarters to seek to redress the historic imbalance in Irish nationalist historiography by underplaying the extent to which the native Irish were indeed subject to colonial domination. Thus, Howe (2000: 233) claims to have revealed 'how poorly the colonial and postcolonial models fit modern Irish experience itself'. Yet, even if the fit is not an exact one, the postcolonial model itself, unlike an ill-fitting shoe, may still have some intrinsic worth. By studying the relationship between sport and national identity and specifically the role of sport in terms of both accommodation and also resistance to British cultural hegemony, we can acquire a deeper and more balanced understanding of the nature of the links between Britain and Ireland in general and, more specifically, of the analytical utility of the concept of postcolonialism in this particular context.

It is undeniable that sport was given an important role in the promotion of British culture in Ireland. Certainly both soccer and rugby can be regarded as having been major elements in the imperial project. Whether or not those Protestant workers in the north-east corner of Ireland who were first to take up the former can legitimately be described as colonizers is open to debate. It is undeniable, however, that their enthusiasm for soccer was linked to their empathetic relationship with the British. Furthermore, when Catholics began to play soccer they were, in part, accommodating themselves to the reality of British sporting diffusion. The modern passion amongst nationalists, both north and south, for English Premiership soccer teams can be taken as further evidence of an ongoing process of cultural assimilation. None of this, however, is to deny the fact that nationalists in Ireland, as elsewhere, have also been able to harness soccer to the demands of cultural resistance. Specifically, northern nationalists have done so by founding symbolically nationalist clubs (Belfast Celtic), by colonizing traditionally non-nationalist clubs (Cliftonville) and by supporting teams that are formally situated outside their own constitutional or quasi-national boundaries (the Republic of Ireland and Celtic).

The case of rugby presents an altogether different set of politico-cultural dynamics. It has been played for well over a century by middle-class Protestants, whom many commentators would be happy to describe as colonizers, and also by middle-class, and some working-class, Catholics in the south of Ireland who critics within the nationalist tradition might argue have not only accommodated themselves to but have also helped to direct the imperialist project. But all of this demands closer scrutiny. Many nationalists who have embraced rugby would argue that in doing so they have been in a strong position to wave the flag of Irish sporting nationalism in the face of British and other international opposition. The position of unionists, moreover, is even more complex. On the one hand, their participation in rugby can be interpreted as a contribution to an ongoing colonial sporting agenda. Alternatively, however, this sporting involvement has also meant that they have been obliged to recognize the national integrity of Ireland.

Finally, Gaelic games superficially present fewer analytical problems. As was noted in the introduction, most commentaries on the political significance of sport in Ireland have identified the importance of Gaelic games with particular reference to their role in counter-hegemonic struggle. What a discussion of Irish sport within the context of the debate on postcolonialism suggests, however, is that while Gaelic games have certainly been part of an anti-colonial movement, they have also allowed Gaels in the Irish Republic to begin to accommodate themselves to a 26-county partitioned Ireland, even though many of their northern counterparts might still cherish the vision of a 36-county unitary state. In a sense, therefore, Gaelic games, like the other sports discussed in this chapter, reflect the paradox that Ireland can actually be described, at the start of the twenty-first century as being, at one and the same time, postnationalist, postcolonial and also colonial.

11

Football and FIFA in the Postcolonial World

John Sugden and Alan Tomlinson

Football as Cultural Politics

The organization in control of world football is FIFA (Fédération Internationale de Football Association). The FIFA story is more than a tale of successful sporting development, however. The growth from 7 member countries in 1904 to 200 at the end of the twentieth century illustrates the game's growing global appeal, and its significance as a barometer of international relations. The growth of nations and nationalism in the postcolonial world, and the use of transnational structures by ambitious individuals and aspiring nations, have been central features of world football and FIFA's rising profile. This chapter locates FIFA's story within debates concerning the contribution of football to the politics and culture of the postcolonial world.

As the world's most popular game, football is unrivalled in its capacity to generate passionate and deeply-rooted feelings of local and national pride or shame. In late modernity, there are few, if any, other social gathering points like football. People congregate around football, either interpersonally, at the game or related events, or intellectually, through the media and other forms of popular communication, to make strong public declarations of who they are, what groups they identify with, what they stand for and who and what they stand against. Football has come to represent distinct sets of values and ideologies, transcending any intrinsic meaning that the game itself might have. It provides a cultural milieu for the working up of quasi-political formulations. 'Quasi-political' refers to the way in which clusters of ideas about communities of power inform and are informed by relationships of domination and oppression in the wider society and which, under certain circumstances, can lead to more formal expressions of political will. Football, because it means so much to so many people, is also a vehicle for the acquisition of power and the expression of status in the international community. In the postcolonial period, football has been a major source for both these levels of expression of national identity and autonomy. We will illustrate this argument as the chapter progresses. Initially, though, it is useful to engage in some conceptual ground-clearing, and to clarify our own modest use of the category 'postcolonial.'

It is not uncommon in cultural and social theory to offer an overview of a field and then to conclude that there is no clear definition of things. This is an evasion, a theoretical and analytical laziness, a form of fence-sitting that abnegates the major task of the social sciences and the theoretical and conceptual debate central to that task. But such an approach has become an orthodoxy in postcolonial theory. Thus an introduction to postcolonial theory by Childs and Williams can conclude by citing Gayatri Spivak's warning that academics must beware claiming any particular expertise. They must, in Spivak's words in her *Outside in the Teaching Machine*, 'resist the tyranny of the specialist' (cited in Childs and Williams 1997: 22). 'After all that has been discussed so far', Childs and Williams (1997: 20) write, 'attempting to conclude would be a particularly rash exercise.' And so they sign off with a combination of nervousness and apologetics, and express a 'hope' that their book 'manages to convey a sense of engagement with thinkers and issues, rather than a mastery of all theoretical areas' (23). There's a kind of reverence here, for thinkers and their concepts, that undermines their very useful earlier discussion, in sections asking when, where, who and what are the postcolonial. There, we are reminded, the simplest answer to the 'when' question is 'after colonialism', and only solid empirical historical work can confirm the specific historicity of particular cases. The 'where' question raises obvious issues of place and 'spatial location', as Childs and Williams put it, and again there is an obvious answer – those areas formerly controlled by colonial powers. Edward Said's (1993) reminder that colonialism was extremely uneven does not, for us, undermine the primary point that it took a grip in particular parts of the world as well as at particular times. The 'who' question is answered by pointing to 'those people formerly colonized by the West'. If we drop the last three words of this answer the whole question is clearer, in that the theoretical issue does not become one solely of Western ethnocentrism. After all, Japan colonized Korea in classically imperialist and brutal fashion. The final question of 'what is the postcolonial' is answered less clearly, in a section swaying between literary examples and the listing of conceptual confusions in cultural theory. Let us offer a simple formulation here. The postcolonial comprises the cultural and political practices and ideologies of those cultures and societies that have emerged from a period of explicit colonial domination. This does not at all imply a supersession of the colonial, and, returning to the when question, the continuation of colonial elements could alternatively be categorized as the neo-colonial (see Hall 1996). The only fuller answer to the 'what' question requires close study of particular contexts and a careful accumulation of comparative and comparable cases.

Postcolonial theory has generated, and in part revived and revitalized, some important concepts that can be borne in mind while working up appropriate case-studies. Prominent among these are alterity and hybridity. Etymologically, alterity derives from the Latin, and refers to difference, diversity and otherness. In literary theory it derives from the work of Mikhail Bakhtin, and can only be understood in relation to the possibility of a dialogue – there is no other without exchange. In postcolonial theory it informs the recognition that there is always a 'possibility for potential dialogue between racial and cultural others . . .' (Childs and Williams 1997: 12).

Hybridity refers to the process whereby transcultural forms are created, in, as Homi Bhabha (1994) has insisted, interdependence and a relation of mutual construction of their emerging subjectivities. Much postcolonial work revolves around the interpretation of literary texts and discourse, rather than institutional forms and practices. Turner has noted that in the work of Edward Said a 'concentration on textuality and textualism . . . an exclusive focus on "textual practices" has negated the social dimension of language and meaning, and confused the materiality of social relations with an alleged materiality of the context' (Turner 1994: 7). In considering two cases of the place of football in post- or neo-colonial contexts, we seek to avoid the dangers of such imbalance or analytical lopsidedness.

FIFA's Place, and Football's Role, in the World Order

In 2001, the FIFA 'family' – as those at its centre consistently refer to FIFA – consisted of around 200 full-member nations. So long as it took part in a FIFA-sponsored competition, each full member was entitled to vote at FIFA's congresses. Regardless of size, longevity of membership or playing status, one member's vote is equal to that of every other FIFA member. For instance, Brazil's or Germany's votes carry no more weight than those from Mali or Armenia. This has had great significance in the internal politics of FIFA.

FIFA recognizes six regional confederations. These are:

- UEFA: Union des associations européennes de football – formed 1954, in 2001 51 members.
- CONMEBOL: Confederacion Sudamericana de Fútbol – formed 1916, in 2001 10 members.
- CONCACAF: Confederacion Norte-/Centroamericana y del Caribe de Fútbol – formed 1961, in 2001 35 members.
- CAF: Confédération Africaine de Football – formed 1957, in 2001 52 members.
- AFC: Asian Football Confederation formed 1954, in 2001 45 members.
- OFC: Oceania Football Confederation – formed 1966, in 2001 11 members.[1]

The languages of the confederations' titles demonstrate the early Spanish, French and English influences across world football's organizational origins, and examination of the tensions between these dominant early influences and emergent powers in the world game is central to understanding FIFA and football's postcolonial role.

At one level, the outer circle of FIFA can be represented, in Weberian terms, as a particularly advanced case of progressive global bureaucratization and rationalization, albeit with a democratic façade. At another, deeper level, FIFA's inner circle is best viewed as a hierarchical organization so steeped in oligarchic and corporate patronage that its organizational coherence has bordered on a form of total power often conveyed in European social thought as 'oriental despotism' (Turner 1994: 29 and 34). The juxtaposition of these two articulations of power illustrates the tensions between FIFA's earlier (and imperialist-based) claims to universalism, and struggles for influence and power within the organization during the period of postcolonial growth in its membership.

FIFA attributes this expansion, in its own internal publication celebrating its ninetieth anniversary *90 Years of FIFA* (Souvenir Edition 1994), to the power of universalism and international diplomacy:

> . . . football embraces such a gigantic family, creating spontaneous human bonds and reconciling peoples all around the globe. In the words of FIFA's President, Dr João Havelange: 'Wherever people can find an outlet for communication and – especially – play, you will always find peace and harmony' (FIFA 1994: 75).

Internationalism, then, through the expansion of the FIFA family and the promotion of harmony among nations and power blocs, is fundamental to FIFA's sense of mission. At one level, this mission can be interpreted as part of a broader twentieth-century project to move towards a world order that, in the wake of two world wars, was more co-ordinated, regulated and 'civilised' (Turner 1994: 105–14). And in this respect FIFA can be revealed as a body with supranational or modernist aspirations.

The missions of more formally politically constituted internationalist organizations, such as the League of Nations between the two world wars, and the United Nations since, have been undone by the pervasive persistence of forms of nationalism. One of FIFA's main problems has been balancing its global ideals with the fact that international football *per se* tends to stimulate and promote parochial forms of nationalism. Sport in general, and football in particular, have proved to be significant theatres for the working-up and expression of national identity, and, in its mobilized form, nationalism. Football and sport create special socio-cultural spaces for this. As John Tomlinson has argued, 'for most people, most of the time, their national identity is not at the forefront of their lived experience' (Tomlinson 1991: 87). We do not routinely spend time wondering or worrying about what nation we belong to, unless there is a perceived threat to that identity, as in times of war (international or civil). It is during such times of jingoistic political rhetoric, emblematic mass rallies and national flag-waving that dormant or apparently passive notions of national identity become mobilized as nationalism.

International football is not war,[2] but because football has been so implicated in the processes through which modern nation-states have been made and proclaimed, international football can act as a surrogate theatre for the working-up of 'passionate nationalism' (Tomlinson 1991: 85). An international football match involving 'our' team intrudes into our daily routine, reminding us with whom we stand with regard to our fellow nationals, and whom we stand against in the international sphere. Sometimes, simply taking part in FIFA competitions can create the conditions for exaggerated displays of nationalism that have meaning beyond the games themselves, and that, under certain circumstances, are fed by and can feed into more central and turbulent currents of international relations. For instance, in one of the Asian qualifying series for the 1994 World Cup Finals, not long after two Gulf wars, Saudi Arabia found itself in a qualifying group with Iran and Iraq. Included in the same group were North and South Korea and Japan, presenting a mind-boggling series of opportunities through which ancient and contemporary national enmities could be flagged.

Other than being admitted as a member of the United Nations, membership of FIFA (and of a comparable body such as the International Olympic Committee) is the clearest signal that a country's status as a nation-state has been recognized by the international community. FIFA claims that when adjudicating the sovereign status of new membership applicants it is guided by decisions already taken by the United Nations. However, this is not always the case. Take the cases of Palestine and Bosnia-Herzegovina, two countries that were given provisional membership of FIFA (and, as such, permission to organize and play international 'friendlies') before their official status as nation-states had been formally recognized by the UN. In the 1990s the whole issue of football, nations and nationalism was thrown into stark relief by events in the Balkans and in the former republics of the USSR. The evidence is convincing, as Edelman (1993) also observes, that new football federations have not simply grown up as a consequence of national fragmentation, but that football has been very significant in the working-up and communication of ideas of nationalism.

FIFA and the Legacy of Imperialism

At the heart of these and many other related issues is the role that football and FIFA have played in nation-building in the postcolonial era. In many respects, until the Second World War there was considerable ambiguity over precisely who ruled world football. When FIFA came into being in 1904 its seven founder members were France, Sweden, Belgium, Denmark, Switzerland, Spain and the Netherlands. England joined in 1905 (an Englishman holding the presidency from 1906 to 1918), but withdrew in 1920, affronted by the idea that other nations might not share its view on cutting off 'football relations with former Central Powers' (Meisl 1960: 301; and see Tomlinson 1986) – these latter being Germany and its allies:

> Almost twenty years before FIFA's formation, in 1886, the four 'home' associations of England, Ireland, Scotland and Wales got together to form the International Board, the remit of which was: 'to discuss and decide proposed alterations in the laws of the game and generally any matters affecting association football and its international relations' (International Board, Minute 7, 1886 minutes) (Sugden and Tomlinson 1998: 10).

The sub-text to this was: 'Britain invented the game and gave it to the world, and we're going to damn well control it!'

Football spread on the industrial and commercial wings of the British Empire. First in Europe and then in South America, British engineers, traders, commercial travellers, military personnel and diplomats introduced football to countries outside the formal embrace of the Empire. Here, where the preferred team sports of upper-class colonial administrators – most notably, rugby and cricket – had not become established as 'the' games to play, as they had in places like South Africa and Australia (Perkin 1989), there was social and cultural 'space' for football to develop as the national game. Beyond the 'informal empire', as Perkin refers to sport's place in British colonial and imperial history, football could flourish. This occurred in countries such as Germany, Russia, Italy, Brazil, Argentina (Sugden and Tomlinson 1994), and Korea (Lee 1997).

While the idea of FIFA was born in Europe, its post-imperial political persona was developed in Latin America. The Americas, north, south and central, were among the first regions to break free from direct colonial rule from Europe. In the United States there was an ambivalence towards embracing the cultural products of the former colonial master, and consequently football failed to develop a strong foothold there (Sugden 1994; Markovits and Hellerman, 2001). On the other hand, because they had not been colonized by the British, football could more easily develop as the national game in countries such as Mexico, Chile and Colombia. In football, the newly independent countries of Latin America discovered a vehicle through which to express national self-determination, firstly within the sub-continent, but eventually on a world stage (Mason 1995).

A major step was taken in 1928 when the International Board admitted four FIFA members with equal voting powers to the four representatives of the home nations. This move was the first formal recognition by the British that 'their game' had become global property and that FIFA had a say in how it should be run. However, if FIFA were to be allowed a say in the affairs of the International Board it was considered of paramount importance that Europe and particularly Britain should have a strong voice within FIFA itself. This they achieved under the guiding hands of Arthur Drewry and Stanley Rous, who between them held the Presidency of FIFA from 1955 until 1974. When FIFA was formed at the beginning of the twentieth century the world's political geography was significantly different from what it was in the century's final decade. The majority of the two hundred or so countries affiliated to FIFA by the end of that century did not exist as independent nation-states when the organization was established. It was this shift in the distribution of power that Rous failed to control. As FA secretary he had kept contact with FIFA during the later years of the UK's period of non-membership from 1928 to 1946–7 (Beck 2000: 108–13). Rous was the architect of the British re-entry into the FIFA fold, also negotiating a UK-specific seat on FIFA's executive board.

At least in part, the deep structure of FIFA was forged through the politics of postcolonialism in Latin America (Sugden and Tomlinson 1998). Similar processes were at work as imperial flags descended in Africa and in Asia after the Second World War. The challenge to this European authority was led by South American associations, who also formed the catalyst for the mobilization of the new and expanding constituencies of Africa and Asia. In postcolonial Africa and Asia football was adopted as a symbol of liberation and/or a source of expression of national autonomy, something over which to drape a new flag of self-rule. In ways largely unseen by the Europeans, for many emergent nations participation in international football, and membership of FIFA, were important political statements. Football contributed to national redefinition in both the African and Asian continents.

Rous and his contemporaries revealed a lack of understanding of how rapidly colonialism was to collapse and what the implications of this were likely to be for what they considered to be their game. In FIFA's regional committee structure, countries that were otherwise politically invisible discovered a political platform for focusing and asserting often newly acquired independence and national identities. However, in considering the reform of FIFA from the mid-1970s onwards, while there was a degree of 'push' from these new national and regional governing bodies such as CAF and the ACF, in equal measure there was the 'pull' of those with vested interests in diminishing European influence – i.e., the South Americans – and it was a combination of both forces that was to lead to the election of the first non-European President of FIFA in 1974. Although the particular postcolonial circumstances were very different across Latin America, Africa and Asia, enough commonalities of interest could be identified by the emerging interest and power groups in those societies to form coherent alliances against dominant first-world and imperialist forces.

Out of Africa: African Football, Colonialism and the Postcolonial Experience

African football is framed totally by colonialism and the postcolonial experience. Football came to Africa on the wings of empires. European colonial administrators, military personnel, diplomats, traders and itinerant workers and fortune-seekers introduced the game throughout the continent in the late nineteenth and early twentieth centuries (Murray 1994: 229–56). In Ghana, for instance the game was introduced by British sailors and developed by the large numbers of British nationals who lived along the cape coast. There were not sufficient numbers of expatriates to keep the game exclusive for a privileged, colonial white elite. Football became popular with the local population, who formed their own teams in opposition to those established by their colonial masters. The semantics and semiotics of clubs with names such as Cape Coast Mysterious Dwarves and Cape Coast Venomous Vipers, formed long before the end of colonialism, indicates that football in Ghana was more than simply a passive replica of the British game (Bediako 1995). Likewise, in Southern Africa, football became a tool of political protest:

> In the soccer crowd there was a refuge for political and nationalist leaders constantly in fear of government spies or arrest. Soccer, popular among both the labouring classes and the African elite, became an ideal tool with which to win mass support from the majority of the population. African political leaders were not slow to exploit soccer in this way (Stuart 1995: 34).

In Egypt and Algeria (Murray 1994: 242–3) football became embroiled in the struggles for independence from Britain and France respectively. Dr Abdel Halim Mohamed of Sudan explained the way football was used in the struggle for independence in his country. The Sudan was used by the British as a training ground for colonial administrators and district commissioners. Almost all who came were public school educated, and the vast majority were graduates of Oxford or Cambridge. The classification of their degrees was not so important as having earned a sporting blue (Mangan 1998). Halim believed that the British used sport in the small number of secondary schools that they set up in the Sudan as a means of disciplining local young intellectuals and dissipating energies that might otherwise have been directed towards political protest. However, because football became so popular with the Sudanese masses that an educated Sudanese elite was able to harness it to a movement for political emancipation:

> We had our social clubs and we were talking about independence. The British accused us of being *afendeya* (elitist and bourgeoisie) – that we were not with the masses of the people, that we do not represent them. As a counter to this we started football clubs as social clubs where we would talk the principles of civics to the masses – that this is their country and that they have the right to independence. This helped to show that while it was we, the intelligentsia, who were the architects of the independence movement, we were backed by the people.[3]

In this regard, throughout Africa, football had a rooted political pedigree that was to become a critical feature of black-national identity in the postcolonial era and would raise the political profile of football in the world in general. In the words of Faouzi Mahjoub (1996), football can 'provide a symbolic parallel for the difficult and tentative steps Africa has made forging ahead in the modern world .'

The Confederation of African Football (CAF) had been formed in 1956 by Egypt, Ethiopia, Sudan, and South Africa – the only independent nations on the continent at that time. The proposal to form an African confederation met stern resistance from the South Americans, who, misreading their own history, viewed the African nations as potential dupes of their former colonial masters. However, with strong support from Sir Stanley Rous and Granatkin of the Soviet Union, CAF was formerly inaugurated at its first constitutional assembly in Khartoum in 1957. In possibly the first use of sport as a political tool in the fight against apartheid, South Africa was suspended from CAF the following year when it insisted on sending either an all-white or an all-black team to the first African Cup of Nations in the Sudanese capital, Khartoum.

As the European powers relinquished and at times lost their colonial authority, newly independent African nations, in the absence of economic and military might, discovered in football a medium through which to register their presence in the international arena both on and off the playing-field. And, as Ebo Quansah points out, 'applications for membership of the United Nations (UN), the Organization of African Unity (OAU) and CAF go hand in hand' (Quansah 1996: 27). In certain respects, African representatives at CAF and FIFA viewed their responsibilities in the same light as colleagues at the OAU and UN: that is, to establish and embellish the bargaining position of African nations in the market-place of international relations, despite the North/South, Arab/Black schisms in any apparent pan-African unity.

Beyond pan-African divisions there are also serious problems within individual African nations, with implications for any understanding of football. Clearly, the history of postcolonial Africa has not been one of a smooth and progressive transition to self-determined democracy. On the contrary, it has been characterized by autocracy, despotism, political disorder and civil war. As the South African writer Rian Milan observes, modern Africa 'is made up of artificial states ruled for the most part by the jumped-up and corrupt heirs of colonialists' (Milan 1997: 33). These 'artificial states', over which a succession of dictators has ruled, are so riven by tribal factionalisms and ethnic rivalries that it has been all but impossible to construct meaningful and durable civil societies – that is institutional frameworks for the working up and maintenance of shared principles of equality and social justice, and counter-balances to the naked power of the state and its functionaries.

The potential liberalization of postcolonial Africa has never really materialized. Immature democratic experiments have, more often than not, perished, to be replaced by a range of authoritarian, military regimes and/or single party systems with little or no effective civil opposition. Jean-François Bayart borrows a metaphor from Cameroon, 'the politics of the belly', to characterize the relationship between the state and immature civil societies in sub-Saharan Africa. He presents a model within which quasi-feudal traditions of power, patronage and exploitation operate in settings of bureaucratic rationality. Under such circumstances the abuse of political power and corruption have flourished and become institutionalized. Bayart works with two models of corruption: the *resources of extraversion* – command over or access to scarce physical and cultural capital; and *positions of predation* – the occupation of roles that provide opportunities for predatory actions, such as extortion. The administration of football in many African countries is illustrative of how both of these models operate (Bayart 1996; Harriss-White and White 1996).

Because football emerged from colonialism as one of the few institutions that captured the imagination of diverse populations, in the context outlined above, it became the target for political interference and economic exploitation by powerful political elites:

> In Africa, where the activities of military dictators and self-imposed iron-fist life presidents have stifled open political debate, the ordinary man's idea of self-expression emanates from the terraces . . . Such is the power of football that, the world over, aspiring and actual rulers, whether constitutionally elected, military dictators or civilian autocrats, have tended to exploit

the game's influence on the populace in order to buy time for their moribund administrations. Governments tend to look upon the game as the public relations wing of the ruling class. Administrators are often appointed without the interests of the game at heart, but according to how sycophantic they are and to the extent they can use the popularity of the game to further the interests of their rulers (Quansah 1996: 26–7).

Examples of heads of state taking an excessive and often manipulative interest in national football affairs would include Nkrumah and Rawlings in Ghana, Babangida and Abacha in Nigeria, Doe in Liberia, Numeiri in Sudan and Mubarak in Egypt.[4] Dr Halim of Sudan recalls giving up his post as president of the Sudanese Football Association:

> In 1959 we had a junta government. They wanted to interfere in the work of the FA. They wanted to select the president and all of the committee members . . . I would not work in this situation. They put in a Minister for Sport who could have been my son! How could I be told what to do by a soldier? (interview with authors, London 12 June 1997).

Despite the manifold intra-continental divisions and problems alluded to above, in its dealings with FIFA, as it grew, CAF managed to present a more or less unified front, and with a growing membership it was wooed by successive pretenders to the FIFA throne – Havelange in 1974, and Sepp Blatter in 1998.

Oroc Oyo, the first secretary of the Nigerian Football Association after independence, recalls the situation back in the early 1970s:

> I remember the 1974 elections very vividly. There was this struggle (*between Rous and Havelange*) and I was in the centre of it. Dr Havelange mounted his campaign in 1971 and he produced a brochure on himself that was circulated around the world. I remember he attended the CAF congress in Egypt 1974. After the congress he invited African delegates to a cocktail party hosted by the ambassador of Brazil in Egypt. All of us were invited . . . The plank of Havelange's campaign was to ostracize South Africa, because this was the clarion call of African football. This was a carrot which Dr Havelange brandished before Africa. So Ganga mustered Africa (interview with authors, Johannesburg 23 January 1996).[5]

In response to the intransigence of the English FIFA boss Stanley Rous on the issue of apartheid in South Africa, a Kenyan delegate responded:

> In his declaration we saw the manifestation of old and dying colonialism. It is of no avail of him to say that the Football Association of South Africa has committed no crime because it is the government which is responsible of the apartheid policy. It is the government which controls the affairs of the F.A.S.A. We in Kenya wish to see that all means possible are used to bring about a change in South Africa so that our brothers there may enjoy the freedom of sports we have.[6]

According to the Brazilian, Peter Pullen, a senior official (Advisor for Special Duties) and a long-time associate of Havelange (recalled by Rous's PA Rose-Marie Breitenstein as 'Havelange's agent in England'), there was a hidden irony in this result. Some time before he launched his own campaign for the FIFA Presidency, Havelange, in his capacity as President of the Brazilian Sport/ Football Federation (CBF), had warned Rous of the increasing power of the Third World. Havelange counselled that Rous should consider changing FIFA's constitution in such a way that the votes of the more established nations of Europe and Latin America would weigh more than those of the newer members from Africa and Asia. Pullen believes that: 'Rous, thinking that he had the votes of the British Commonwealth nations in the palm of his hand, turned down Havelange's proposal – a decision that was to haunt him after the Frankfurt congress' (interview with authors, Fukuoka Japan, 5 September 1995). Havelange's victory signalled a sea-change in the affairs of FIFA as, largely through the intervention of the Africans, the balance of power in world football shifted from the northern to the southern hemisphere. Almost a century earlier, the British Prime Minister, Gladstone had commented that one day Britain's African colonies would become as 'millstones around our necks .' In the early 1970s, Gladstone's words resounded within FIFA's European inner circle, a situation that the Latin Americans were more than happy to exploit to propel their man into the President's seat. African nations have gone on to challenge at the highest levels, with Cameroon and Nigeria the outstanding performers in World Cup and Olympic tournaments and post-apartheid South Africa emerging strongly, and with administrators of integrity such as Issa Hayatou (of Cameroon, president of CAF) sufficiently respected to be widely accepted as a front-runner for the FIFA presidency itself. But the development has been extremely uneven.

Extreme poverty and political instability have been the most serious obstacle to the development of football in Africa, and regularly countries are forced to withdraw from international competitions because national federations do not have the money to send their teams abroad. In the qualification series of the 1996 African Cup of Nations, a combination of civil war and lack of funds led to 16 countries dropping out. Mali let it be known that, owing to economic problems, they would not be able to take part in the World Cup qualifiers for France 1998. This situation, according to Maradas, is not helped by the approach of international aid agencies and the like:

The main problem for football on this continent are the very weak African economies. With so much poverty, we simply cannot afford to fund football properly. The situation is made worse through the stance taken by the World Bank which has very strict criterion for money lending and equally strict monitoring procedures. It is not permitted to spend money on sport while money is borrowed from and owed to the World Bank (Maradas 1996: 16).

The financial misery of African football is accentuated through the corruption that so often goes hand in hand with the administration of football on the continent. Unlike so many other spheres of interest in Africa, football, because it is so popular, generates income through grants from sponsorship deals, television contracts, gate receipts and government subsidies. However, quite often the money that should be spent on football development ends up in the pockets of corrupt administrators and government officials. Stadium tragedies in South Africa and Ghana in 2001 attest to the maladministration of ticket allocations and crowd control, and unaccounted cash flows and revenues. Maradas refers to this as 'the cancer of African football'. We could present material in support of this claim from almost every sub-Saharan African country, comparable to the documented cases of Zaire, Cameroon and South Africa (see Sugden and Tomlinson 1998: Chapter 6).

Africa may, from time to time, produce teams of world-beating potential and impact, such as Cameroon in Italia '90 or Nigeria, Olympic champions in 1996, and Cameroon, Olympic champions in 2000. And, yes, Africa may indeed one day win the World Cup. But, so long as 'the politics of the belly' continues to characterize the administration of football in Africa – with critical resources controlled with no accountability, by ruthlessly self-seeking individuals – the tremendous potential for sustained development across the continent will never be realized. Add to this the flow of talent from the continent to the lucrative performance pastures of North America and Europe (Bale and Maguire 1994), and the potential for development is still further threatened. There is nothing particularly new in this, as Mahjoub (1999) has illustrated in tracking the contribution of North African footballers to French football, from the entry of the nineteen-year-old Moroccan Larbi Ben Barek into the French game in 1938, through to the impact of Zinedine Zidane, born of Algerian parents who had moved to the area of Marseilles in the 1960s. But as nations acquired their independence, in many footballing nations the idealism of the postcolonial dawn would be lost in the pragmatics of survival and an endemic culture of corruption, combined with an intensifying sporting cosmopolitanism that acts as an exploitative market favouring corporate interests and the most powerful societies and economies at the heart of the global market-place.

Eastern Promise: Football Development in Postcolonial Asia

The roots of football in Asia are comparable to those in South America and Africa, shaped by British imperialist and commercial influences. Thus, in the South Asian sub-continent, the oldest established football association was the Calcutta-based Indian FA (1893) (though the All India Football Federation was not established until 1937). In South-East Asia football made some early institutionalized impact, Singapore's football association dating from 1892. Little detail is known of this body's history, but the Football Association of Singapore (1997) is certain that 'the game was dominated by the British companies and the British forces that were stationed in Singapore during the colonial days', and that 'Inter-Business Houses football matches started in the early part of the twentieth century', involved in which 'there were many expatriate players, mostly from England .' Occupying forces and international business were the seminal influences on what was then known as the SAFA (Singapore Amateur Football Association). Indeed, this legacy lives on, at least in the sphere of tradition and cultural heritage, in the context of Singapore's modern professional league, the S-League, modelled explicitly upon Japan's J-League, but with deeper historical roots. The top and bottom clubs in the Pioneer Series B programme of 14 matches during Singapore's inaugural professional season in 1996 were, respectively, Singapore Armed Forces Football Club, and Police FC (Football Association of Singapore 1996). Much had happened in Asian football in the intervening century to indicate that, though tradition might live on in matters of nomenclature and labels, the meanings, motivations and aspirations underlying the game at the end of the twentieth century were a world apart from those that stimulated the pioneers of the game in the continent. The scale of this transformation and growth was captured by the tigerish comments on Asian football by Peter Velappan, general secretary of the Asian Football Confederation (AFC), in December 1996: 'Football is a serious business. We need to reorientate our thinking to treat Asian soccer as a product which needs to be researched, produced and marketed on a planned and sustained basis through every available means throughout the continent' (Velappan 1996: 1).

Football in Asia has acquired – in this seriously developed, produced and marketed form – a wider global profile, in line with some very ambitious objectives. For Velappan, increasing success in FIFA tournaments at world-class level – particularly in younger age-group categories – has demonstrated genuine development and authentic potential. This has been so much the case that Velappan believes that 'by 2,005, Asia will be the equal to Brazil in terms of standards.'[7] Much of this notable pace of development has required the promotion and management of change – organizational and cultural as well as sporting – in and among the 44 (as of 1996) member associations of the confederation. The AFC's own modernization – driving 'towards a more professional approach to football management and an improved and efficient communications system' – has generated a set of objectives for itself and its member associations:

The following measures are now being initiated within the AFC to further **enhance** its image:

- The push towards well-structured national associations
- Professional management of the Associations
- An effective communications system between the Confederation and National Associations
- Well-structured professional leagues
- Coach Education Programme
- Youth Development Programme
- Referees Development Programme
- Promotion of the game through the Media, TV and newsletters
- Sports medicine and its contribution towards high-level performance
- Stadia Security
- Fair Play drive

With the above in view, FIFA and AFC have been working very closely in assisting the National Associations through the introduction of various programmes, seminars, study tours, and inspection visits. This is to ensure that the National Associations are professionally managed, the leagues well structured and the various programmes implemented (Velappan 1996).

This is ambitiously framed. It proposes a new era of professionalized and more systematically developed football politics and culture, in which FIFA and the Confederation can work together to lead the transformation of a cross-continental sporting infrastructure. This assumes that between them the two federations can operate as a successful facilitators of supranational initiatives. They are global initiatives – despite the relatively low profile of Asian football in the football world's biggest showcase, the World Cup – because of the sheer scale of the confederation's brief, geographically, demographically, politically and culturally.

The Asian presence in world football at its highest levels was most dramatically announced by North Korea's successes in the World Cup in England in 1966, most notably its defeat of Italy (Tomlinson 1994: 24–5). But that was prompted above all by the sporting imperatives of a Communist régime (other social formations were developing their football cultures and systems much more unevenly), and by that country's opportunistic response in going to England when the mass of Asian and African nations withdrew from the qualifying rounds. The succeeding thirty years saw some outstanding successes in football development in very different national contexts. In November 1996, according to the Coca-Cola/FIFA Asian rankings, the more prominent Asian national sides were as follows (for this purpose, only those Asian nations featuring in FIFA's top 100 World Ranking are listed): [8]

FIFA/Coca-Cola Asian Rankings, November 1996

Asian Ranking	Country	World Ranking	Change: Oct.– Nov. '96
1	Japan	22	−2
2	Saudi Arabia	40	0
3	South Korea	46	−1
4	Thailand	57	−3
5	Qatar	64	−2
6	UAE	69	+4
7	Iran	77	−6
8	China	78	−12
9	Kuwait	79	+7
10	Oman	88	0
11	Malaysia	92	0
12	Singapore	94	−1
13	Lebanon	99	−2
14	Myanmar	100	−2

Five years on, the rankings remained similar. Saudi Arabia stood at 27th in the overall FIFA rankings, Japan 33rd, Korea 37th, Iran 49th. It is striking, in these rankings, that (apart from Thailand and Iran) the top ten is dominated by either Arab Gulf states in the Middle East (Saudi Arabia, Qatar, United Arab Emirates, Kuwait and Oman), or established or aspirant superpower societies of the Far East (China, Japan and Korea). Thailand's ranking was based in part upon its prominence within the South-east Asia region – the ASEAN (Association of South-east Asian Nations) grouping, having triumphed in the inaugural Tiger Cup. Its bubble, though, was soon to be burst at the Asian Cup in the UAE, where it suffered confidence-shattering defeats at the hands of Saudi Arabia (0–6), Iran (1–3), and Iraq (1–4). Iran re-emerged as a regional power, in the wake of persisting problems even six years after the end of the Iran–Iraq war. But the dominant regions, performing frequently and consistently enough to make a mark in world rankings, were the oil-rich societies of the Gulf, and the thrusting capitalist and emerging tiger economies of the Far East. Performance in the World Cup finals has also reflected such patterns.

Asian national sides did not immediately follow up the 1966 success of the Korean Democratic People's Republic. As the AFC General Secretary reflected: 'Asia did not take the cue that Asian teams had the potential and the capability to take on the best in the world. Asia continued to slumber' (Velappan 1996: Section 2). To put this point less poetically, but in a more explanatory way – no other Asian side was as yet supported by a centrist infrastructure, in the North Korean case along para-Soviet lines; nor were any yet undergirded by a supportive infrastructure from within a capitalist economy, or a corporatist alliance of social, political and economic interests. It is the societal type, and the deployment of resources within the society, that has promoted football enough to heighten levels of aspiration and raise levels of performance – along with an increased presence within FIFA and confederational organization, administration and politics (Stamm and Lamprecht 1996: 7–11). Along with CAF, AFC has doggedly pursued increased representation on the executive committee of FIFA. Many Asian countries were to experience, in periods of postcolonial independence and adaptation, the same type of developmental problems as were newly independent African nations. The collapse of empire also meant the withdrawal of forms of organization and resources. Football could hardly be immune from this. Unless newly formed nations could provide substantial resources, and scrupulous and efficient administration, there was little chance of their reaching world-class performance levels. The record of Asian teams in World Cups after 1966 testifies to this basic but critical point:

Finishing Position of Asian Sides in World Cup Finals

World Cup	Year	Asian Team	Finishing Position
West Germany	1974	Korea Republic	16/16
Spain	1982	Kuwait	21/24
Mexico	1986	Korea Republic	20/24
Italy	1990	Korea Republic	22/24
Italy	1990	United Arab Emirates	24/24
USA	1994	Korea Republic	20/24
USA	1994	Saudi Arabia	12 (or 8)/24
France	1998	Iran	3rd in its group with 3 points
France	1998	Saudi Arabia	Bottom (4th) in its group with 1 point
France	1998	Korea Republic	Bottom of its group with 1 point
France	1998	Japan	Bottom of its group with 1 point (31/32)

Clearly, on the levels of performance among the established, developed elite of world footballing nations, Asian sides have been the minnows in the global sea. Only the USA finished below Japan in the overall 1998 table. But the resounding fact for Asian football remains – whatever the level achieved, anticipated or predicted – that its leading countries have *systematically* produced the continent's elite squads, in some cases in astoundingly short-term phases of development. China's vast resources, for instance, could be harnessed behind sport, so enabling its footballers to set up a training camp in the Brazilian jungle, in the belief that there was something to be learned from proximity to and immersion in the football culture that had produced the most successful international side in the history of the World Cup (Bernstein 1995). Documented cases of the UAE and South Korea, as well as Japan, show the powerful combination of state sponsorship underlying the ambitious and rapid growth of football in such societies.

In such societies – widely different in political profile – alliances of the state and private-sector interests have ensured that the development of football has been seen as a serious political commitment and cultural project. This has contributed to the raising of the global profile of emerging states such as the UAE and South Korea, and also for Japan – as stated by Ryo Nishimura, of Japan's World Cup 2002's Communications Department – to the post-Second World War project of rehabilitation (interview with authors, Tokyo Japan, 21 March 1997).

The Third World, as has been shown in the previous section in the context of Africa, was promised much by Havelange in his drive for the FIFA presidency. This is not to say that Asia had not benefited from FIFA during Sir Stanley Rous's leadership of FIFA. Velappan describes Rous's contribution: 'mainly on the technical development programmes. With his assistance we organized the Asian academies for coaches, referees and always he had a very ready and open heart to receive whatever Asia's needs were' (interview with authors, Abu Dhabi, UAE, 17 December 1996). Rous's relationship with FIFA's Asian constituency was not exclusively technical and administrative. His stated aim was 'to maintain the sporting unity of football', even wherever 'politics were apt to intrude as in the Djakarta games of 1962' (Rous 1978: 161). In this case, Israel and Taiwan were refused visas to enter Indonesia, and all Rous's diplomacy could not get the bans lifted. Rous's solution to the Israel problem was to work towards the relocation of its national association into Europe. In a letter, marked confidential, to the AFC secretary Koe Ewe Teik in Penang, Malaysia, in September 1970, Rous voiced privately his view of how the problem might be solved, and new allies within FIFA carefully courted:

In view of the possible 'bloks' in FIFA becoming more solid I wish to talk to you, when we next meet, about strengthening the position of Asia. Is there any possibility of you eventually succeeding one of the present members? You have done so much to develop football throughout Asia that you ought to become one of the leaders within FIFA. Do you agree that in the Olympic Games and the World Cup, in future, we should put Israel in a European group? If we do, I am told by the leaders of Kuwait and Bahrain, more Arab countries would participate and we might be able to find influential leaders in those states.[9]

So in appropriate circumstances, Sir Stanley was not averse to playing Jew off against Arab. Such negotiations developed over the next two years, and the Kuwait Football Association proposed to the AFC that 'Israel be excluded from future AFC tournaments'. Z. Bar-Sever, Chair of the Israel Football Association, registered his astonishment at this proposal, in a letter to Rous dated July 1972, recounting his association's long service to the cause of Asian football, and its representation of the continent at the Olympic Games of 1968, and the World Cup finals of 1970 (both in Mexico):

You will agree that this ridiculous proposal is against the principles, objects and ideal of the A.F.C., as stated in the A.F.C. statutes. It seems that those who are demanding equality in sports are, themselves, ruthlessly ruining the term and aim of sportsmanship and fairness, and are trying again and again to involve politics with sports. [10]

The Israeli condemned the Kuwaiti proposal as a mockery of the first principle of 'world sporting organizations . . . that there will be no racial or any other discrimination in sport'. Clearly, behind his own resolute defence of FIFA statutes, Rous was not above some political pragmatism of his own. Israel was actually ejected from the AFC in 1976, two years after the end of his presidency, and 'flitted from Europe to Oceania in search of a home' (Oliver 1992: 377), before stabilizing its affiliation in UEFA in 1992. Rous himself had been willing to recognize the pressing claims of the emergent Arab nations, and sacrifice Israel on an altar of FIFA *realpolitik*.

Velappan recalled the 1974 campaign for the FIFA presidency: 'I think Sir Stanley did not take the election too seriously. He didn't believe in campaigning. But Dr Havelange and his people did a lot of groundwork, and specially promising Asia and Africa many benefits, such as more places in the World Cup, more places in the Olympics and also the introduction of youth tournaments, technical aid programmes and so on, and obviously he carried the day. He has achieved all that, he expanded the World Cup, he introduced the youth tournaments for the Under-17 and the Under-20 years, the women's tournament, and now the FUTSAL development programmes. And so he has given enormous contribution to football and I am sure in 1998 when he officially retires everyone will be very very thankful for his contribution' (interview with authors, Abu Dhabi, UAE, 17 December 1996).

It could be said that FIFA itself, via the confederation, has also been used as a means of internationalizing a nation and a figure – such as Sheikh Zayed of the UAE, appending the Asian Cup to his solipsistic celebration of the nation's birthday; or Dr Mong Joon Chung of South Korea, boss of Hyundai heavy industries, representing the intricate intertwining of political, economic and sports interests as he manipulated support for election on to FIFA's executive committee. So, by the end of the century, where stood the peoples' game among more than half of the world's population? In many ways it depends where you looked. The big guns of the Far East, the toothless tigers of December 1996, were certainly on a different plane to the societies of South-East Asia; and what, really, united them with the nations and countries of the Middle East? As a widely experienced European coach noted, the Middle East and the Far East have limitless resources but restricted potential; some societies of South-East Asia have massive potential, but problematic infrastructures and limited resources.[11] Such a persistently uneven development of the game worldwide in such circumstances would reiterate the dominance of the traditionally powerful centres of world football, reminding us of the local and regional hierarchies that have continued to characterize the game's global culture. South Korea and the Gulf States (Saudi Arabia, Kuwait and Qatar in 2001) provided the ACF delegates to the FIFA executive committee, and were able to influence decisively decisions of the import of who would host the 2006 World Cup, backing Germany in an ultimate Europe–Asia alliance that was to snatch the decision from South Africa's grasp. This is not to say that the most well-resourced and focused nations are not improving, and Japan's close battle with France in a 2001 international tournament was evidence of this, auguring well for Asian aspirations in the 2002 World Cup in Korea and Japan.

Conclusion: Postcolonial Effects in the Re-shaping of World Football Politics

Our consideration of the place of football in selected postcolonial societies and cultures has avoided the mistakes of lopsided concentrations upon the cultural at the expense of the social, and has focused rather upon the materiality of social relations within the global football culture, and the institutional manifestation of that reality, FIFA and the world football federations. At the same time, we recognize the potential generality of Said's assertion that: 'Cultural experience or indeed every cultural form is radically, quintessentially hybrid, and if it has been the practice in the West since Immanuel Kant to isolate cultural and aesthetic realms from the worldly domain, it is now time to rejoin them' (Said

1993: 68). Our study of global sports culture has sought never to isolate such key realms.

But football as a sports practice has remained remarkably homogeneous during its worldwide expansion. This has meant that, where football has been developed, there may be preferences of style or preferred influences and predecessors, but it has kept a single identifiable form. It has been able to express an otherness of identity precisely by bringing heterogeneous cultures together around shared values ambitions, by creating a common meeting-ground in the sporting sphere. It has been largely immune from any process of cultural hybridization that cultural forms of a different kind might undergo. Yet cases show that the place and meaning of football in a society can vary widely. It is open to cultural and political forms of appropriation. It can mean different things in different places.

Overall, football can be viewed as both a symbol of economic and cultural imperialism, and as a forum for resistance by the Third World to first-world domination or hegemony. It can operate in extraordinarily complex ways, bolstering internal political cultures whilst also promoting the global ambitions of football bodies and administrators. Žižek has noted how 'each universal ideological notion is always hegemonized by some particular content which colours its very universality and accounts for its efficiency' (1997: 28). Football in postcolonial cultures, around the FIFA-promoted ideologies of universal participation and fair play and youth, has expressed both a tendency to keep power in the hands of an elite, and a tolerance of 'the Other's identity, conceiving the Other as a self-enclosed "authentic" community towards which . . . the multiculturalist maintains a distance rendered possible by his privileged universal position' (Žižek 1997: 44). And in this way there may indeed have been a kind of implicit racism of the variety talked of by Žižek, in the way that FIFA has recognized cultural difference in non-interventionist and permissive fashion. In some very direct, and also in some subtle and ideologically complex ways, FIFA has played a critical role in the brokerage of forms of neo-imperialism and so in the reshaping of football politics in the postcolonial context.

Notes

1. This list is compiled from the *FIFA Directory* 2001, and contemporaneous federational websites.
2. Though it can stimulate conflict. In 1969 hostilities between El Salvador and Honduras were ignited in the course of World Cup qualifying matches. Though

the war lasted only 100 hours, 6,000 people lost their lives, and 50,000 their homes and fields. See Kapuscinski (1994: 23).

3.   Abdel Hamil Mohamed, interview with authors, London, 12 June 1997. Dr Halim has been the President of the Sudanese Football Association; a co-founder and former President of CAF; a member of the FIFA Executive; and a member of the IOC.

4.   Yorkshire Television Archive, Sports Cultures Archive for Investigative Research (SCAIR), Chelsea School Research Centre, University of Brighton.

5.   Jean-Claude Ganga is a veteran dealmaker on the pan-African sports politics scene. His style and his morals hit world headlines during the Olympic (IOC) scandals when these were exposed in early 1999. Ganga was one of the seven IOC members expelled for misconduct (that is, bribery and corruption).

6.   Rous papers, SCAIR.

7.   Rous papers, SCAIR

8.   The table is from *Asian Football Confederation News*, Vol. 3, No. 1/97, January 1997, p. 6. Our thanks to AFC marketing Ltd., Hong Kong, publisher (on behalf of the Asian Football Confederation) of *Asian Football Confederation News*.

9.   Rous papers, SCAIR.

10.   Rous papers, SCAIR.

11.   Authors' interview with German Otto Pfister, Abu Dhabi, UAE, 15 December 1996. At the time Pfister was coach to the Bangladeshi national side.

Bibliography

Ahmad, A. (1995) 'The Politics of Literary Postcoloniality'. *Race and Class* 36: 1–20.

Alomes, S. (1999) '"The One Day in September": Grass Roots Enthusiasm, Invented Traditions, Contemporary Commercial Spectacle and the Australian Football League Finals', School of Australian and International Studies seminar, Deakin University, Geelong, 3 September.

Alter, J. (1992) *The Wrestler's Body: Identity and Ideology in North India*, Berkeley, CA: University of California Press.

Anderson, C. (2000) *Convicts in the Indian Ocean: Transportation from South Asia to Mauritius 1815–1853*, Basingstoke: Macmillan.

Anderson, I. (1993) 'Black Suffering, White Wash', *Arena*, June–July: 23–25.

Andrews, Anderson and W. Atkinson (eds) *Ngariarty: Kooris talkin*, Melbourne: Latrobe University.

Anthias, F. and Yuval-Davis, N. (1992) *Racialised Boundaries: Race, Nation, Generation, Colour and Class and the Anti-racist Struggle*, London: Routledge.

Appadurai, A. (1993) 'Number in the Colonial Imagination', in C. A. Breckenridge and P. van der Veer (eds) *Orientalism and the Postcolonial Predicament: Perspectives on South Asia*, Philadelphia: University of Pennsylvania Press.

—— (1996) 'Playing With Modernity: The Decolonization of Indian Cricket', in C. A. Breckenridge (ed.) *Consuming Modernity: Public Culture in Contemporary India*, Minneapolis, MN: University of Minnesota Press.

Appiah, K. A. (1991) 'Is the Post- in Postmodernism the Post- in Postcolonial?'. *Critical Inquiry* 17: 336–57.

—— (1997) 'Is the "Post-" in "Postcolonial" the "Post-" in "Postmodern"?', in A. McClintock, A. Mufti and E. Shohat (eds), *Dangerous Liaisons: Gender, Nation and Postcolonial Perspectives*, pp. 420–44, Minneapolis, MN: University of Minnesota Press.

Arnold, D (1993) *Colonizing the Body: State Medicine and Epidemic Disease in Nineteenth Century India*, Delhi: Oxford University Press.

Ashcroft, B., Griffiths, G. and Tiffin, H. (1998) *Key Concepts in Post-colonial Studies*, London: Routledge.

Atkinson, W. and Poulter, J. (1993) 'The Origins of Aboriginal Football Skills', in I.

Augoustinos, M., Tuffin, K. and Rapley, M. (1999) 'Genocide or a Failure to Gel? Racism, History and Nationalism in Australian talk'. *Discourse and Society* 10: 351–78.

Australian Associated Press (1995) 'Kickett Tells of Magpie taunt', *Herald-Sun*, 18 May, The Herald and Weekly Times Limited: 2.

Australian Bureau of Statistics (1995) *Sports Attendance*, Cat no. 4174.0. Canberra.

Australian Football League (1995) *Football Record,* 30 June 1995–2 July, Melbourne: Progress Printers.

Bairner, A. (1996a) 'Sportive Nationalism and Nationalist Politics. A Comparative Analysis of Scotland, the Republic of Ireland and Sweden'. *Journal of Sport and Social Issues,* 20 (3): 314–34.

—— (1996b) 'Ireland, Sport and Empire', in K. Jeffery (ed.) *'An Irish Empire'? Aspects of Ireland and the British Empire,* Manchester: Manchester University Press.

—— (1999) Review of Joseph M Bradley (1998) *Sport, Culture, Politics, and Scottish Society: Irish Immigrants and the Gaelic Athletic Association,* Edinburgh: John Donald in *International Review of the Sociology of Sport,* 34, No. 2: 191–2.

—— (2000) 'Sport and Peace: An Uneasy Dialogue', in E. Slater and M. Peillon (eds) *Memories of the Present. A Sociological Chronicle of Ireland, 1997–1998,* Dublin: Institute of Public Administration.

—— (2001) *Sport, Nationalism and Globalization. European and North American Perspectives,* Albany, NY: SUNY Press.

—— and Darby, P. (1999) 'Divided Sport in a Divided Society. Northern Ireland', in J. Sugden and A. Bairner (eds) *Sport in Divided Societies,* Aachen: Meyer and Meyer.

Baker, A. and Boyd, T. (eds) (1997) *Out of Bounds: Sport, Media, And The Politics of Identity,* Bloomington, IN: Indiana University Press.

Bale, J. and Maguire, J. (eds) (1994) *The Global Sports Arena: Athletic Talent Migration in an Interdependent World,* London: Frank Cass.

—— and Sang, J. (1996) *Kenyan Running, Movement Culture, Geography and Global Change,* London: Frank Cass.

Barker, B. (1997) *Getting Government To Listen: A Guide to the International Human Rights System for Indigenous Australians,* East Sydney: The Australian Youth Foundation.

Barnes, T. and Gregory, D. (eds) (1997) *Reading Human Geography,* London: Arnold.

Barnett, C. (1995) 'Awakening the Dead: Who needs the History of Geography? *Transactions of the Institute of British Geographers,* 20, 4, 417–19.

Barnett, E. E. (1990) *My Life in China, 1910–1936,* Michigan: Michigan State University.

Bates, C. (1995) 'Race, Caste and Tribe in Central India: The Early Origins of Indian Anthropometry' in P. Robb (ed.), *The Concept of Race in South Asia,* Delhi: Oxford University Press.

Baucom, I. (1996) *Out of Place; Englishness, Empire and the Locations of Identity,* Princeton, NJ: Princeton University Press.

Bayart, J.-F. (1996) *The State in Africa: The Politics of the Belly,* New York: Addison Wesley.

Beck, P. (2000) *Scoring for Britain – International Football and International Politics, 1900–1939,* London: Frank Cass.

Bediako, K. (1995) *The National Soccer League of Ghana: The Full Story,* Accra: Buck Press.

Belich, J. (1986) *The New Zealand Wars and the Victorian Interpretation of Racial Conflict*, Auckland: Auckland University Press.

Bell, C. (1996) *Inventing New Zealand: Everyday Myths of Pakeha Identity*, Auckland: Penguin Books.

Berghorn, F., Yetman, N. and Hanna, W. (1988) 'Racial Participation and Integration in Men's and Women's Intercollegiate Basketball: Continuity and Change, 1958–1985'. *Sociology of Sport Journal* Vol. 5: 107–24.

Bernstein, K. (1995) 'Born in China, Made in Brazil', *Independent on Sunday Magazine*, 9 July: 8–11.

Bhabha, H. K. (1994) *The Location of Culture*, London/New York: Routledge.

Birrell, S. (1989) 'Racial Relations Theories and Sport: Suggestions for a More Critical Analysis'. *Sociology of Sport Journal* Vol. 6: 212–27.

Blainey, G. (1990) *A Game of Our Own: The Origins of Australian Football*. Melbourne: Information Australia.

Blake, B. (1995) 'A Name Change?', *The Age*, 16 August, David Syme & Co.: 16.

Blake, M. (1999) 'Arjuna's Sound Bite', *Age*, Sport 6, 6 May.

Boehmer, E. (1995) *Colonial and Postcolonial Literature*, Oxford: Oxford University Press.

Bose, M. (1986) *A Maidan View: The Magic of Indian Cricket*, London: Allen and Unwin.

—— (1990) *Cricket Voices: Interviews with Mihir Bose*, London: Kingswood.

Botham, I. (1995) *Botham: My Autobiography*, London: CollinsWillow.

Boyle, R. and Haynes, R. (1996) 'The Grand Old Game: Football, Media and Identity in Scotland'. *Media, Culture and Society* 18: 549–64.

Brass, P. (2001) 'The Production of Hindu–Muslim Violence in Contemporary India', presented at *Representing the Body in Colonial and Post-Colonial South Asia*, (symposium at Purdue University, 24 February 2001).

Bremer, R. (with Tom Brooking) (1993) 'Federated Farmers and the State', in Brian Roper and Chris Rudd (eds), *State and Economy in New Zealand*, pp. 108–27, Auckland: Oxford University Press.

Brock, P. and Kartinyeri, D. (1989) *Poonindie: The Rise and Destruction of an Aboriginal Agricultural Community*, Adelaide: Aboriginal Heritage Branch, Department of Environment and Planning.

Brohm, J.-M. (1978) *Sport A Prison of Measured Time*, London: Ink Links.

Bromberger, C. (1995) *Le match de football: Ethnologie d'une passion partisane à Marseille, Naples et Turin*. Paris: Editions de la Maison des sciences de l'homme.

Broome, R. (1979) 'Professional Aboriginal Boxers in Eastern Australia 1930–1979'. *Aboriginal History* Vol. 4, No. 1: 49–70.

Broome, R. with Jakomos, A. (1998) *Sideshow Alley*, St Leonards, NSW: Allen and Unwin.

Brower, J (1972) 'The Racial Basis of the Division of Labor among Players in the National Football League as a Function of Stereotypes', Paper presented at the annual meeting of the Pacific Sociological Association, Portland, Oregon.

Brownell, S. (1995) *Training the Body for China: Sports in the Moral Order of the People's Republic*, Chicago IL: The University of Chicago Press.

—— (2000) 'Why Should an Anthropologist Study Sports in China?', in Noel Dyck (ed.), *Games, Sports and Cultures*, 43–63. Oxford: Berg

Brydon, D. (2000) *Postcolonialism: Critical Concepts in Literary and Cultural Studies*, London: Routledge.

Buckland, C. E. (1976) *Bengal Under the Lieutenant-Governors: Being a Narrative of the Principal Events and Public Measures during their Periods of Office, from 1854 to 1898*, Vol. II, 2nd edn, New Delhi: Deep Publications.

Budd, M. A. (1997) *The Sculpture Machine: Physical Culture and Body Politics in the Age of Empire*, New York: New York University Press.

Burton, A (2001) 'Thinking Beyond the Boundaries: Empire, Feminism and the Domains of History'. *Social History* 26 No. 1, January: 60–71.

Butler, J. (1997) *Excitable Speech: A Politics of the Performative*, New York: Routledge.

Butlin, N. G. (1983) *Our Original Aggression, Aboriginal Populations of Southeastern Australia, 1788–1850*, Sydney: George Allen & Unwin.

Campbell, Sir G. (1893) *Memoirs of My Indian Career*, ed. Sir C. E. Bernard, London: Macmillan.

Carrington, B. (1998) 'Sport, Masculinity, and Black Cultural Resistance'. *Journal of Sport and Social Issues* 22: 275–98.

Cashman, R. (1980) *Patrons, Players and the Crowds: The Phenomenon of Indian Cricket*, Delhi: Longman.

—— (1992) 'Symbols of Imperial Unity: Anglo Australian Cricketers, 1877–1900,' in J. A. Mangan, (ed.) *The Cultural Bond: Sport, Empire, Society*, pp. 128–41. London: Frank Cass.

—— (1995) *Paradise of Sport: The Rise of Organised Sport in Australia*, Melbourne: Oxford University Press.

—— and Hughes, A (1998) 'Sport', in Philip Bell and Roger Bell (eds), *Americanization and Australia*, pp. 179–92. Sydney: UNSW Press.

Castles, S., Kalantzis, M., Cope, B., and Morrissey, M. (1990) *Mistaken Identity, Multiculturalism and the Demise of Nationalism in Australia*, 2nd edn, Sydney: Pluto Press.

Chabal, P. (1996) 'The African Crisis: Context and Interpretation', in R. Werbner and T. Ranger (eds) *Postcolonial Identities in Africa*, London/New Jersey: Zed Books Ltd.

Chapple, G. (1984) *1981: The Tour*, Auckland: W. H. and A. H. Reed.

Childs, P. and Williams, R. J. P. (1997) *An Introduction to Post-Colonial Theory*, London: Prentice Hall/Harvester Wheatsheaf.

Chiou, Bian, Song, Qiang and Zhang, Zang Zang (1997) *China Can Say No (Chinese)* Hong Kong: Mingpao News.

Chow, Rey (1993) *Writing Diaspora: Tactics of Intervention in Contemporary Cultural Studies*, Bloomington, IN: Indiana University Press.

—— (1997) 'Can One Say No to China?' *New Literary History* 28: 147–51.

Chowdury-Sengupta, I. (1995) 'The Effeminate and the Masculine: Nationalism and the Concept of Race in Colonial Bengal', in P. Robb (ed.) *The Concept of Race in South Asia*, Oxford: Oxford University Press.

Chritcher, C. (1979) *Football Since the War: A Study in Social Change and Popular Culture*, Birmingham: Centre for Contemporary Cultural Studies.

Chryssides, H (1993) *Local Heroes*, North Blackburn, Victoria: Collins Dove.

Churchill, W. (1994) 'Crimes against humanity'. *Cultural Survival Quarterly*, winter: 36–9.

Clark, M. T. (1972) *Pastor Doug: The Story of Sir Douglas Nicholls, Aboriginal Leader*, Melbourne: Lansdowne Press.

Clarke, J. (1978) 'Football and Working Class Fans: Tradition and Change', in R. Ingham, (ed.) *Football Hooliganism*, London: Inter-Action Imprint.

Coakley, J. (1994) 'Using Social Theories: What Can They Tell Us about Sports in Society?'. *Sport in Society: Issues and Controversies*, St Louis, IL, Mosby.

Cohen, J. (1985) 'Strategy or Identity: New Theoretical Paradigms and Contemporary Social Movements'. *Social Research*, Vol. 52, No. 4: 663–716.

Connerton, P. (1989) *How Societies Remember*, Cambridge: Cambridge University Press.

Connolly, R. (1997) 'The Revolutionary', *The Sunday Age*, 27 April, David Syme & Co.: 17.

Coolwell, W. (1993) *My Kind of People: Achievement, Identity and Aboriginality*, St Lucia, Queensland: University of Queensland Press.

Crace, J. (1992) *Wasim and Waqar: Imran's Inheritors*, London: Boxtree.

Critcher, C. (1979) 'Football since the war', in C. Critcher, J. Clarke and M. Johnson (eds) *Working Class Culture*, London: Hutchinson.

Cronin, M. (1996) 'Defenders of the Nation? The Gaelic Athletic Association and Irish National Identity'. *Irish Political Studies*, 11:1–19.

—— (1999) *Sport and Nationalism in Ireland*, Dublin: Four Courts Press.

Crotty, M., Crotty, R., Habel, N., Morre, B. and O'Donoghue, M (1993) *Social Justice in Today's World: Finding a Just Way*, Melbourne: Collins Dove.

Crush, J. (1994) 'Postcolonialism, Decolonisation and Geography' in A. Godlewska and N. Smith (eds.), *Geography and Empire*, Oxford, Blackwell, 333–50.

Curry, M. (1996) *The Work in the World*, Minneapolis, MN: University of Minnesota Press.

Dalglish, K. (1996) *Dalglish: My Autobiography*, London: Hodder and Stoughton.

Daly, J. (1994) '"Civilising" The Aborigines: Cricket at Poonindie, 1850–1890', *Sporting Traditions: Journal of the Australian Society for Sports History* Vol. 10, No. 2: 59–67.

Davies, R. (1994) 'Irish Cricket and Nationalism'. *Sporting Traditions* 10, 1994: 77–96.

Davis, L. (1990) 'The Articulation of Difference: White Preoccupation with the Question of Racially Linked Genetic Differences Among Athletes'. *Sociology of Sport Journal* Vol. 7: 179–87.

Davis, M. (1997) 'Stynes Says He, Too, Is Casualty of Abuse', *The Australian*, 29 May, Nationwide News Pty Limited: 22.

—— (1998) 'Fight against Racism Being Won', *The Australian*, 19 June, Nationwide News Pty Limited: 20.

Dawson, J. (1981[1881]) *Australian Aborigines: The Language and Customs of Several Tribes of Aborigines in the Western District of Victoria, Australia*, Canberra: Australian Institute of Aboriginal Studies (1981 edition, originally published 1881).

De Boeck, F. (1996) 'Postcolonialism, Power and Identity: Local and Global Perspectives from Zaire', in R. Werbner and T. Ranger (eds) *Postcolonial Identities in Africa*, London: Zed Books Ltd.

De Bolfo, T. (1995) 'Player Plea for Code on Abuse', *Herald-Sun*, 18 May, The Herald and Weekly Times Limited: 2.

de Certeau, M. (1984) *The Practice of Everyday Life* Berkeley, CA: University of California Press.

De Cillia, R., Reisigl, M. and Wodak, R. (1999) 'The Discursive Construction of National Identities'. *Discourse and Society*, 10: 149–159.

de Jong, P. (1986) 'Kicking and Struggling into the Twentieth Century: Making Sense of New Zealand Rugby'. *Sites* 12: 29–42.

—— (1987) '"The Old Rugby Grows on You": The Making of a Game in a Small New Zealand Town'. *Sites* 14: 35–56.

Derrida, J. (1985) 'Racism's Last Word'. *Critical Inquiry* 12: 290–9.

Deutchman, I. and Ellison, A. (1999) 'A Star Is Born: The Roller Coaster Ride of Pauline Hanson in the News'. *Media, Culture and Society* 21: 33–50.

Dimeo, P. (1999) 'Race, Colonialism and the Emergence of Football in India', in M. Allison, J. Horne and L. Jackson (eds) *Scottish Centre Research Papers in Sport, Leisure and Society, III*, University of Edinburgh.

—— (2000) 'Racism, Football and Cultural Difference: The Experience of Scottish Asians', Unpublished Ph.D., University of Strathclyde.

—— (2001) 'Football and Politics in Bengal: Colonialism, Nationalism, Communalism' in Mills, J. and Dimeo, P. (eds) *Soccer in South Asia: Empire, Nation, Diaspora*, London: Frank Cass.

Dirlik, A. (1994) 'The Postcolonial Aura: Third World Criticism in the Age of Global Capitalism'. *Critical Inquiry* 20: 328–56.

Donegan, L. (1999) 'Blair Needs Briefing in Gaelic Because It's Not His Field', *Guardian*, 22 June.

During, S. (1995) 'Postmodernism or Postcolonialism Today' in B. Ashcroft, G. Griffiths and H. Tiffin (eds.), *The Post-Colonial Studies Reader*, London: Routledge, 125–9.

Edelman, R. (1993) *Serious Fun: A History of Spectator Sports in the USSR*, Oxford: Oxford University Press.

Edwards, H. (1969) *The Revolt of the Black Athlete*, New York: The Free Press.

Eitzen, D. and Tessendorf, I. (1978) 'Racial Segregation by Positions in Sport: The Special Case of Basketball'. *Review of Sport and Leisure*, Vol. 3: 109–38.

Elias, N. and Dunning, E. (1986) *Quest for Excitement. Sport and Leisure in the Civilizing Process*, Oxford: Basil Blackwell.

Erwin, A. (1989) 'Sport: The Turning Point', in C. Roberts (ed.), *Sport and Transformation: Contemporary Debates on South African Sport*, Cape Town: Township Publishing Co-Operative.

Evans, G. (1979) 'Differences in recruitment of black and white football players at a Big-Eight University'. *Journal of Sport and Social Issues*, Vol.3: 1–9.

Fan, Hong (1997) *Footbinding, Feminism and Freedom: the liberation of women's bodies in Modern China*, London: Frank Cass.

Fanon, F. (1986) *Black Skin, White Masks*, London: Pluto Press.

—— (1990) *The Wretched of the Earth*, London: Penguin Books.

Farrell, N. and Mooney, F. (1998) 'British Soldiers "Would Enjoy Gaelic Football"', *Irish News*, 30 May.

Fei Xiaotong (1985) *America and Americans (Chinese)* Beijing: Sanlian Books.

FIFA (1994) *90 Years of FIFA – Souvenir Edition*, Zurich: FIFA.

Fine, B. (1999) 'A Question of Economics: Is It Colonising the Social Sciences', *Economy and Society*. 28: 403–25.

Fiske, J. (1992) 'The Cultural Economy of Fandom', in Lisa A. Lewis (ed.), *The Adoring Audience: Fan Culture and Popular Media*, pp. 30–49, London: Routledge.

Fitzgerald, R. and Spillman, K. (eds) (1988) *The Greatest Game*, Richmond: William Heinemann, Australia.

Flanagan, M. (1998) *The Call*, St Leonards, NSW: Allen and Unwin.

Fleming, S. (1991) 'Sport, Schooling and Asian Male Youth Culture', in G. Jarvie (ed.), *Sport, Racism and Ethnicity*, London:The Falmer Press.

Foley, D. (1990) 'The Great American Football Ritual: Reproducing Race, Class, and Gender Inequality'. *Sociology of Sport Journal*, Vol.7: 111–35.

Football Association of Singapore (1996) *S-League Ball – Gala Dinner & Awards Presentation '96*, 15 November: Singapore: Football Association of Singapore.

—— (1997) *A Brief History of the FAS*, Singapore: Football Association of Singapore.

Foucault, M. (1973) *The Birth of the Clinic: An Archaeology of Medical Perception*, New York: Vintage Books.

—— (1989) *Madness and Civilization: A History of Insanity in the Age of Reason*, London: Routledge.

Fox, R. (1985) *Lions of the Punjab: Culture in the Making*, London: Berkeley & Los Angeles: University of California Press.

Gandoulou, J. D. (1989) *Dandies à Bacongo: le culte de l'élégance dans la société congolaise contemporaine*, Paris: l'Harmattan.

Ganter, R. (1999) 'Letters from Mapoon: Colonising Aboriginal Gender', *Australian Historical Studies*, 30 No. 113, October: 267–85.

Gardiner, G. and Bourke, E. A. (2000) 'Indigenous Populations, "Mixed" Discourses and Identities'. *People and Place*, Vol. 8 no. 2: 43–52.

Garland, J. and Rowe, M. (1999) 'Selling the Game Short: An Examination of the Role of Antiracism in British Football'. *Sociology of Sport Journal* 16: 35–53.

Gatting, M. and Patmore, A. (1988) *Leading from the Front*, London: Macdonald Queen Anne.

Geddes, B. and Crick, M. (eds) (1997) *Global Forces, Local Realities: Anthropological Perspectives on Change in the Third World*, Geelong: Deakin University Press.

Gelder, K. and Jacobs, J. M. (1998) *Uncanny Australia: Sacredness and Identity in a Postcolonial Nation*, Carlton, Victoria: Melbourne University Press.

George (1997) 'Full Points to Carey Comment', *Herald-Sun*, 2 May, The Herald and Weekly Times Limited: 20.

Ghosh, B. (1998) 'The Postcolonial Bazaar: Thoughts on Teaching the Market in Postcolonial Objects', *Postmodern culture,* http://muse.jhu.edu./journals/postmodern_culture/v000/0.1ghosh.html

Gikandi, S. (1996) *Maps of Englishness,* New York: Columbia University Press.

Gilbert, H. and Thompkins, J. (1996) *Post-Colonial Drama: Theory, Practice and Politics,* London: Routledge.

Given, J. (1995) 'Red, Black, Gold To Australia: Cathy Freeman & The Flags'. *Media Information Australia* 75: 46–56.

Glendinning, M. (1999) 'China Set For Twenty-First Century Success'. *Sport Business Magazine,* January.

Godwell, D. (1999) 'A Handshake Will Not Defeat Racism', *The Age,* 2 April, David Syme & Co.: 11.

Graham, D. (1994) 'Polly Farmer: Still Giving It All to the Game', *The Age,* 9 September, David Syme & Co.: 1.

Green, A. (ed.) (1997) *Can't Bat, Can't Bowl, Can't Field: The Best Cricket Writings of Martin Johnson,* London: CollinsWillow.

Gren, M. (1994) *Earth Writing,* Gothenburg: Department of Geography, Gothenburg University.

Gregory, D. (1994) *Geographical Imaginations,* Oxford: Blackwell.

Grossberg, L. (1992) 'Is There a Fan in the House?: The Affective Sensibility of Fandom', in Lisa A. Lewis (ed.), *The Adoring Audience: Fan Culture and Popular Media,* pp. 50–65, London: Routledge.

Grow, R (1998) 'From Gum Trees to Goalposts, 1858–1876', in Rob Hess and Bob Stewart (eds), *More than a Game: An Unauthorised History of Australian Rules Football,* pp. 4–28, Melbourne: Melbourne University Press.

Gu Shiquan (1989) *A Modern History of Sport in China (Chinese* Beijing: Beijing University of Physical Education.

Gu Shiquan (1990) 'Introduction to Ancient and Modern Chinese Physical Culture' in H.G. Knuttegen, O. Ma and C. Wu (eds.), *Sport in China,* Champaign: Human Kinetics.

Guha, R. (1998) 'Cricket and Politics in Colonial India'. *Past and Present* 161: 155–89.

Gupta, A. and Ferguson, J. (1992) 'Beyond "Culture": Space, Identity, and the Politics of Difference'. *Cultural Anthropology* 7(1): 6–23.

Guttmann, A. (1978) *From Ritual to Record,* New York: Columbia University Press.

Hadfield, W., Pegler, T. and Burke, B. (1999) 'Contrite Everitt Bans Himself'. *The Weekend Australian,* 10–11 April: 67.

Haigh, G. (2001) *Sports Factor,* ABC Radio National, 11 May.

Hall, M. A. (1985) 'Knowledge and Gender: Epistemological Questions in the Social Analysis of Sport'. *Sociology of Sport Journal* Vol. 2: 25–42.

Hall, S. (1995) 'New Cultures for Old', in D. Massey and P. Jess (eds), *A Place in the World: Places, Culture and Globalisation,* pp. 175–213, Oxford: Oxford University Press.

—— (1996) 'When Was the Post-Colonial?', in I. Chambers (ed.) *The Post-Colonial Question,* London: Routledge.

Hallinan, C. (1991) 'Aborigines and Positional Segregation in Australian Rugby League'. *International Review for Sociology of Sport*. Vol. 26, No. 2: 67–78.

—— Bruce, T. and Coram, S. (1999) 'Up Front and Beyond the Centre Line: Integration of Australian Aborigines in Elite Australian Rules Football', *International*

Hampton, K. and Mattingley, C., *Survival in Our Own Land,* Sydney: Hodder and Stoughton.

Hargreaves, J. (1986) *Sport, Power and Culture*, New York: St Martins Press.

—— (1992) 'Olympism and Nationalism: Some Preliminary Considerations', *International Review for the Sociology of Sport* 27 (1): 119–37.

—— (2000) *Freedom for Catalonia? Catalan Nationalism, Spanish Identity and the Barcelona Olympic Games*, Cambridge: Cambridge University Press.

Harris, B. (1989) *The Proud Champions*, Crows Nest, NSW: Little Hills Press.

Harriss-White, B. and White, G. (eds) (1996) *Liberalisation and the New Corruption*, *IDS Bulletin*, 27 (2).

Haughey, J. (1998) 'Brave Celtic Get Right Result', *Irish News*, 9 November.

Hawke, S. (1994) *Polly Farmer: A Biography*, South Fremantle: Fremantle Arts Centre Press.

Hay, R. (1994) 'British Football, Wogball or the World Game? Towards a Social History of Victorian Soccer', in John O'Hara (ed.) *Ethnicity and Soccer in Australia*, Studies in Sports History Number 10, Campbelltown: Australian Society for Sports History: 44–79.

—— (1997) 'The Migrants' Game: Soccer in Australia: International and Domestic Perspectives', British Society of Sports History, annual conference, Keele University, 12–13 April.

—— (1998) 'Croatia: Community, Conflict and Culture', in Mike Cronin and David Mayall (eds) *Sporting Nationalisms*, pp. 49–66, London: Cass.

Hazeldine, I. (1994) 'Aspects of Racism in the Australian Context: Issues of Definition and Action'. *Australian Journal of Human Rights*, Vol. 1 (1): 149–68.

Hedgcock, M. (2000) 'Australian Rules Football', in Richard Cox, Grant Jarvie and Wray Vamplew (eds), p. 27, *Encyclopedia of British Sport*, Oxford: ABC-Clio.

Hibbins, G. (1989) 'The Cambridge Connection: The Origin of Australian Rules Football', *International Journal of the History of Sport* 6: 172–92.

Hoberman, J. (1987) 'Sport and Social Change: The Transformation of Maoist Sport'. *Sociology of Sport Journal* 4: 156–70.

—— (1997) *Darwin's Athletes: How Sport Has Damaged Black America and Preserved the Myth of Race*, Boston: Houghton Mifflin Co.

Hollinsworth, D. (1997) 'The Work of Anti-racism', in G. Gray and C. Winter (eds), *The Resurgence of Racism: Howard, Hanson and the Race Debate*, Monash University, Victoria, Monash Publications in History, Vol. 24: 129–38.

Holt, R. (1989) *Sport and the British: A Modern History*, Oxford: Clarendon Press.

Hopcraft, A (1978) 'Football Man' quoted by J. Clarke, 'Football and Working Class Fans: Tradition and Change', in R. Ingham, (ed.), *Football Hooliganism*, London: Inter-Action Imprint.

Howe, S. (2000) *Ireland and Empire. Colonial Legacies in Irish History and Culture,* Oxford: Oxford University Press.

Howell, R. and Maxwell, L. (1986) 'The Effects of Acculturation on the Aborigines: A Case Study of the Sport of Cricket', in J. Mangan, J. and R. Small (eds), *Sport, Culture, Society: International, Historical and Sociological Perspectives,* Proceedings of the 8th Commonwealth and International Conference, Glasgow, Scotland: 14–19.

Howell, S. (1995) 'The Black Experience', *The Sunday Age,* 3 September, David Syme & Co.: 15.

Huang, Chichung (1997) *The Analects of Confucius: A Literal Translation with an Introduction and Notes,* Oxford: Oxford University.

Hughes, K. (1998) 'Political Football Is a Difficult Game', *Ireland on Sunday,* 8 November.

Hughson, J. (1997) 'Football, Folk-dancing and Fascism: Diversity and Difference in Multicultural Australia'. *Australian and New Zealand Journal of Sociology* 33, No. 2: 167–86.

Human Rights and Equal Opportunity Commission (1997) *Bringing Tthem Home: National Inquiry into the Separation of Aboriginal and Torres Strait Islander Children from their Families,* Commonwealth of Australia, Canberra: Australian Government Publishing Service.

Illingworth, R. and Bannister, J. (1996) *One-man Committee: The Controversial Reign of England's Cricket Supremo,* London: Headline.

Indian FA (1993) *Role, Achievements of the Indian Football Association (W.B.) in the Promotion and Development of the Game of Football in India,* West Bengal: IFA.

Irish News (1998) 'Club Used as Political Pawn', 14 November.

—— (1998) 'Peace Should Ban rule 21', 1 June.

Jackson, S. (1998) 'A Twist of Race: Ben Johnson and the Canadian Crisis of Racial and National Identity'. *Sociology of Sport Journal* 15: 21–40.

Jaireth, S. (1995) 'Tracing Orientalism in Cricket: A Reading of Some Recent Australian Cricket Writing on Pakistani Cricket'. *Sporting Traditions* 12: 103–20.

Jakubowicz, A., Goodall, H., Martin, J., Mitchell, T., Randall, L. and Seneviratne, K. (1994) *Racism, Ethnicity and the Media,* St. Leonards: Allen and Unwin.

James, A., Hockey, J. and Dawson, A. (eds), *After Writing Culture,* London: Routledge.

James, C. L. R. (1994) *Beyond a Boundary,* London: Serpent's Tail.

JanMohamed, A. R. (1985) 'The Economy of Manichean Allegory: The Function of Racial Difference in Colonialist Literature'. *Critical Inquiry* 12, 59–87.

Jarvie, G. (1985) *Class, Race and Sport in South Africa's Political Economy,* London: Routledge & Kegan Paul.

—— (1991) *Sport, Racism and Ethnicity,* London: The Falmer Press.

—— and Walker, G. (eds) (1994) *Scottish Sport in the Making of a Nation: Ninety Minute Patriots?,* Leicester: Leicester University Press.

Jeffery, K. (1996) 'Introduction', in K. Jeffery (ed.) *'An Irish Empire'? Aspects of Ireland and the British Empire,* Manchester: Manchester University Press.

Jenkin, G. (1979) *Conquest of the Ngarrindjeri,* Adelaide: Rigby.

Jensen, J. (1992) 'Fandom as Pathology: The Consequences of Characterization', in Lisa A. Lewis (ed.) *The Adoring Audience: Fan Culture and Popular Media*. pp. 9–29, London: Routledge.

Jobling, I. (1988) 'The Making of a Nation through Sport: Australia and the Olympic Games from Athens to Berlin, 1898–1916'. *Australian Journal of Politics and History* 34: 160–72.

Jones, M. (1994) 'Empowering Victims of Racial Hatred by Outlawing Spirit-Murder'. *Australian Journal of Human Rights* Vol.1 (1): 299–326.

Jones, R. (ed.) (1985) *Archaeological Research in Kakadu National Park*, Canberra City, A.C.T.: National Parks and Wildlife Service.

Kapuscinski, R. (1994) 'The Soccer War', in *The Best of Granta Reportage*, London: Granta Books, in association with Penguin Books.

Kell, P. (2000) *Good Sports: Australian Sport and the Myth of the Fair Go*, Sydney: Pluto Press Australia Ltd.

Kennedy, D. (1996) 'Imperial history and post-colonial theory'. *Journal of Imperial and Commonwealth history* 24, No. 3, September 1996.

Kibberd, D. (1997) 'Modern Ireland: Postcolonial or European?', in S. Murray (ed.) *Not On Any Map. Essays on Postcoloniality and Cultural Nationalism*, Exeter: University of Exeter Press.

Kidd, B. (1992) 'The Culture Wars of the Montreal Olympics', *International Review for the Sociology of Sport* 27 (2): 151–64.

Kirshenblatt-Gimblett, B. (1998) 'Black Box/White Cube: The Museum as a Technology', paper presented to 'Culture Shocks', Te Papa Tongarewa/Museum of New Zealand, Wellington, July.

Klein, A. (1991) *Sugarball: The American Game, the Dominican Dream*, New Haven, Yale University Press.

Knight, L. (1990) 'Mourie Happy in Official Limbo' *Dominion Sunday Times*, March 11: 11.

Knuttgen, H. G., Ma, Q. and Wu, Z. (eds) (1990) *Sport in China*, Champaign, IL: Human Kinetics Books.

Koebner R. and Schmidt, H. D. (1964) *Imperialism: The Story and Significance of a Political Word, 1840–1960*, Cambridge: Cambridge University Press.

Krotee, M. (1988) 'Apartheid and Sport: South Africa Revisited'. *Sociology of Sport Journal* Vol. 5: 125–35.

Langton, M. (1994) 'Aboriginal Art and Film: The Politics of Representation'. *Race and Class* Vol. 35, No. 4: 86–106.

Lapchick, R (1981) *Broken Promises*, New York: St Martins Press.

Lee, J.-Y. (1997) 'World Cup Co-Hosting and the Korean Society', in Proceedings of *How Sport Can Change the World*, international conference of the Japan Society of Sport Sociology, Ritsumeikan University, Kyoto, Japan, 26–28 March.

Lefebvre, H. (1991) *The Production of Space*, Oxford: Blackwell.

Lemon, A. (1987) *The History of Australian Thoroughbred Racing. Volume one. The Beginnings – to the First Melbourne Cup*, Melbourne: Classic Reproductions.

Leslie, S. (1916) *The End of a Chapter*, Heinemann: London.

Leviatin, D. (1993) 'The Evolution and Commodification of Black Basketball Style'. *Radical History Review,* Vol. 55: 154–64.

Licudi, A. and Raja, W. (1997) *Cornered Tigers: A History of Pakistan's Test Cricket,* St John's: Hansib Caribbean.

Lippmann, L. (1994), *Generations of Resistance: mabo and Justice,* Melbourne: Longman Cheshire.

Long, M. (1997) 'Despite Racial Setbacks, I Still Have My Dream', *The Age,* 23 April, David Syme & Co.: B16.

Lovell, N. (1998) 'Introduction: Belonging in Need of Emplacement?', in Nadia Lovell (ed.), *Locality and Belonging,* pp. 1–24, London:Routledge.

Mackenzie, J. M. (1995) *Orientalism: History, Theory and the Arts,* Manchester: Manchester University Press.

MacLean, M. (2000) 'Football as Social Critique: Protest Movements, Rugby and History in Aotearoa/New Zealand 1970–1985'. *International Journal for the History of Sport* 17(2/3): 255–77.

—— (forthcoming) '"Almost the Same But Not Quite . . . Almost the Same But Not White": Maori and Aotearoa/New Zealand's 1981 Springbok Rugby Tour'. *Kunapipi.*

MacMunn, Sir G. (1933) *The Martial Races of India,* London: Sampson, Low, Marston & Co. Ltd.

Maguire, F. and Gordon, M. (1999) 'Elliot Slur on "Forgotten Race"', *The Age,* 10 March, David Syme & Co.: 1–2.

Maguire, J. (1999) *Global Sport: Identities. Societies. Civilizations,* Cambridge: Polity Press.

Mahjoub, F. (1996) 'Rendez-vous à Soweto', *Balafon,* Air Afrique, January/February.

—— (1999) 'France-Maghreb – From Ben Barek to Zidane: From Assimilation to Integration', *CAF News,* Number 67: 3–11 (Confédération Africaine de Football).

Malkki, L. H. (1995) *Purity and Exile: Violence, Memory and National Cosmology among Hutu Refugees in Tanzania.* Chicago, IL: The Chicago University Press.

Malthouse, M. (1999) 'Racists Need a Spell on Sideline', *The Australian,* 8 April, Nationwide News Pty Limited: 18.

Mancini, A. and Hibbins, G. M. (eds) (1987) *Running with the Ball: Football's Foster Father,* Melbourne: Lynedoch Publications.

Mandell, R. (1984) *Sport: A Cultural History,* New York: Columbia University Press.

Mandle, W. F. (1973) 'Games People Played: Cricket and Football in England and Victoria in the Late Nineteenth Century'. *Historical Studies* 15: 511–35.

—— (1979) in 'Sport as Politics: The Gaelic Athletic Association, 1884–1916', in Richard Cashman and Michael McKernan (eds), *Sport in History,* St Lucia, Queensland: University of Queensland Press.

—— (1987) *The Gaelic Athletic Association and Irish Nationalist Politics 1884–1924,* London: Christopher Helm.

Mangan, J. A. (1998) *The Games Ethic and Imperialism: Aspects of the Diffusion of an Ideal,* London: Frank Cass.

Mao, Zedong (1975) *Selected Works of Mao Zedong Volume II*, Oxford: Pergamon Press.

Maradas, E. (1996) 'The Long Road to South Africa'. *African Soccer Magazine (Special Souvenir Edition)* January: 16–17.

Markovits, A. S. and Hellerman, S. L. (2001) *Offside: Soccer and American Exceptionalism*, Princeton, NJ: Princeton University Press.

Markus, A. (1994) *Australian Race Relations, 1788–1993*, Sydney: Allen and Unwin.

Marqusee, M. (1997) *War Minus The Shooting: A Journey through South Asia during Cricket's World Cup*, London: Mandarin.

Masanauskas, J., Heaney, C. and Probyn, A. (1997) 'Call for Stronger Line against Footy Racism', *Herald-Sun*, 25 April, The Herald and Weekly Times Limited: 3.

Mason, T. (1995) *Passion of the People? Football in South America*, London: Verso.

Mbembe, A. (1986) 'Pouvoir des morts et langage des vivants: les errances de la mémoire nationaliste au Cameroun'. *Politique Africaine* 22: 37–72.

—— (1992) 'Provisional Notes on the Postcolony'. *Africa* 62: 3–37.

—— and Roitman, J. (1995) 'Figures of the Subject in Times of Crisis'. *Public Culture* 7: 323–52.

McAsey, J. (1993) 'The Off-field Fight with Footy Racists', *The Weekend Australian*, 1 May, Nationwide News Pty Limited,: 7.

McCann, E. (1998) 'Politics Take Precedence Over Sport', *Sunday Tribune*, 1 November.

McCarthy, M. (1999) *Passing It On. The Transmission of Music in Irish Cultures*, Cork: Cork University Press.

McConville, C. (1998) 'Footscray, Identity and Football History'. *Occasional Papers in Football Studies* 1: 48–58.

McCorquodale, J. (1987) *Aborigines and the Law: A Digest*, Canberra: Aboriginal Studies Press.

McCusker, E. (1998) 'Rule 21 May Go If RUC Review Is "Acceptable"', *Irish News*, 1 June.

McGuiness, P. (1992) *Australian*, 27 May 1992.

McKay, A. (2001). 'Kicking the Buddha's Head': India, Tibet and Footballing Colonialism' in P. Dimeo and J. Mills (eds) *Soccer in South Asia: Empire, Nation, Diaspora*, London: Frank Cass.

McKay, J. (1990) 'Sport, Leisure and Social Inequality in Australia', in David Rowe and Geoff Lawrence (eds), *Sport and Leisure: Trends in Australian Popular Culture*, Sydney: Harcourt Brace Jovanovich.

McKendry, B. (1999) *Champions. The Players' Story*, Belfast: Irish Rugby Football Union (Ulster Branch).

McKew, M. (2001) Seven-thirty report, ABC, 19 April.

McLeod, J. (2000) *Beginning Postcolonialism*, Manchester: Manchester University Press.

McMichael, G. (1998) 'Sectarian Thugs Rule in Nationalist Areas', *Ireland on Sunday*, 22 November.

McNamara, L. (1998) 'Long Stories, Big Pictures: Racial Slurs, Legal Solutions and Playing The Game'. *The Australian Feminist Law Journal* 10: 85–108.

McTaggart, S. (1982) 'Graham Mourie: Far from the Sporting Crowds' *NZ Listener* November 6: pp. 14–15.

Meisl, W. (1960) 'The F.I.F.A.', in A. H. Fabian and D. Green (eds) *Association Football*, London: The Caxton Publishing Company Limited.

Memmi, A. (1970 and 1990 edn.) *The Colonizer and The Colonized*, Boston: Beacon Press.

Milan, R. (1997) 'Stop the Slaughter: Give Africa Back to the Tribes', *Sunday Telegraph*, 8 June, p. 33.

Miles. R. (1984) *Racism*, London: Routledge.

Mills. J. (2000) *Madness, Cannabis and Colonialism: The 'Native-only' Lunatic Asylums of British India, 1857–1880*, Basingstoke: Macmillan.

—— (2001) 'The Historiography of South Asian Sport', in J. Mills, J. and P. Dimeo, (eds), *Sport in South Asia*, Special Issue of *Contemporary South Asia*.

—— and Dimeo, P. (2001) ' Introduction: Empire, Nation, Diaspora', in P. Dimeo and J. Mills (eds), *Soccer in South Asia: Empire, Nation, Diaspora*, London: Frank Cass.

Mirzoeff, N. (1995) *Bodyscape*, London: Roputledge.

Mohanty, C. T. (1991) 'Under Western Eyes: Feminist Scholarship and Colonial Discourses', in C. Mohanty, A. Russo, and L. Torres (eds), *Third World Women and the Politics of Feminism*, Bloomington, IN: University of Indiana Press.

Mongia, P. (1996) *Contemporary Post-colonial Theory*, London: Arnold.

Montagu, A. (1974) *Man's Most Dangerous Myth: The Fallacy of Race*, New York: Oxford University Press.

Mookerjee, S. (1989) 'Early Decades of Calcutta Football', *Economic Times: Calcutta 300*, September: 146–57.

Moore, B. (1994) *The Australian Construction of Racism*, Adelaide: University of South Australia, unpublished paper.

Moore, K. (1989) '"The Warmth of Comradeship": The First British Empire Games and Imperial Solidarity'. *International Journal of the History of Sport*, 6.

Moore-Gilbert, B. (1997) *Postcolonial Theory. Contexts, Practices, Politics*, London: Verso.

—— Stanton, G. and Malet, W. (ed.) (1997) *Postcolonial Criticism*, London: Longman.

Mulvaney, D. J. and Golson, J. (eds) (1971) *Aboriginal Man and Environment in Australia*, Canberra: Australian National University Press.

—— and Harcourt, R. (1988) *Cricket Walkabout: The Australian Aborigines in England*, 2nd edn, South Melbourne: Macmillan in association with the Dept. of Aboriginal Affairs.

Murray, B. (1994) *Football: A History of the World Game*, Aldershot: Scolar Press.

Murray, S. (1997) 'Introduction', in S. Murray (ed.), *Not On Any Map. Essays on Post-coloniality and Cultural Nationalism*, Exeter: University of Exeter Press.

Myers, K. (1998) 'An Irishman's Diary', *Irish Times*, 19 August.

Nadel, D. (1993) 'Aborigines and Australian Football: The Rise and Fall of the Purnim Bears'. *Sporting Traditions Journal of the Australian Society for Sports History* Vol. 9, No. 2: 47–63.

Nandy, M. (1990) 'Calcutta Soccer', in S. Chaudhuri (ed.), *Calcutta: The Living City, Vol. II: The Present and Future*. Calcutta: Oxford University Press.

National Research Institute of Martial Arts (1996) *A History of Chinese Martial Arts* (Chinese) Beijing: The People's Physical Education Publishing House.

ni Fhlathuin, M. (1997) 'Anglo-India after the Mutiny: The Formation and Breakdown of National Identity', in S. Murray (ed.), *Not On Any Map. Essays on Postcoloniality and Cultural Nationalism*, Exeter: University of Exeter Press.

Niall, J. (2000) 'Aborigines in Football: It Would be a Sorry Game Without Them', *The Sunday Age*, 5 March, David Syme & Co.: 16–17.

Nkwi, P. N. and Vidacs, B. (1997) 'Football: Politics and Power in Cameroon', in G. Armstrong and R. Giulianotti (eds), *Entering the Field: New Perspectives on World Football*, Oxford: Berg.

Ntonfo, A. (1994) *Football et politique du football au Cameroun*. Yaoundé: Editions du CRAC.

O Muilleoir, M. (1998). 'N' neart go cur le chile', *Andersonstown News*, 21 November.

O'Brien, C. C. (1980) *Neighbours*, London: Faber and Faber.

O'Dowd, L. (1990) 'New Introduction', in A. Memmi, *The Colonizer and the Colonized*, London: Earthscan Publications.

Oldfield, S. (1995) 'Long's Abuse Claim to Test Code of Conduct', *The Age*, 28 April, David Syme & Co.: 1.

Oliver, G. (1992) *The Guinness Book of World Soccer – The History of the Game in Over 150 Countries* (2nd edn) Enfield/London: Guinness Publishing Ltd.

Olsson, G. (1991) *Lines of Power/Limits of Language*, Minneapolis, MN: University of Minnesota Press.

Oslear, D. and Bannister, J. (1996) *Tampering with Cricket*, London: CollinsWillow.

Outlaw, L. T. Jr (1999) 'On Race and Philosophy', in S. Babbitt and S. Campbell (eds), *Racism and Philosophy*, pp. 50–75, London:Cornell University Press.

Parisi, P. (1998) 'The *New York Times* Looks at One Block in Harlem: Narratives of Race in Journalism'. *Critical Studies in Mass Communication* 15: 236–54.

Park, G. (1995) *Nga Ururoa: Ecology and History in a New Zealand Landscape*, Wellington: Victoria University Press.

Parkes, P. (1996) 'Indigenous Polo and the Politics of Regional Identity in Northern Pakistan' in J. MacClancey (ed.), *Sport, Identity and Ethnicity*, Oxford: Berg.

Parkin, D. (1998) 'Foreword', in Nadia Lovell (ed.), *Locality and Belonging*, pp. ix–xiv, London: Routledge.

Pascoe, R. (1995) *The Winter Game: The Complete History of Australian Football*, Melbourne: Text Publishing Company.

Perkin, H. (1989) 'Teaching the Nations How to Play: Sport and Society in the British Empire and Commonwealth'. *The International Journal of the History of Sport*, 6 (2): 145–55.

Perry, J (1993) 'The Quick and the Dead: Moral Turpitude and the Stawell Easter Gift', *Australian Cultural History*. Crimes and Trials, 12, 1993.

Perry, R. E. (1921) *The Sikhs of the Punjab*, London: Drane's.

Pieterse, J. N. and Parekh, B. (eds) (1995) *The Decolonization of Imagination: Culture, Knowledge and Power*, London: Zed Books Ltd.

Pile, S. and Thrift, N. (1995) 'Introduction', in Steve Pile and Nigel Thrift (eds) *Mapping the Subject: Geographies of Cultural Transformation*, pp. 1–12, London: Routledge.

Plymire, D. C. (1999) 'Too Much, Too Fast, Too Soon: Chinese Women Runners, Accusations of Steroid Use, and the Politics of American Track and Field'. *Sociology of Sport Journal* 16: 155–73.

Poulter, J (1993) 'The Origins of Australian Rules Football', in Peter Burke and Leo Grogan (eds), *This Game of Ours*, St Andrews: pp. 64–7, Eatwarlflemsd.

Pratt, M.L. (1995) 'Scratches on the Face of the Country' in H.L. Gates (ed), *Race, Writing and Difference,* Chicago: University of Chicago Press.

Quansah, E. (1996) 'Football is More than a Game', *Africa Today* 2 (1): 26–8.

Quayson, A. (2000) *Postcolonialism. Theory, Practice or Process?*, Cambridge: Polity Press.

Read, P. (1996) *Returning to Nothing: The Meaning of Lost Places*, Cambridge: Cambridge University Press.

Rees, P. (1994) 'Less Abused – and Proud of It', *The Sunday Age*, 10 April, David Syme & Co.: 5.

Reynolds, H. (1987) *Frontier,* Sydney: Allen and Unwin.

Reynolds, H. (1999) *Why were we not told?*, Ringwood: Penguin.

Rice, G. (ed.) (1992) *Oxford History of New Zealand* 2nd edn, Wellington: Oxford University Press.

Rigney, D (1997) *'The Construction and Maintenance of Racism in Sport: Nunga* Perspectives on Australian Rules Football', Master of Education thesis, University of South Australia, unpublished.

Riordan, J. and Jones R. (eds) (1999) *Sport and Physical Education in China*, London: E. & F. N. Spon.

Ritzer, G. (1998) *The McDonaldization Thesis: Explorations and Extensions,* London: Sage.

Rive, R. (1981) *Writing Black,* Cape Town: David Philip.

Rose, D. (1985) *Employment and the Economy (Planning Paper No. 21),* Wellington: New Zealand Planning Council.

Ross, J. (ed.) (1996) *One Hundred Years of Australian Football, 1897–1996*, Ringwood: Penguin.

Rosselli, J. (1980) 'The Self-image Effeteness: Physical Education Nationalism in Nineteenth Century Bengal'. *Past and Present*, 86: 121–48.

Rous, S. (1978) *Football Worlds: A Lifetime in Sport*, London: Faber and Faber.

Rowe, D. (1998) 'Play Up: Rethinking Power and Resistance in Sport', *Journal of Sport and Social Issues* 22: 241–51.

—— and Lawrence, G. (1996) 'Beyond National Sport: Sociology, History and Postmodernity'. *Sporting Traditions* 12: 3–16.

Ryan, L. (2001) 'Postcolonialism and the Historian: The Aboriginal History Wars', *Australian Historical Association Bulletin* 92, June: 31–7.

Ryan, S. (1996) *The Cartographic Eye,* Cambridge: Cambridge University Press.

Sackett, L. (1993) 'A Post-modern Panoptican: The Royal Commission into Aboriginal Deaths in Custody'. *Australian Journal of Social Issues* 28 (3): 229–44.

Sage, G. (1990) *Power and Ideology in American Sport: A Critical Perspective,* Champaign, IL: USA, Human Kinetics.

Said, E. (1986) 'Orientalism Reconsidered' in Francis Barker *et al.* (eds), *Literature, Politics and Theory,* London: Methuen.

—— (1989) 'Representing the Colonized: Anthropology's Interlocutors'. *Critical Inquiry* 15.

—— (1993) *Culture and Imperialism,* London: Vintage.

—— (1995) *Orientalism,* London: Penguin Books.

Sampson, A. (1987) *Black And Gold: Tycoons, Revolutionaries and Apartheid,* London: Coronet Books.

Sandercock, L. and Turner, I. (1981) *Up Where, Cazaly?: The Great Australian Game,* Sydney: Granada.

Sayle, J. (1999) 'The Gendered Sublime in Memory and Desire'. *Illusions* 28: 17–23.

Schneider, J. and Eitzen, D. (1986) 'Racial Segregation by Professional Football Positions 1960–1985'. *Sociology and Social Research,* Vol. 70: 259–61.

Sen, S. (2000) *Disciplining Punishment: Colonialism and Convict Society in the Andaman Islands,* Delhi: Oxford University Press.

Sheahan, M. (1995) 'It's Time the Axe Fell', *Herald-Sun,* 2 May, The Herald and Weekly Times Limited: 13.

Sinha, M. (1995) *Colonial Masculinity: The 'Manly Englishman' and the 'Effeminate Bengali' in the Nineteenth Century,* Manchester: Manchester University Press.

Sissons, R. (1985) Review of Christopher Douglas, *Douglas Jardine: Spartan Cricketer, Sporting Traditions,* 1, No. 2: 106–7.

Smith, P. (1995a) 'Racism Rules', *The Age,* 3 June, David Syme & Co.: 7.

—— (1995b) 'AFL Is Out of Step in Attempt to Solve Race Row', *The Age,* 8 May, David Syme & Co.: 1.

—— and Lyon, K. (1999) 'Race Code to be Widened', *The Age,* 27 March, David Syme & Co.: 1.

Soja, E. (1989) *Postmodern Geographies: The Reassertion of Space in Critical Social Theory,* London: Verso.

—— (1996) *Thirdspace: Journey to Los Angeles and Other Real-and-Imagined Places,* Oxford, Blackwell.

Spivak, G. C. (1987) *In Other Words: Essays in Cultural Politics,* London: Routledge.

—— (1990) *The Post-Colonial Critic: Interviews, Strategies, Dialogues,* London: Routledge.

—— (1995) 'Can the Subaltern Speak?' in: B. Ashcroft, G. Griffiths, and H. Tiffin (eds), *The Post-Colonial Studies Reader,* London: Routledge

Sporting Globe, Saturday, 11 March 1933.

Spurr, D. (1993) *The Rhetoric of Empire,* London: Duke University Press.

Stamm, H.-P. and Lamprecht, M. (1996) 'Factors Governing Success in International Football', *FIFA Magazine,* August: 7–11.

Stepan, N. (1982) *The Idea of Race in Science*, Connecticut, USA: Archon Books.

Stokes, J. (1985) *The Sociology of Sport with Particular Reference to Australia*, Adelaide: CSIRO, Division of Human Nutrition.

Stone, D. (1999) 'Making Up For Years of Stolen Time', *The Sunday Age*, 28 March, David Syme & Co.: 4.

Struna, N. (1984) 'Beyond Mapping Experience: The Need for Understanding the History of American Sporting Women'. *Journal of Sports History* Vol.11, No. 1: 120–33.

Stuart, O. (1995) 'The Lions Stir: Football in African Society', in S. Wagg (ed.) *Giving the Game Away: Football, Politics and Culture on Five Continents*, Leicester: Leicester University Press.

Sugden, J. (1994) 'USA and the World Cup: American Nativism and the Rejection of the People's Game', in J. Sugden and A. Tomlinson (eds), *Hosts and Champions: Soccer Cultures, National Identities and the USA World Cup*, Aldershot: Ashgate Publishing Ltd.

—— and Bairner, A. (eds) (1999) *Sport in Divided Societies*, Aachen: Meyer and Meyer.

—— and Tomlinson, A. (eds) (1994) *Hosts and Champions: Soccer Cultures, National Identities and the USA World Cup*, Aldershot: Ashgate Publishing Ltd.

—— and Tomlinson, A. (1998) *FIFA and the Contest for World Football: Who Rules the Peoples' Game?*, Cambridge: Polity Press.

Tatz, C. (1987) *Aborigines in Sport*, The Australian Society for Sports History, Flinders University of South Australia.

—— (1995a) 'The Sport of Racism'. *Australian Quarterly*, Autumn: 38–48.

—— (1995b) *Obstacle Race: Aborigines in Sport*, Kensington: New South Wales University Press.

—— (1999) 'Genocide in Australia', *Australian Institute of Aboriginal and Torres Strait Islander Studies Research Discussion Paper*, 8: 10.

—— and Tatz, P (2000) *Black Gold: The Aboriginal and Islander Sports Hall of Fame*, Canberra: Aboriginal Studies Press.

Taylor, K (2001) 'Cricketer Clark to Lodge an Unusual Bet', *Age*, News, 19 April: 5.

Teo, P. (2000) 'Racism in the News: A Critical Discourse Analysis of News Reporting in Two Australian Newspapers'. *Discourse and Society*, 11: 7–46.

Terry, S. (ed.) (1981) *Energy Development in Taranaki: Are We on the Right Track?* Wellington: Environment Group Inc.

Thomas, W. (1838–9) *Brief Remarks on the Aborigines of Victoria*, Melbourne: Latrobe Library, MS 7838.

Thompson, E. P. (1977) *Whigs and Hunters: The Origins of the Black Act*, Harmondsworth: Penguin.

Thornton, R. (1996) 'The Potentials of Boundaries in South Africa: Steps Towards a Theory of the Social Edge', in R. Werbner and T. Ranger (eds) *Postcolonial Identities in Africa*, London: Zed Books Ltd.

Tierney, M (1976) *Croke of Cashel*, Dublin: Gill and Macmillan.

Tomlinson, A. (1986) 'Going Global: The FIFA Story', in A. Tomlinson and G. Whannel (eds) *Off the Ball: The Football World Cup*, London: Pluto Press.

—— (1996) 'Olympic Spectacle: Opening Ceremonies and Some Paradoxes of Globalization'. *Media, Culture and Society* 18: 543–601.

—— and Whannel, G. (eds) (1984) *Five Ring Circus: Money, Power and Politics of the Olympic Games*, London: Pluto Press.

Tomlinson, J. (1991) *Cultural Imperialism – A Critical Introduction*, London: Pinter.

Touraine, A. (1985) 'An Introduction to Social Movements', *Social Research*, Vol. 52, No.4: 749–87.

—— (1992) 'Beyond Social Movements'. *Theory, Culture and Society*. Vol. 9: 125–45.

Trouillot, M.-R. (1992) 'The Vulgarity of Power'. *Public Culture* 5: 75–81.

Trust and Fear Not (1885) *Ought Natives to be Welcomed as Volunteers?*, Calcutta: Thacker, Spink & Co.

Turner, B. S. (1994) *Orientalism, Postmodernism and Globalism*, London: Routledge.

Vamplew, W., Moore, K., O'Hara, J., Cashman, R. and Jobling, I. (1992) *The Oxford Companion to Australian Sport*, Melbourne: Oxford University Press.

Vansittart, E. (1915) *Gurkhas: Handbooks for the Indian Army*, Calcutta: Government Printing.

Velappan, P. (1996) *Asian Football in the New Millennium*, presented at a Media Seminar held in conjunction with the XIth Asian Cup, Abu Dhabi, United Arab Emirates, 14 December.

Vertinsky, P. (1994) 'Gender Relations, Women's History and Sports History: A Decade of Changing Enquiry, 1983–1993'. *Journal of Sports History*, Vol. 2, No.1: 1–24.

Vidacs, B. (1998) 'Football and Anti-colonial Sentiment in Cameroon', *Mots Pluriels* 6, htttp://www.arts.uwa.edu.au/MotsPluriels/MP698bv.html

Viti, D. (1995) 'Blacks Have Thin Skin', *Herald-Sun*, 5 September, The Herald and Weekly Times Limited: 15.

Waitangi Tribunal (1996) *The Taranaki Report: Kaupapa Tuatahi*, Wellington: Waitangi Tribunal.

Walker, C. (1992) 'Native Ability', *Inside Sport*, August: 59–65.

Wang, Hui and Yu, Kwok-leung (1998) *Post-ism in the Nineties (Chinese)* Hong Kong: The Chinese University of Hong Kong.

Wang, Ning (1997) 'Postcolonial Theory and the "Decolonization" of Chinese Culture'. *A Review of International English Literature* 28: 33–47.

Wang, Zhen and Olson, E. G. (1997) 'Present Status, Potential and Strategies of Physical Activity in China', *International Review for the Sociology of Sport* 32: 69–85.

Ward, A. (1997) *Rangahaua Whanui National Overview Report*, Wellington: Waitangi Tribunal.

Warren, I. (1997) 'Racism and the Law in Australian Rules Football: A Critical Analysis'. *Sporting Traditions* 14: 27–53.

Webster, D. (1988) *Looka Yonder! The Imaginary America of Populist Culture*, London: Routledge.

Werbner, R. (1996) 'Introduction. Multiple Identities, Plural Arenas', in R. Werbner and T. Ranger (eds) *Postcolonial Identities in Africa*, London: Zed Books Ltd.

Whimpress, B (1992) 'Few and Far Between: Prejudice and Discrimination among Aborigines in Australian First Class Cricket 1869–1988', *Journal of the Anthropological Society of South Australia* Vol. 30, No. 1–2: 57–70.

—— (1999) *Passport to Nowhere: Aborigines in Australian Cricket, 1850–1939,* Sydney: Walla Walla Press.

Wilmot, E. (1991) 'Dilemma of Mind'. The Inaugural David Uniapon Lecture, Kaurna Higher Education Centre, University of South Australia, Adelaide.

Wilson, C. (1991) 'Racism on the Field: AFL Football's Shameful Secret', *The Sunday Age*, 25 May, David Syme & Co.: 6.

Wilson, D. (1998) 'Time to Play the Right Game', *Andersonstown News*, 14 November.

Winks, R. W. (1954) *These New Zealanders*, Christchurch: Whitcombe and Tombs.

Wolpert, S. (1997) *A New History of India*, 5th edn, New York and Oxford: Oxford University Press.

Xie, Ming (1997) 'The Postmodern as the Postcolonial: Re-cognizing Chinese Modernity'. *A Review of International English Literature* 28: 11–32.

Xie, Shaobo (1997) 'Rethinking the Problem of Postcolonialism'. *New Literary History* 28: 7–19.

Yetman, N. and Eitzen, D. (1972) 'Black Americans in Sports: Unequal Opportunity for Equal Ability'. *Civil Rights Digest* Vol. 5: 20–34.

—— Berghorn, F. and Thomas, F. (1982) 'Racial Participation and Integration in Intercollegiate Basketball, 1958–1980', *Journal of Sport Behaviour* Vol. 5, No.1: 44–56.

Zizek, S. (1997) 'Multiculturalism, or, the Cultural Logic of Multinational Capitalism" *New Left Review* 225: 28–51.

—— (1999) *The Ticklish Subject: The Absent Centre of Political Ontology*, London: Verso.

Index